ALSO BY DON STAP

Letter at the End of Winter (poems)

A Parrot Without a Name

Alfred A. Knopf   New York   1990

A Parrot
Without a Name

*The Search for the Last
Unknown Birds on Earth*

DON STAP

For my teachers

Robert Mezey, Richard Schramm, Brooke Hopkins,
and Roy Healy

THIS IS A BORZOI BOOK
PUBLISHED BY ALFRED A. KNOPF, INC.

Copyright © 1990 by Don Stap
Map copyright © 1990 by George Colbert

Grateful acknowledgment is made to Charles Scribner's Sons, an imprint of Macmillan Publishing Company, for permission to reprint excerpts from *Tropical Nature* by Adrian Forsyth and Ken Miyata. Copyright © 1984 by Adrian Forsyth and Ken Miyata. Reprinted by permission.

Library of Congress Cataloging-in-Publication Data

Stap, Don.
A parrot without a name : the search for the last unknown
birds on earth / Don Stap. — 1st ed.
p.   cm.
ISBN 0-394-55596-1
1. Birds—Peru.   2. Rare birds—Peru.   3. Bird watching
—Peru.   I. Title.
QL689.P5S7   1990
598.2985—dc20   89-43291
CIP

Manufactured in the United States of America
First Edition

Contents

Acknowledgments

John O'Neill and Ted and Carol Parker opened their doors to me over a period of four years. Their graciousness and good companionship in travel went far beyond common courtesy. They took time out of busy schedules and important work to share their lives with me, and my gratitude, heartfelt as it is, seems inadequate. Ted Parker and O'Neill also read the manuscript and made suggestions that improved many parts of the book. If any errors in fact remain, they are mine.

The members of the 1987 Cordillera Divisor expedition were good enough to put up with a journalist looking over their shoulders, and more; my sincere thanks to them all: Angelo Capparella, Paul and Mara Freed, Pete Marra, Al Gentry, Camilo Díaz, Donna Schmitt, Tony Meyer, Gabriel Ballón, Cecilia Fox, Manuel and Marta Sánchez, and Magno Lazón. (The expedition was generously supported by the National Geographic's Fund for Research and Exploration.) Others at LSU were very kind as well, in particular Van Remsen and Tom Schulenberg, both of whom helped me find my way around Peru on separate occasions. I would like to thank Catherine Cummins and Tristan Davis also. John Fitzpatrick at Chicago's Field Museum spoke with me several times about his own excellent fieldwork in Peru. Mary LeCroy at the American Museum of Natural History showed

Acknowledgments

me the type specimen of *Tolmomyias flaviventris* from 1831 and helped me locate several rare books (excerpts of which were translated for me by Mrs. Anna Greif and novelist Stephen Becker), and Mark Robbins at the Academy of Natural Sciences of Philadelphia located some of M. A. Carriker's journals for me. Many other people took time to talk with me, including Roger Tory Peterson, John Terborgh, Manuel Plenge, John Farrand, and James Gulledge.

Several people read the manuscript in progress and made very helpful comments, most notably Stuart Dybek, whose encouragement and advice from the very beginning of the project were invaluable, and Peter Matthiessen, whose good faith and practical suggestions both inspired and prodded me when I most needed it. I'm also grateful to my good friend John Ray for his insights and comments on an early draft of the manuscript.

In addition, I would like to thank Victor Emanuel, to whom I will always be grateful for pointing me in the direction of Peru in the first place. In Lima, Beatrice Berger and Beatríz Cavero of Panorama Viajes/Turismo SA went out of their way to solve travel problems for me more than once, providing that inestimable comfort any traveler in a foreign land most appreciates—a reassuring smile. Peter Jensen, who operates Explorama Tours in Iquitos, was also very kind, providing lodging and transportation.

On the home front, Stuart Omans of the University of Central Florida was particularly helpful and supportive, and I'm grateful to the Division of Sponsored Research at the university for a research grant that helped me set aside time to read and travel. Provost Richard Astro, Rick Schell, and Dan Jones were quick to provide assistance; and I also appreciate the capable and cheerful help I received from Steve Andrews, Colin Kemp, and Allison Romansky, whose hands-on guidance with computer software and laser printers saw me through the many drafts of the manuscript.

Finally, I can think of no adequate way to thank Kristine and Benjamin, except to say what they already know too well—that they were there with me, always, amidst the tangle of vines and lianas and sentences.

Prologue

In January 1984 I accompanied a birdwatching tour in south Texas organized by Victor Emanuel Nature Tours (VENT). The outing was led by Victor Emanuel himself, one of the country's most knowledgeable birdwatchers. I was on the tour not only because I was an occasional birdwatcher but also because I had contracted to write a magazine article about Victor, who was renowned as much for his enthusiasm for birding as his skill at finding and identifying uncommon birds. When in passing conversation one day Victor mentioned that a little-known lodge in Peru, the Explorer's Inn, would make a good subject for a travel article, I made note of it. Talk to Ted Parker at Louisiana State University, he told me. Parker, Victor explained, led VENT tours in Peru and probably knew more about the Explorer's Inn than anyone else.

Three months later I phoned Parker, introduced myself, and asked him about the Explorer's Inn. In the middle of a rambling, spirited description of the place, Parker told me that in addition to taking birdwatchers to the Explorer's Inn he also used it as a base for several ongoing ornithological studies. His work there, he said, was connected with the Louisiana State University Museum of Natural Science, which had led the way in South American bird studies since the

1960s, when a graduate student named John O'Neill discovered several new species of birds in Peru. These discoveries had greatly surprised ornithologists everywhere, who had assumed that virtually all the species of birds in the world had already been found. Parker gave me a brief account of LSU's bird study program in Peru and then suggested I get in touch with O'Neill, who was now Coordinator of Field Studies at LSU. The Explorer's Inn, I decided, could wait.

By July I had spoken with O'Neill and exchanged several letters. Subsequently, O'Neill invited me to join an LSU expedition. In the past, the LSU ornithologists had ruled out taking any outsiders with them on their extended treks into isolated areas of Peru, but as O'Neill explained in a letter, "I am very worried that we are near the end of really pioneering, basic expeditions to discover what is actually in a wild part of this earth. There are few wild places left and the political situation around the world is such that we may not be able to do this sort of work too much longer. I want to see such work well documented."

My own interest in birds went back to my childhood in rural Michigan, where the most exotic and colorful bird I knew was the Baltimore Oriole. For both the birdwatcher and journalist in me, this was a once-in-a-lifetime opportunity, so on a visit to Baton Rouge later that year I made plans to accompany the next LSU expedition, set for the summer of 1985. When the time arrived, however, the expedition had to be canceled because of lack of funds. I went to Peru that summer anyway, met up with Parker, who was working alone at a study site in northern Peru, and got a heady introduction to neotropical ornithology. A year later, the expedition was again stalled, and O'Neill seemed frustrated but not deterred. Finally, in the summer of 1987, with a grant from the National Geographic Society, O'Neill's long-planned expedition got under way. On June 11, I flew to Lima, and three days later on to Pucallpa, a frontier town in eastern Peru where the LSU group was gathering.

A Parrot Without a Name

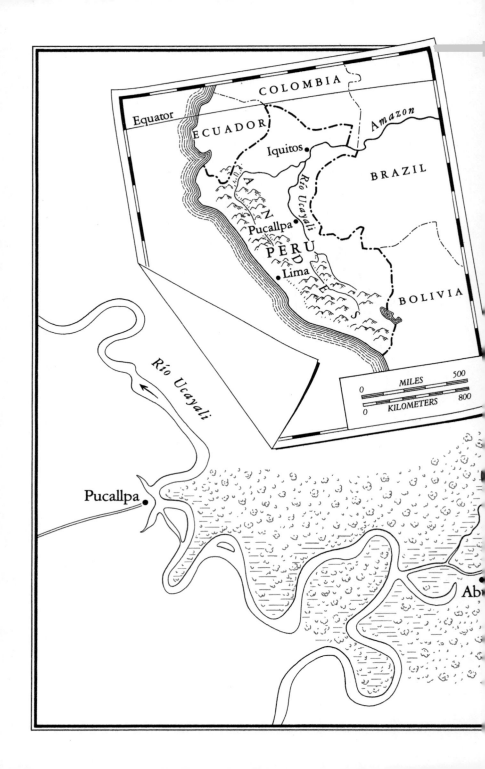

The
Orange-throated
Tanager

 John O'Neill has been in Pucallpa for two days, checking the gear and buying supplies. Some of the expedition members arrived with O'Neill, others came in today, and we are still expecting botanist Al Gentry, who has chosen to drive his jeep from Lima, crossing the Andes on the Trans-Amazon highway. The highway dead-ends here in Pucallpa, though a hundred miles to the east, just over the Brazilian border, it picks up again and from there wanders roughly three thousand miles eastward to the Atlantic Ocean. When the last section between Pucallpa and Brazil is completed, it will be possible to drive across the continent. The highway is halted here by the Río Ucayali, a river as formidable as the Mississippi. This is good, because when a bridge is eventually constructed and the bulldozers attack the jungle to the east, the untouched tropical wilderness—which is the destination of O'Neill's expedition—will be exposed to development, and destruction of the rainforest will almost certainly follow as it has in similar cases all over South America. Half of the earth's original five billion acres of rainforest has been decimated, most if it in the last two hundred years.[1] We are losing ground, quite literally—fourteen million acres

a year—and by the turn of the century we may have destroyed as many as one-third of the species of plants and animals in Latin America alone.[2]

Peru is one of the poorest countries in South America, and, except for Lima, there isn't a Peruvian city anywhere that has one foot firmly in the twentieth century. One senses that only the greatest effort keeps Pucallpa from being reclaimed by the jungle that surrounds it. It is a dusty, heat-bitten town of rusting tin roofs and noisy motorbikes. The shops and cafés are concrete or brick, usually painted a dull green or mustard, a crudely lettered sign above the door. Furnishings are sparse and the rooms are always dimly lit. At its edges Pucallpa disintegrates into muddy, refuse-filled shantytowns. Approaching the area by air is like coming across a dirty penny in an old green rug.

O'Neill is eager to get out of Pucallpa. He stands near the door of the Gran Hotel Mercedes, above him a wobbly ceiling fan stirring the humid tropical air that comes in off the streets.

"Get another box of crackers," he says to Pete Marra, an LSU graduate student. "And maybe some vanilla wafers if you can find them."

Pete scribbles this onto his list. Though over a dozen trunks of equipment were brought in from the United States, O'Neill prefers to buy many of the supplies here—they are cheaper, and then too this is a way of supporting the Peruvian economy, something O'Neill can point to when he negotiates with the Peruvian government for permits to collect birds.

The expedition's supplies now fill an extra room in the hotel and weigh well over a ton. Altogether we need food for fifteen people for two and a half months. Tomorrow we hope to leave Pucallpa and head east-southeast by river, first on the Río Ucayali, then the smaller Río Abujao, and then, as soon as we can hire enough dugout canoes, proceed northeast up the Río Shesha, a minor river that does not appear on most maps. Our destination is an isolated cluster of low mountains that rises unexpectedly out of the lowlands stretching for hundreds of miles north, south, and east of them. To the west, more than a hundred miles away, are the foothills of the Andes, which, it appears, is where these low mountains belong. They have been separated from the Andes by the lowlands in between since the time the Andes mountain range was formed ten thousand years ago. The Cordillera Divisor, as the cluster is known, is a geological oddity. This in turn makes it a unique habitat that holds the promise of rare, even unknown, animals. Furthermore, the rainforest around the Cordillera Divisor is one of the largest unexplored areas on earth, approximately 300,000 square miles of wilderness—an area three times larger than Wyoming. No one, except a few local people, has ever been to these mountains.

The purpose of O'Neill's expedition is to observe and collect as many birds as possible from the Cordillera Divisor and surrounding area. Little is known about many of the birds in this region of Peru, and such a collection will help fill in the blank spaces on a zoogeographical map. Until recently ornithologists have had to assume that the birds in this area were the same as in similar habitats elsewhere in Peru, a dubious assumption, as O'Neill's expeditions have proven over and over again. And though he is reluctant to say it too loudly, O'Neill hopes to find a new species in the Cordillera Divisor. If anyone dared expect such a thing it would be O'Neill—since 1961 he has been involved in the discovery of eleven new species of birds in Peru. While others are trying to save endangered species, O'Neill is adding new birds to the list of the world's known avifauna.

The Río Shesha is a small river, bound to be only a foot or two deep this time of year, and since no one uses the river on a regular basis it will be clotted with deadfall. It might take us a week to get upriver to the spot where it draws nearest the Cordillera Divisor. If the water is low we will have to pole upriver in the canoes. If we are lucky, it will be just deep enough to use small motors. Two weeks ago, before he left the United States, O'Neill got word that the rainy season had lasted longer than usual and the Shesha was a few inches higher than it might otherwise have been.

This morning, however, the expedition is in limbo. Several trunks of supplies that were supposed to arrive on the plane from Lima yesterday didn't show up. While Pete Marra heads off to look for crackers and vanilla wafers, O'Neill will stay at the hotel and call a travel agent he knows in Lima to ask her if she can apply some pressure on the Peruvian airline to get the LSU cargo on today's flight to Pucallpa. He must also call Irma Franke, Curator of Birds at Peru's Museo de Historia Natural, to ask if LSU's permit to collect birds has been approved. The official permits needed for an expedition, which O'Neill has been getting without much difficulty for twenty years, have been a major headache this year—as has customs. Three weeks ago Sunday, when Pete Marra and Angelo Capparella first arrived in Peru with the expedition's supplies, the customs officials at the Lima airport impounded everything. Angelo, who had just finished his doctorate at LSU, had done fieldwork in Peru in previous years and was familiar with the procedures, but this startled him. O'Neill had sent Pete and him ahead with the gear, expecting them to spend about a week in Lima and then get everything to Pucallpa where they would spend several more days making final arrangements. Now the customs officials were saying they wouldn't allow any of this stuff to enter Peru, and what was in all these trunks and bags anyway?

For a day or two the fate of the entire expedition was in doubt. In the States, O'Neill made anxious phone calls to everyone involved. In Lima, Angelo and Pete were told to make a list of everything they had brought with them, then they would open the trunks with the customs officials, take everything out, make a second list, and compare the two. The chore and ensuing discussions took three days. Once this was completed, they were advised that it was against the law to bring perishable items into the country—they might have to leave all the food behind. Angelo, with the help of Irma Franke, did some negotiating. The customs officials eventually came to understand that LSU had a long-standing agreement with Peru about such expeditions, but Peruvian nationalism had been running especially high since 1985 when Alan García, a young social democrat, was elected President. Under García there was more scrutiny of Peru's national resources leaving the country, and, of course, the government officials O'Neill had dealt with in the past had been replaced when García came to power. In the end, to save face (which O'Neill believes was the only real problem all along), the customs officials let LSU donate all the perishable items to the Museo de Historia Natural, then they politely turned their backs while the museum sent these same items to Pucallpa with the two Peruvian students who were on the expedition. O'Neill called everyone to say the expedition was only delayed by a week. Airline reservations could be changed, but meanwhile the water level in the Río Shesha was certainly dropping.

Early this morning, Angelo Capparella left Pucallpa with Manuel Sánchez, a Peruvian who has assisted LSU expeditions since 1967. The two of them hired a speedboat to take them up the Río Ucayali to the mouth of the Río Abujao, and then on to a small village of the same name. At Abujao they will ask about the water level in the Shesha and try to hire several canoes and guides, so that when we all finally get to Abujao we can start upriver as soon as possible. With the speedboat, Angelo hopes to cut a two-day round trip to one day and get back tonight; if they do, and if the cargo arrives from Lima this afternoon, we can all get going tomorrow. O'Neill is still standing in the lobby of the hotel, momentarily looking lost. What was he going to do next? He is a man who checks off his days bit by bit on the lists he keeps. "In Baton Rouge I wake up in the middle of the night to write things down," he once told me. "That's why I love getting away on expeditions. At the end of the day I'm physically tired and mentally relaxed, and I sleep straight through the night."

O'Neill looks at himself with the same analytical eye he applies to his work. He knows that he can be generous to a fault, taking on so many projects that he has little time for the work he values most, but still he has trouble saying no. Thus, the restless nights. He is forty-five years old, short, and widening at the waistline. His haircut and neatly trimmed mustache haven't changed much since the 1950s, except that his dark hair is now liberally flecked with gray. He speaks with the traces of a Texas drawl, and he is careful to say what he means and to say as little as possible if he can say nothing good. He is, if anything, considerate and exact. And his forthright friendliness is as apparent when he speaks of a longtime department secretary as it is when he mentions one of his more well-known colleagues such as Roger Tory Peterson. This, of course, makes him popular with the graduate students at LSU, who turn to him frequently for advice on their studies. He gives most questions careful consideration, often more than they deserve. When he stops to think about something, his face sometimes loses all expression, as it has now.

But suddenly, he changes gears, turning on his heel and bustling off to make the phone calls to Lima. O'Neill has already transformed the hotel into LSU's headquarters. His Spanish is fluent (he can get by in two Indian languages as well), and he has a way with people, making friends easily and negotiating for what he needs with patience and persistence. Señor Theo Inversini, the owner of the Gran Hotel Mercedes, has offered to help in any way he can. The hotel is luxurious by Peruvian standards, especially for Pucallpa. The lobby is spacious; there is a large dining room where the food is very good and a pretty courtyard with a new swimming pool. Though the ceiling fans work on only one of three speeds and the shower spits out water of dubious origin, the rooms are clean and comfortable. And each evening a mild breeze cleanses the air.

After the phone calls, neither of which was conclusive, there are some letters to be mailed. The post office, O'Neill has been told, is several blocks west. We walk along under a hazy blue sky filled with circling vultures. There is enough rotting garbage strewn about to keep the homely black birds fit and happy for years to come. We pass through a small, crowded marketplace where clothes are laid out on boxes, pots and pans stacked on the sidewalk, and watches and jewelry displayed in neat rows on planks. In an empty lot a crowd of people surrounds three cages. An American cougar paces unhappily in one, a bear sits in another, and a raucous group of monkeys bounce about in the third. A sign above the cages announces that this is the American Circus.

At the post office O'Neill sends a batch of letters he has collected from the group to friends and family in the States, the last they will hear from us until we reemerge from the jungle over two months from now. O'Neill himself is divorced, each year renting out a room of his house in Baton Rouge to a graduate student. Most of the ornithologists at LSU who are engaged in fieldwork in South America are single or, if they are married, childless. O'Neill plays down the dangers of the yearly expeditions, but it is difficult, no doubt, for those left behind to endure months of unbreakable silence.

With the letters mailed, we return to the hotel and wait for the afternoon flight from Lima. If the supplies arrive and Angelo Capparella and Manuel Sánchez get back from Abujao with good news, we may still leave tomorrow. By noon everyone else has returned to the Gran Hotel Mercedes as well. In a restaurant across the street we push two tables together and order lunch. With Angelo and Manuel off to Abujao, there are thirteen of us. O'Neill sits at the head of the table. Pete Marra, just finishing his M.A. at LSU, is the youngest member of the expedition and the only one with no experience in the tropics. Paul and Mara Freed are herpetologists from Houston where Paul is in charge of a section of reptiles at the Houston Zoo. They have been to Africa and Central America in recent years, but never to South America and never on an expedition of this nature. Al Gentry, who arrived a short while ago, is a botanist at the Missouri Botanical Gardens with extensive experience in South America. He is accompanied by his Peruvian colleague Camilo Díaz; but Gentry and Díaz will have only two weeks to do a quick floral survey of the Cordillera Divisor before Gentry has to return to the States. Tony Meyer, a former M.D. who now leads birding tours for Victor Emanuel Nature Tours, has been asked along in part because of his medical expertise, but also because of his field experience and knowledge of vocalizations. He will tape-record bird songs and make behavior observations, copies of which he'll turn over to Ted Parker of LSU, whose specialty is vocalizations. The final American on the trip is Donna Schmitt, a biology teacher from New Mexico who has experience on previous

LSU expeditions and is valued for her exceptional skills at preparing specimens. Cecilia Fox and Gabriel Ballón, the two Peruvian ornithology students, have also arrived. O'Neill is more than pleased to have them on the expedition since whatever hope there is for conserving Peru's natural resources surely rests with its students. It is ironic that Peruvian students are learning about their country's flora and fauna from American zoologists, though in a different way the Americans in turn have learned much from Peruvian villagers and Indians near the American study sites. Cecilia and Gabriel, for their part, are friendly and enthusiastic. Cecilia has a wide, toothy smile, and she enjoys making jokes, though they are sometimes hobbled by her imperfect English. The last two members of the expedition are Manuel's wife, Marta, a small, quiet woman with Indian features, and Magno, their young nephew, who will assist with the work around camp.

Now O'Neill wonders aloud how Angelo and Manuel are doing, and he worries over the money they put out for the speedboat, 450 intis, or about 20 dollars. Expedition funds are running low because of the extra expense Angelo and Pete incurred by staying three weeks in Lima while they negotiated the permits. O'Neill asks Pete how many intis he has on him and how many Angelo took with him. He has dollars he needs to exchange for intis before we leave Pucallpa; he's been holding on to them because the exchange rate grows more favorable with each day. He decides he will ask Theo Inversini at the hotel if he'll take the dollars for intis. The black market rate is always better than the bank rate.

Donna Schmitt, who has just taken a mouthful of fried rice, suddenly grimaces and holds her jaw. As politely as she can, she spits something out into her napkin. Upon inspection, it turns out to be a big metal staple. "A tooth seems loose," she says. She feels about with her finger. "It doesn't hurt, but I can wiggle it."

O'Neill takes a look. The tooth appears to be fractured.

"Really, it doesn't hurt though," Donna repeats, but her face reflects the thoughts that must be racing through her mind. Pucallpa is no place to be searching for a reliable dentist. There are still dentists in South America working with drills powered by a foot treadle.

"Well, it wouldn't be good to take a chance with it in the jungle," O'Neill says.

In an instant, the expedition's plans have changed. O'Neill has taken this latest setback in stride. "In Peru it is best to count on things not going as you hope and be happy when they do," O'Neill wrote in a memo that he sent to each expedition member. Now, he decides that he will call an orthodontist friend in Lima and then see if they can get Donna on this afternoon's flight. Maybe she can get the tooth repaired tomorrow morning and get back in the afternoon. That would only hold things up a day. Somehow, it's doubtful that things will go that smoothly, but O'Neill heads back to the hotel with Donna to make the calls while the rest of us linger over our food, inspecting our own portions of rice.

2

 In 1498, on Columbus's third voyage to "the New World," his fleet was anchored off the coast of Venezuela, a distant shoreline that the explorer took to be just another island. Because it was Sunday, and, as his son Ferdinand recorded, "from motives of piety [he] did not wish to set sail that day," Columbus sent several small boats ashore. Thus, the first Europeans set foot on the continent of South America.[1] During the next two centuries the Spanish crisscrossed South America in search of gold and slaves, often accompanied by missionaries seeking to expand God's kingdom. Increasingly, those who returned to Europe brought back specimens of the extraordinary birds they had come across. In the 1700s the first scientific expeditions were sent to the New World tropics, and by the nineteenth century major expeditions had been launched by many European states. From 1799 to 1804, Baron Alexander von Humboldt made his famous journey (one of the first major scientific explorations of South America), during which he explored the sources of the Amazon River, discovered off the coast of Peru the cold-water current that is now known as the Humboldt Current, and made basic observations about physical geography and meteorology

12

that helped lay the foundations for those sciences. From 1812 to 1824, an Englishman named Charles Waterton made four trips to South America, collecting thousands of floral and faunal specimens. A French botanist, August de Saint-Hilaire, journeyed throughout the continent from 1816 to 1822 and returned to France with specimens of 2,005 birds, 6,000 insects, 125 quadrupeds, 35 reptiles, 58 fish, and 7,000 plants.[2] Ten years later Darwin undertook his epoch-making voyage aboard the *Beagle,* and in 1848 two other English naturalists, Henry Walter Bates and Alfred Russel Wallace, set out to emulate Darwin. Bates spent eleven years exploring Amazonian Brazil, returning to England in 1859 with a collection of 14,707 species of animals (the great majority of them insects), of which 8,000 turned out to be new to science—an average of two new species per day.[3]

This is the kind of thing present-day zoologists shake their heads at with wonder, and surely a bit of envy. From 1830 to 1900, 230 new species of birds were discovered in Peru alone. After 1900 the number of new birds found in Peru each decade dropped steadily until only two new birds were listed from 1941 to 1950.[4] Less than fifty years after Bates's death the zoological exploration of South America had come to a halt. Ernst Mayr, a distinguished ornithologist at the Harvard Museum of Comparative Zoology and world expert on avian species, felt certain there were few birds left to be discovered. "It is safe to say," Mayr wrote in 1945, "that practically all the widespread species of birds in the world have been discovered, whether they be rare or common."[5] In 1951 the German ornithologist Erwin Stresemann went a bit further, dropping the qualifier "widespread." He wrote: "Birds are, at present, the best studied of any class in the animal kingdom. By now the number of bird species, and, for that matter, the number and distribution of the geographical races have been all but completely determined."[6] Mayr and Stresemann were saying what nearly everyone in the ornithological community felt: the heyday of exploration and discovery was long gone.

Twenty-six years ago, John O'Neill ignored this prevailing wisdom and set off on a trip that would change the course of neotropical ornithology. In 1961 O'Neill had just finished his freshman year at the University of Oklahoma, where he had gone to study under George "Doc" Sutton, a well-known ornithologist and bird painter. At a local bird club meeting, Sutton introduced him to a journalism professor, Dr. John Whitaker, and his wife. A short while later, when the Whitakers made plans to spend a year in Lima, where Dr. Whitaker would be working under a Fulbright scholarship, they invited the young O'Neill to visit them during his summer vacation. O'Neill recalled: "A lot of times people say things like that just to be polite, but those poor people didn't have a second chance!" A native of Texas, O'Neill had already been to Mexico a few times on short birding jaunts that had whetted his appetite for tropical birds. Nothing in North America could compare with the spectacular variety of birds in the tropics.

As friendly and polite as he was eager, O'Neill got along well with the Whitakers. After two months in Lima, during which much of O'Neill's bird collecting consisted of picking up dead seabirds off the beach, the Whitakers decided to visit some pre-Inca ruins at Trujillo in northern Peru and then fly on to Pucallpa. O'Neill was excited at the chance to see more birds, and to be "in the wild." Once in Pucallpa, Dr. Whitaker was stricken with a recurrence of the emphysema that had plagued him for several years. A long drive on dusty roads had precipitated an attack that sent him to a local hospital operated by missionaries. O'Neill, with a twinge of guilt, rejoiced in his sudden opportunity. While Whitaker was trapped in Pucallpa for ten days recovering, O'Neill hiked in the jungle around the town, gun in hand, and collected birds, none of which, of course, he had ever seen before.

Once back at Oklahoma, he showed his collection of bird skins to Sutton, who marveled at the number and variety of species the inexperienced O'Neill had found. Sutton immediately referred O'Neill to another of the deans of American ornithology, George Lowery of LSU, who was keenly interested in building a collection of neotropical avifauna and had several graduate students doing fieldwork in Central

America. Lowery was ecstatic. Nearly every species O'Neill had brought back was new to the LSU collection; there were even three new families of birds represented.

Not surprisingly, O'Neill went back to Peru the next summer, this time with a National Science Foundation grant and the official support of Lowery and LSU. Then, in 1963, on his third trip, a missionary by the name of Mildred Larsen, who had earlier befriended him, asked him to dinner one evening at her home. At the end of the evening she brought out a bag and handed it to O'Neill somewhat apologetically. Here were a few bird skins she had gotten from some Indians up north. She thought O'Neill might have some use for them, but they weren't in very good shape, she was sorry to say. O'Neill opened the bag and took the birds out one by one. He recognized the first three species, but the fourth one didn't register. It was a tanager— that much he knew—a beautiful black-and-cream–colored bird the size of a blackbird, whose most striking feature was its brilliant orange throat. There were roughly fifteen hundred known birds in Peru at the time, but there was no field guide of any kind to refer to.

A month later, back at Oklahoma, O'Neill looked through all the scientific papers on tanagers and turned up nothing like it. Lowery, to whom the birds had been shipped, searched the literature as well, also with no results. In October, on a trip to New York City, Lowery went to the American Museum of Natural History to compare O'Neill's tanager with those in the museum's collection, the largest collection of bird specimens in the world. A few days later he wrote back to O'Neill: "Caramba! The tanager is unquestionably a new species and probably a member of an undescribed genus." Lowery gushed on excitedly, describing how "the bird caused more excitement in the Department of Birds than anything else in many a moon," and noted with glee, "One after another the 'experts' came into the place where we were working and would pick up the tanager and carry it over to the 'first series' [case]. But one after the other came away muttering exclamations." The American Museum, after all, was the preeminent zoological museum in the country. Frank Chapman, formerly a director of the museum, had been to Peru and written two books on birdlife in the regions he'd studied. And Curator of Birds John Zimmer had spent nearly twenty-five years examining specimens of Peruvian birds in minute detail, publishing a series of sixty-six papers on his work, which today is still considered the first place to look for taxonomic data on Peruvian avifauna. Now, barely twenty-one years old and not yet a college graduate, John O'Neill had discovered a bird new to science, an accomplishment that stunned the ornithological community. It was the first new tanager—a particularly colorful and conspicuous family of birds—in thirty-four years.

Although Lowery had not set foot in South America, he shared in the glory of describing the new species because he had overseen O'Neill's trip to Peru and because O'Neill simply did not have enough experience to write such an important article by himself. Together O'Neill and Lowery named and described the species: *Wetmorethraupis sterrhopteron,* the Orange-throated Tanager.

One of the most striking traits of the tanager was the orange feathers on the throat, which were stiff and waxy, a peculiarity that set it apart from all other genera of tanagers (though Lowery and O'Neill noticed that some male birds of the genus *Spindalis* had a few waxy feathers on the throat). The Orange-throated Tanager's bill was also considerably larger than that of other related genera, so Lowery assured the young O'Neill that they could safely consider the bird a new genus as well as a new species. In giving the bird its generic name, *Wetmorethraupis,* they honored Dr. Alexander Wetmore, a distinguished ornithologist with the American Museum of Natural History and one of Lowery's mentors. Lowery, in fact, had made the mistake of assuming a bit too much responsibility for the new species. Wanting to honor Wetmore, Lowery had written to him, informing him that he and O'Neill were going to erect a new genus in his name. O'Neill, who had not agreed to any such thing, was furious and let Lowery know it. Lowery, as director of the LSU Museum of Natural Science, might have given O'Neill a good lecture at this point about not overstepping his bounds as a lowly college student, but instead Lowery wrote a long apologetic letter and offered to call Wetmore and retract the honor. Considering the embarassment this would have caused Lowery, O'Neill relented, so *Wetmorethraupis* it was. They decided that *sterrhopteron,* Greek for "stiff feather," was a good descriptive species name.[7]

When O'Neill and Lowery published their description of *Wetmorethraupis* a year later in April 1964, neither of them had seen the bird alive; no ornithologist had. Thinking on that now, it seems odd that a new bird was introduced to the world without anyone having seen the glint in its eye as it perched on an exposed branch in early morning, or watched as the bird flew off into the blue sky and shrank to an infinitesimal, finally an imaginary, dot that held the eye longer than common sense would demand. The scientific classification of birds, however, depends on measurable characteristics and reasonable speculation, not on the beauty of birds. Most of the birds from South America have been "discovered" by ornithologists who never saw them alive, and in many cases never set foot on the continent. Twentieth-century taxonomists have usually been stay-at-home types who spend their days in the lab bent over trays of specimens looking for a clue to taxonomic relationships that someone else missed.

But not O'Neill. Jubilant over the publication of his paper and his graduation from the University of Oklahoma, he took off for Peru again. Though he planned to do graduate work at LSU under Lowery, he gave himself a full year in Peru to get to know the country and the birds better. His first order of business was to see *Wetmorethraupis.* John Farrand, who graduated from the University of Oklahoma at the same time and later worked as a natural history editor in New York, went with O'Neill, the two of them arriving in Lima in late May. They made their way north to the Department of Amazonas, where they met two missionary colleagues of Mildred Larsen's. They were to visit several villages of the Aguaruna Indians who knew exactly where to find the bird they called *inchítuch.* O'Neill, of course, wanted to be the first ornithologist to see "his" new bird.

He and Farrand first traveled to several other places with the

17

missionaries, seeing dozens of birds new to them. "I had an old pair of binoculars that were hard to focus," Farrand told me one afternoon, "and I complained some about them. We'd gotten a bit testy at being together so much, and John finally gave me his good binoculars one day as if to say, 'Here, you need these more than I do.' "

So it was that O'Neill was carrying Farrand's old field glasses on the day that the Aguaruna led them up into the hills looking for the Orange-throated Tanager. When a flock of birds moved noisily through the high branches late in the morning, O'Neill and Farrand froze and looked up. Farrand saw the bird first, by a split second, saying "there he is" just as O'Neill was trying to get Farrand's binoculars in focus on the same spot. Farrand remembers O'Neill's exact words on the momentous occasion: "Aw, shit."

Such lapses in decorum aside, O'Neill and Farrand got along well enough to travel together for several more months. O'Neill had arranged to visit people he'd met in previous years and had obtained introductions to Americans living in places he had not yet seen. He zigzagged across Peru, much of the time with Farrand and another ornithologist friend, Alan Feduccia. When Farrand and Feduccia went home, O'Neill continued scouting alone. On a flight from Pucallpa to an Indian village to the southeast, O'Neill remembers looking out the plane window and seeing a stunted mountain range known as the Cordillera Divisor sticking up out of the Amazon basin as if a piece had been torn from the Andes and set off by itself. What birds would be in mountains like that? he wondered.

3

 O'Neill has called Lima and spoken to a Peruvian orthodontist he has known since his first years in Peru, who will call a colleague of his and arrange an emergency appointment for Donna, now hurriedly separating a few items she needs to take with her to Lima. She will leave everything else behind in case the expedition must set off without her. O'Neill flags down a taxi and together they head off for the airport.

When I mention to Tony Meyer that I'd like to track down a fossil left in Pucallpa twenty-seven years ago by writer Peter Matthiessen, Tony is immediately interested. In April 1960, after six months of trekking all over South America, a journey splendidly recounted in *The Cloud Forest,* Peter Matthiessen was ending his adventure with an excursion on the Río Mapuya, a small river about 150 miles south of here. Matthiessen was in search of a giant fossil rumored to be resting in the muddy banks of the river. After weeks of river travel and much skepticism, he found the fossil, just where his guide, a man from Pucallpa named César Cruz, had said it would be. The fossil was the upper jaw of a giant reptile the American Museum of Natural History later determined to be a crocodile that was probably nearly thirty-five feet in length. It was "so large and heavy that it [took], if not six men, at least four strong men to lift it," Matthiessen wrote.[1]

Matthiessen and Cruz took the fossil back to Pucallpa, hoping to ship it to Lima and then to the United States, where paleontologists could study it. But just as they were about to do so, the local police confiscated it, having heard from a third party, Victor Macedo, that it belonged to him. Matthiessen spent a week in Pucallpa trying to get the matter cleared up, but finally had to leave with only photographs of the fossil. Later that year, the poet Allen Ginsberg saw the fossil, still sitting in the police yard, but since then, no one Matthiessen knew had seen or heard of it.

Tony and I begin our search by asking the clerks at the hotel lobby if they've ever heard of the fossil or of César Cruz, who would now be in his seventies. As Tony asks them—his Spanish is quite good, mine nearly nonexistent—the two clerks begin shaking their heads no, but then one repeats the name Cruz and Tony quickly turns to me to say they know of a César Cruz, an old man who lives not far from the hotel. We should ask about him at the Café Blasito, where the owner knows Cruz. We head off down the street—eight blocks north, we were told—and after asking directions once more, we find the Blasito. In the back of the place a man acknowledges that he knows Cruz but says Cruz no longer lives in Pucallpa—he has moved to Lima. He does, however, know of a Señor Rivas, a sculptor who knows Cruz and might know something about the fossil. Rivas lives just two doors down the street.

We knock at the second door, and a small woman opens it and invites us to sit down on a wooden bench in the entranceway while she goes to get Rivas. The house is small and dark, as are nearly all the dwellings in Peruvian towns, and though the walls are rough masonry and unfinished boards, there is something pleasant about this place. In front of us is a sculpture in wood—a sea serpent, it appears to be, five feet high and maybe seven feet long, all of it carved from one piece—and we can see the outlines of several other works in the room beyond. They look mysterious and interesting—a work of art is the last thing anyone would expect to find in Pucallpa.

Several minutes pass before Rivas appears, but he comes in smiling, wiping his hands on a rag. He is a handsome man in his late forties, vigor in his face and light in his dark eyes. When Tony asks him about Cruz, Rivas says immediately that he knows Cruz and has heard of the fossil—it is still in Pucallpa. The conversation continues as Tony asks the whereabouts of the mandibula and about Cruz, who Rivas says has not moved to Lima at all, but lives just a few doors down. Rivas begins drawing a map of how to get to the Tambo Cultural, where the fossil is now kept. His hands are gnarled—even scarred, it seems—but the strength in them from his work chiseling wood is evident.

When he is done with the map we cannot help but ask to see some of his sculptures, and he gladly takes us to a back room where there are a dozen finished pieces propped against the walls. They are all imaginative and forceful renderings of people and animals and folktales. There is one nearly life-sized sculpture of a woman giving birth, a stunning work of art. The baby is half out of the mother, and because it is all one piece of wood the effect of the baby being part of the mother—both the oneness and impending separation—is powerful. In referring to the birth, Rivas uses an idiomatic expression—*dar luz*—which, translated literally, means that the mother is "giving light."

He leads us into his workroom and shows us the current project: the figure of a woman carved from a giant cedar log. It will be the figurehead on the prow of an Austrian medical ship that travels up and down the Ucayali. I look again at Rivas's hands and arms and see more clearly scars on both. He tells us that ten years ago a tree he was cutting fell on him, tearing open both forearms and severing the nerves. He had an operation but was told he should not think about continuing his sculpting. He'd be lucky if he could ever move his fingers again at all. He did rehabilitation exercises for months—he demonstrates them for us—and finally restored some of the movement in his hands, and eventually by constant effort got enough muscle and nerve control back to hold his chisels and hammer.

Now, we take the map and with Rivas walk down the street a short distance. At the locked gate to an alleyway Rivas calls out for Cruz, but there's no answer. We go back into the Blasito and when Rivas questions the owner again, he now says that Cruz is in the United States for a relative's wedding. Rivas, however, says that more likely he is in Lima visiting someone. In the space of an hour we've accumulated four explanations of Cruz's whereabouts, but what we've lost in translation is anyone's guess. We do, however, know the name of the doctor—Ulises Reategeci—who has the fossil at the place Rivas has mentioned, the Tambo Cultural. We thank Rivas for his help and set off down the broken sidewalk, heading west. The air is humid, the sun beating down, and at Tony's pace—a jaunty clip—we are soon sweating profusely. There are only a few thin, strung-out clouds in the sky, and everywhere vultures riding the updrafts. The houses and shops grow dirtier and more ragged the farther we go from the center of town. After seven blocks we hit a wide paved street where we are to turn south. A few minutes later we reach a main intersection where the Tambo Cultural is supposed to be, but on the corner is nothing more than a drab little building with a window open to the street, from which a boy is selling soft drinks and candy. We are parched after our walk, so we ask for two Inca Colas, a Peruvian soft drink that is the color of lime Kool-Aid but does not taste quite as good. Often it is served warm, since refrigeration is a great luxury here; but when we are handed the bottles, they are quite cold and we chug them down like ten-year-olds.

But where is the Tambo Cultural and Dr. Ulises Reategeci? Tony asks the boy, who says that this *is* the Tambo Cultural. He tells us to go around to another door, where he meets us and shows us in. We wait in the entranceway while he goes to get the doctor. Fifteen minutes pass before Reategeci appears. A short, squat man, he has a three-day beard and a suspicious look in his eye. His hair is greasy black. Perspiration is running down his cheeks and his once white shirt is stained with sweat and dirt. He looks like a doctor as played by Peter Lorre. Tony carefully explains who we are and that Señor Rivas has directed us here. We'd like very much to see the fossil and take some pictures of it, Tony tells him. Our doctor stands, unblinking, and says that this fossil never belonged to any American named

Matthiessen, that it now belongs to someone named Raul de los Ríos, without whose permission we cannot look at it, though it sits in the very next room. Our luck has run out, it seems, but we ask where we might find de los Ríos. He lives about eight blocks north—this is as specific as the doctor gets.

Off we go back down the road we've just been on. We pass Rivas's street, block four, and continue counting, but a few feet farther the street disintegrates. There are no distinct cross streets and the road has turned to mud. On our right is a row of houses, on our left a shantytown. The refuse from both lies in something too uneven to be called a ditch. Human waste and rotting fruit rinds line both sides of the road and in places form piles in the middle, so that we must find our way around them, jumping back and forth across the ditch, trying not to slip into it. When we come upon a woman outside her house, Tony asks the whereabouts of de los Ríos. She tells us we are going the right way. Another dozen houses, perhaps, and we'll find him. We count houses, stop again when we see someone else, and are told we have to go back a few houses. This routine continues until we have gone back and forth several times, narrowing down the possibilities. Finally we end up at a two-story structure that may be de los Ríos's house. We knock and a man comes to the door. He looks hot and tired, but he is indeed Señor Raul de los Ríos, and he invites us in.

He is friendly but cautious, and as he tells us about the fossil he repeats several times that he is the rightful owner. When Tony asks him about the original dispute over ownership, de los Ríos explains that Victor Macedo eventually was declared the owner of the mandíbula, negating Matthiessen and Cruz's claim, and that he, de los Ríos, a friend of Macedo's, kept the fossil for him, later purchasing it. He tells us he has official documents to prove his ownership. For some time he collected artifacts and put on natural-history exhibitions, taking the fossil once to Lima, where there were people who wanted to buy it, but he refused to sell. He has left it in the charge of the doctor, who, de los Ríos now exclaims, is a "complete fool" for not showing it to us. He's "not in touch with reality," de los Ríos says. He is supposed to show the fossil to people, not keep it hidden. As de los Ríos talks, he cools himself with a fan made of vulture feathers. We are sitting at a table in a room with a dirt floor and nothing more than an out-of-date calendar on one wall. Tony tells him how much we would like to see the fossil. He cannot go with us, he says, but he will write something that we can take to the doctor. He disappears into the next room and is gone for some time, appearing finally with an elaborate letter instructing the doctor to show Señores Meyer and Stap the fossil. As we leave, I take some pictures of him in front of his house. He has on grimy pants and an old green shirt that hangs loosely on him, but he stands erect and tries to present the best possible pose. The late afternoon sun shines on him and he squints, but keeps his head up and looks directly into the camera.

With our letter of permission in hand, we hustle back to the doctor's office where we are greeted as coldly as before. Dr. Reategeci leads us through a courtyard where he has been playing chess with another man and into his office, a small dirty room. On the floor along the west wall is a heavy wooden crate the size of a footlocker, though only half the height. He tells us to go ahead and have a look and then leaves the room. The crate is dusty, suggesting no one has touched it in some time. The top planks are loose so we lift them off and set them against the wall. And there it is, the jawbone of a crocodile that was perhaps big enough to swallow a man whole.

If the entire creature had somehow been preserved—all thirty-five feet of him—he would not fit in this or any other room in the house. The sockets from which teeth once protruded are twice as thick as my thumb. I try to picture a crocodilian head, teeth as long as butcher's knives protruding from that familiar, crooked smile that is as funny as it is menacing, bubble eyes bulging from a forehead as broad as a moose's, a body like the trunk of an oak tree. Such an animal would hardly be out of place today in South America where it would fit appropriately into the big rivers that rule the continent. We stand and stare at the fossil. The sockets are mostly filled with a copper-colored sediment. I kneel and run a hand over the smooth, petrified stone that fills the crocodile's immense palate. The mandibula is too heavy for the two of us to lift, and we strain just to roll it onto its side. It strikes me that if the fossil were where it belonged, in a museum, I'd not have the opportunity to examine it like this, to feel its tooth sockets and take measure of it by its heft. Nevertheless, it should be in a display case rather than this box with clumps of dirt and gum wrappers in the corners. Other than Matthiessen and Ginsberg, we are the only Americans ever to have seen it. It has rested here for the last twenty-five years, as hidden from the world as it was for thousands of years in the mud of the Río Mapuya.

Like many Latin American countries Peru does not have the resources, financial or otherwise, to properly handle its great archeological treasures. Efforts to do so have been inconsistent. The condition of the research area of the Museo de Historia Natural is pitiful. The bird skin collection is housed in a poorly lit room with cracked outer walls that do not come all the way to the ceiling. The gaps let in the weather and destructive vermin. And until Irma Franke recently took over as Curator of Birds, the position had been vacant for more than ten years. (Perhaps Cecilia or Gabriel will one day replace Prof. Franke.)

Tony and I linger near the fossil for half an hour, not knowing what to do except take in as much as we can since we will surely never see it again. The excitement I felt at locating the mandibula has dissipated rather quickly. Getting here was more than half the adventure, and the knowledge that the fossil will remain here for who knows how long has left me feeling at loose ends. When a young woman enters the room, Tony, remembering for a moment that he is a doctor, asks her if the X rays an assistant hung up a moment ago are hers, and when she nods yes, Tony says, "Let's get out of here." She has an advanced case of tuberculosis, Tony tells me, and her persistent cough may well be filling the room with bacteria.

When we leave, the afternoon is nearly over. The sun is low in the sky and it blazes our backs as we return to the hotel to tell the others about the fossil.

25

By dinnertime O'Neill has returned from the airport. Donna is on her way to Lima, though whether she'll be able to get a seat on the return flight tomorrow is questionable.

"Well, we'll find out tomorrow," O'Neill says.

In any case, there's no sign yet of Angelo and Manuel. They weren't at all certain they would make it back from Abujao tonight. The sun has already set. No one envies Angelo and Manuel being on the Ucayali at night in a speedboat swerving around flotsam.

Around the dinner table the talk is full of anticipation over getting into the jungle. Paul Freed, who is bouncing with energy, has already been crawling around in the plants beside the swimming pool looking for lizards and frogs. Pete jokes that he wants to get a close-up photo of a *Bothrops,* the generic name of one of South America's deadliest snakes.

"Let's try not to use up all the antivenin the first week," Tony says.

A discussion ensues about the antivenin and potential allergic reactions to it. Pete says that he believes he's allergic to some farm animals. Tony makes a mock horrified face. Antivenin is made from horse serum, and if one is allergic to horses then the antivenin is going to be worthless; an allergic reaction might be more serious than the snakebite. Tony tells Pete that he's a goner if he gets bitten, and then teases him about it. Pete, who has an easy smile and plenty of enthusiasm, laughs and kids around with "Dr. Tony," but he slips in a few serious questions—the point has not been lost on him entirely.

O'Neill does not enter the conversation. He has seen enough of the jungle to know that it's unlikely that anyone will step on a *Bothrops.* In twenty-six years, he has had only one close call with a snake. He's pragmatic about the risks of such expeditions, taking every reasonable precaution but showing no fear of the jungle's notorious dangers. He scoffs at the public's distorted image of a jungle. Nevertheless, he is one of only a handful of zoologists still engaged in "old-time" expeditions. While other zoologists explore the "frontiers" of science by plotting out theories on a computer, O'Neill is still bushwhacking his way into areas where no one has set foot before, staying for months at a time, and coming out with birds the scientific world did not know existed.

4

 O'Neill hardly looks like an ornithologist about to set off for ten weeks in the jungle. Around the LSU campus he usually wears gray slacks, dress shoes, and a shortsleeved sports shirt. He does not worry about trying to look like either the distinguished professional or the intrepid explorer. His professional reputation is firmly established. His work on South American avifauna has created a new foundation on which all other ornithologists stand when they look at neotropical birds. It is virtually impossible to find a major paper of the last fifteen years on neotropical ornithology that does not have a reference to O'Neill.

Since O'Neill's discovery of the Orange-throated Tanager, other museums have renewed their interest in South America. Chicago's Field Museum, which had a long history of work in South America that lapsed during the 1950s, hired John Fitzpatrick, who had done his undergraduate work under Ernst Mayr at Harvard. Fitzpatrick, now head of the Bird Division at the Field Museum, has been involved in the discovery of several new species of birds from Peru, including some co-authored with O'Neill. Each year Fitzpatrick returns to the same general area where he is surveying the birds isolated on

27

several mountain ridges of different altitudes. John Terborgh of Princeton has also done extensive work in Peru. Terborgh directs a study site in Manu National Park—one of the largest parks in the world—in southern Peru. Terborgh and his associates at Manu are engaged in a wide range of studies, one being a ten-year avifaunal survey of a section of this primary rainforest, the first long-term survey of birds in any area of Peru. There are a handful of other knowledgeable ornithologists working regularly in South America, but there were probably more ornithologists fighting over how best to save the California Condor than are engaged in neotropical studies.

O'Neill's discovery of the Orange-throated Tanager in 1963 was followed by the Selva Cacique (1965), then the Black-faced Cotinga (1966), Elusive Antpitta (1969), Pardusco (1976), Long-whiskered Owlet (1977), Cinnamon-breasted Tody-tyrant (1979), Ochre-fronted Antpitta (1983), Inca Wren (1985), Cinnamon Screech Owl (1986), and Ash-throated Antwren (1986). (To be fair, several of these new species descriptions were co-authored by a colleague.) As if that wasn't enough, O'Neill is one of the country's finest natural-history painters. His paintings appear in numerous field guides and have been exhibited worldwide, products of a talent that has earned him the respect of fellow artists such as Roger Tory Peterson and Guy Tudor, whose own paintings—gifts or trades—grace the walls of O'Neill's red brick home in a quiet neighborhood of Baton Rouge.

The house is filled with items O'Neill has picked up in South America, everything with its own place on a crowded shelf or table on which O'Neill's two cats tiptoe despite repeated threats. The kitchen table has been removed and in its place is a tall cage with a ragged African Gray Parrot named Pigpen. O'Neill has had the bird for twelve years and gives it plenty of attention, but the parrot has plucked out most of its body feathers, apparently in anxiety fits over O'Neill's yearly trips to Peru. At first light each day Pigpen lets loose with a truly amazing repertoire of household sounds: an ear-splitting rendition of a catfight followed by musical phrases from various backyard songbirds or the sound of water burbling down a drain, then partial conversations with animals and people long since departed—"Wanna go out?" he asks the ghost of a dog—topped off with a perfect imitation of a Volkswagen backing out of the driveway. When O'Neill wanders over to the cage, the bird is likely to admonish him with an O'Neill maxim: "Work work work."

O'Neill usually spends his mornings on campus, discussing the work of graduate students, answering letters, and preparing reports before returning home in the afternoon to paint. Foster Hall, which houses the LSU Museum of Natural Science, is an undistinguished three-story building capped by a Spanish tile roof of meager slope. At the front of the building is a courtyard shaded by live oaks where art students, whose classes meet on the third floor, often sit with sketch pads in their laps. Foster Hall has a sleepy air about it, an anonymity. Maybe it is the quiet courtyard or the officious pillars that nearly hide the face of the building. Or maybe it is because the only students who hang out there are serious about either art or birds, and what could be more anonymous than that?

The undergraduate zoology students are aware of the peculiarity of their endeavors. These are, after all, kids who, on finding a freshly killed bird in the road, feel a secret excitement over the opportunity it will give them to practice their dissecting technique. At the back of the building is a battered shed with screened front where the skeletons of recently deceased mammals are hung to dry. The smell that lingers about the sidewalk must make the place notorious. A crudely painted sign hangs on the shed: Dead Things R Us.

The front entrance to the building leads directly into the museum's public exhibit—one large room with glass cases containing the fauna native to Louisiana. The birds and mammals appear faded, the labels look a hundred years old, and the ambience is particularly antique, even for a museum. The stuffed heads of bison, elk, and moose jut out like trophies from the wall above the exhibit cases, and at one end of the room a large case holds a Bengal tiger—Mike, the LSU Tigers' original team mascot, who died in 1956. You can push a button and hear Mike roar.

A PARROT WITHOUT A NAME

Behind the exhibit area is "the range"—the specimen collection. The range is separated from the public exhibition area by two heavy metal doors. Inside, the high ceiling is strung with fluorescent lamps that are supplemented by two frosted-glass skylights. Three rows of specimen cases dominate the area, which is roughly fifty by eighty feet. Each case is bigger than an oven. They are stacked three high and placed back-to-back, the three rows running nearly the length of the room, much as bookshelves in a library. The cases are uniformly army green, set on a green industrial tile floor. The interior walls are brick painted something between gray and white. Along the back wall is a row of semi-opaque windows.

It seems funny that on the floor directly above is an art workroom, airy and undivided, the windows lifted open. But here in the range, direct sunlight is not desirable. Bird feathers retain their color quite well in general, but over decades they do lose something. Dark colors edge into brown and browns tend toward rusty red, a phenomenon known as "foxing." The range, though not really dark, is dull, toneless. Its colors, in palettes any art student would envy, are locked away in shallow trays. For a visitor, O'Neill will pull out a tray of small tanagers to illustrate the point: canary yellow, turquoise green, opalescent blue, bronze-gold, copper and chestnut, and dark cobalt blue— a dazzling iridescence that runs together like a rainbow in a pool of oil. The birds lie belly-up in neat, tight rows, data tags tied to their withered legs, which are crossed as if in repose. They are stuffed with cotton that protrudes slightly from the eye sockets, a jarring image and a stark reminder that this is science, not art.

The LSU collection is the fourth largest university-related collection of bird specimens in the United States, but funding is inadequate and space is a serious problem (the cafeteria at the American Museum of Natural History is larger than the entire LSU range). The general condition of the LSU range seems summed up by the sad-eyed gaze of a moose that looks down from the west wall. Along the outer wall, every third or fourth window has a yellowed sign taped to it: Functional Window. A new word processor occupies a narrow room that was made by knocking out a doorway and tapping into what had been dead space between two walls. As in most research museums an odd array of items is scattered about the room: a couple of dozen plastic bags of small skeletons; a collection of vials with stomach contents; a ratty stuffed rhea atop one of the specimen cases; and, of course, maps and bird paintings hanging from every available space. This does not present any real problem, but the specimen cases themselves are so full—birds laid in sideways and crossways—that no more room exists for the bird skins that have been collected in the last two years. And the metal door of the "type case," where the museum keeps the ideal individual bird from which a new species has been described— something like the printer's plate for a ten-thousand-dollar bill—is held shut by slipping a piece of paper between the door and frame.

O'Neill's response to the situation has always been bemusement and sarcasm. When George Lowery died in 1978, O'Neill was appointed director of the museum, but he resigned the position four years later to get back to research and painting; he grew up with a passion for birds, not paperwork. For several years the museum drifted into further disrepair, and though part of his current responsibility is to raise money for the museum, O'Neill has not been particularly suc- cessful. The very thing that has brought some glory to the museum— the extensive fieldwork—has left it without an effective director. Though each curator has taken a turn as director, no one really wants the job and the university has not yet seen the wisdom of hiring a full-time administrator. J. V. "Van" Remsen, Curator of Birds, received a National Science Foundation grant to buy new specimen cases, but, until the art department gives up some of its classrooms upstairs as promised several years ago, there is nowhere to put the cases. These worries are exactly what O'Neill is happy to leave behind him when he heads off on an expedition.

5

 In the morning there's a flurry of activity. Late last night Angelo knocked on my door. He and Manuel had gotten back from Abujao a few minutes earlier and conferred with O'Neill, who decided we should leave first thing in the morning. Be up and ready to go by five-thirty, Angelo told me. Now, all the gear is being piled in one corner of the lobby. From there it will be loaded into Al Gentry's jeep. It will take several trips in the jeep to get all the stuff down to the river and onto the boat, so Cecilia and Mara will go with the first load and stay on the boat to guard things there. O'Neill is rushing back and forth, making certain no one has forgotten anything. He has to pay the hotel bill and exchange dollars for intis, and once again he is counting the intis that he has divided up among himself, Angelo, and Pete. In the midst of this activity I retreat to make a phone call to the States, and when I return O'Neill comes hustling over. Did I have a large green duffel bag? he wants to know. Did I already bring it downstairs? Was it with the other bags? Someone from the street came in a moment ago, picked up one of the bags, and walked out the door with it. Three people, including O'Neill, were keeping an eye on the gear, but no one caught

on until the man had rounded the corner of the street. When Manuel went after him he was already half a block away, then round another corner, and gone. What hits me first is that while I conscientiously divided up most of my belongings—half my shirts in one bag, half in another—the bag that has been lost contained all of my toiletries and medicines and all the books I brought along to read in camp, where, I know from experience, the days can sometimes grow long. My notebooks, binoculars, and camera are safe because they are in my daypack, which never leaves my side, and I realize that my tent and sleeping bag are in the army duffel that is still here, so I try to reason that it could be worse. I remember that a new Buck knife was in the stolen bag—whoever has it now will be happy, I'm sure. And then I realize that I've lost my sleeping pad. And my underwear—I'm left with only what I'm wearing. O'Neill is not going with us this morning. He'll stay behind and wait for Donna to return and then catch up with us in Abujao. Thus, he can shop around and buy a few items for me.

By nine o'clock the last bags have been taken to the river, and we say a hasty farewell to O'Neill, hop into a taxi, and are off, arriving at the river moments later. The Ucayali is the major highway in this region. On the bank above the water a shantytown and marketplace have settled into the mud. To get to the river we must sidestep down the sloppy bank, about a forty-foot drop, trying to avoid the piles of rotting fish and fruit. Vultures stand about in groups of three or four, picking at the refuse. At the waterline there are dozens of boats of all sizes crowded together, some that have just arrived from somewhere with bananas and papayas, others getting ready to leave, and more than a few that appear to be neither coming nor going, whose owners loll about and look content to sit around for another day or two. We have hired one of the numerous *colectivos,* or river taxis, that have daily routes up and downriver, from which Mara is now waving and shouting something to the effect that it's about time we got here. She and Cecilia have been sitting here for three hours already in the middle of this miserable scene. The boat is forty feet from bow to stern, maybe eight feet wide, with wood seats built along each side and covered by a tin roof, the sides open to the breeze. Our gear is stacked three and four bags high down the center, and we must squeeze into a seat and turn our feet at odd angles to fit into the spaces below. Camilo has gone back to town with Al Gentry's jeep, which he will store at the hotel, so we wait for half an hour before he returns, our excitement mitigated by knowing that we are going to be all day on the Ucayali in these cramped quarters.

At ten forty-five we shove off. In five minutes we are well away from Pucallpa, a big outboard motor sending us upriver and far beyond hotels and telephones and motorbikes and dusty streets. A string of islands runs the length of the Ucayali, so that it is virtually impossible to ever see both banks of the river at the same time, but even so the river is expansive, diminished only a little by the low sky that hangs over us this morning. The Ucayali begins south of here where it is fed by the Río Urubamba, which itself originates over 600 miles away near Lake Titicaca, at 12,500 feet, the highest lake in the world. To the north, nearly as far away, the Ucayali empties into the Amazon, the greatest river on earth: 4,000 miles long, more than a thousand tributaries (ten of them larger than the Mississippi), one-fifth of all the fresh water on earth flowing at a rate that would fill Lake Ontario in three hours. As is the case with nearly all the major rivers in Peru, the banks here are dark mud that rises vertically 40 feet or more, atop which are thatched-roof dwellings on stilts surrounded by fruit trees and other garden crops in little plots known as *chacras.* In the wet season the river may rise above these banks, and it is sometimes possible for the local people to paddle a canoe up to their doorstep. The Ucayali River, like the Amazon, acts as a major distribution barrier for many Peruvian birds. Because some species occurring on one side of the river are so closely related to another species on the other side, ornithologists have theorized that river formation in South America was a primary factor in the evolution of species. As rivers grew wider, two populations of a single species would no longer cross the open space and thus, over time, they split into two distinct species. Angelo's Ph.D. dissertation deals with several pairs of such sibling species, which he examined biochemically as a way of predicting how closely the species might be related.

Where the river has left mudflats, there are, occasionally, rice paddies, whose pale green grass riffles in the breeze. Vultures are wheeling high above us and swifts and swallows sweep past. Pete has his binoculars in hand, calling out one bird after another, nearly all of which he is seeing for the first time. Until now he has known these birds only by the specimens in the museum. A pair of Large-billed Terns comes up on our right, flying alongside us for a few seconds, then veering off across the open water. The first hour goes quickly. At noon we pass an immense sandbar a couple of hundred yards to our right where two Indian women walk peacefully along with baskets atop their heads. They are the only figures in the landscape. Because the sandbar is part of an island that appears uninhabited—an isolated desert in this most unlikely of places—I wonder where they are going. They look like characters in a Fellini film, with no past or future.

The drone of the outboard motor carries us into the afternoon. The river, after a while, grows dull. The distant banks look the same, young trees of uniform height making the "green wall" that so many previous travelers have referred to. From this distance it appears lifeless. The day is hot, the sky has opened up, and the sun is softened only a little by a few high, thin clouds. A pleasant breeze swirls around us. As we come round a bend in the river and head east momentarily, Angelo, who has been scanning the horizon with his binoculars, says, "Look—there they are!" Far off, through the haze, we can see what at first looks like a mass of clouds rising out of the jungle. But as I look hard at this phenomenon, its edges become more distinct. There are slopes rather than billows, and peaks instead of white crowns. We all have our binoculars raised, though for a minute or two no one says anything. Then, Angelo speaks again.

"Well, that's where we're going." He looks at Al Gentry. "What do you think of them?"

"They look awfully far away," Gentry says, smiling.

For half an hour the Cordillera Divisor remains within sight; then the river takes a ninety-degree turn and the near bank blocks our view. The conversation has dissolved and everyone seems preoccupied with trying to find a restful position for the remainder of the trip. The time passes slowly. About an hour before sunset, a river dolphin breaks the surface—once, twice, and then is gone. A little later we pass by several piranha jumping above the water in shallow arcs. Late in the afternoon we arrive at the mouth of the Río Abujao, turn in, and leave the Ucayali behind. The Abujao, though it cannot compare at all with the Ucayali, is still as much as two hundred feet wide here. It will be another hour now, maybe two, before we reach the village. The sun sinks below the tree line, a deep smudge of tropical orange that makes a broad brush stroke across the sky. The river has a silver cast to it and the air has cooled down quickly.

By six o'clock it is quite dark and there's no sign of the village. We've all grown restless, even the few local people who have come with us. A boy climbs onto the tin roof and walks noisily above our heads from the stern to the prow, where he now stands with the boatman, who, throughout the trip, has been watching the current and the islands and now and then signaling a change of course to the driver at the outboard behind us. Another long forty-five minutes pass; then there is a sudden shout and the outboard is cut back as we aim for the left bank. By now it's pitch-black. Someone is holding a lantern on the shore, and Angelo and Pete have dug out their flashlights and are shining them at the mud landing—if that's what it is—of Abujao. Everyone is standing up, anxious to get off and use their legs again. Angelo and Pete are both shouting at us to watch our bags. Then Angelo says we should sit tight, let the local people all get off first so we can see what goes with them, and then we will unload; but of course two or three people are already up, standing in the way, another boy is running over the roof where no one can see him, someone else has ahold of one of our bags and seems to be volunteering to help, and Manuel, who is already ashore, is suggesting we start unloading right away while he goes to look for additional help. Tony asks if we can afford to pay for this help, and that sets Angelo to figuring, but then he abruptly stops and says that Manuel knows what he's doing—in cases like this it is always best to defer to him. We also have to pay the owner of the *colectivo,* so Pete and Angelo are comparing who has what in intis. It's best to save as many small-denomination bills as possible, since from now on the people we meet will not be able to change any larger bills.

"So, are we coming or going?" says Paul.

We begin climbing off the boat, jumping from the prow onto the bank. Each of us has a bag or two of personal items, so we look for a place to set them down, but even with several flashlights shining here and there it's impossible to get a sense of what surrounds us. The darkness is profound. All I can tell is that from the waterline the bank rises at a forty-five-degree angle for several feet and then becomes a nearly vertical wall of mud about twenty feet high. Getting the trunks to the top of the bank is going to be a chore. I stand off to one side, having found a small foothold, waiting to see how we are going to go about this. Angelo suggests that Cecilia and I stay here to watch the supplies as they come off the boat. Mara will guard them at the other end, wherever that is, and everyone else will lug them up the bank. Because my bag was stolen this morning, everyone is particularly concerned about how easily something could disappear in this darkness. It's less likely for that to happen in such a small village, but it seems better at this point to be extra cautious. Manuel returns to say he's found a place to store the gear, on the porch of the local bar; so the labor begins.

Many of the villagers have lined up atop the bank to watch the spectacle, and they get their money's worth. The show lasts for nearly an hour. At the bar, a thatched-roof, open-sided structure, the trunks and bags have been piled all over the porch. The spectators have followed us and are now lingering about the edges of the building. Since Marta has stayed behind with O'Neill to wait for Donna, Manuel will cook dinner. He asks Angelo for the items he will need: spaghetti-sauce mix, noodles, sardines, the big pot, water, et cetera.

A PARROT WITHOUT A NAME

Pete gets out his list of what's what. The numbered list of items corresponds to numbers written on each trunk or bag. All of the items are in separate trunks, and we quickly realize that no one thought to stack the trunks with the numbers visible, nor is there any way to get at many of the trunks without crawling over the others. They have all been packed together two or three high. Paul makes the most of this. He is not too tired or hungry to joke about the predicament ("Hey, Pete, that's real specific—it says here that trunk number twenty-one contains 'food' "), and in fact we are all too giddy to be frustrated by the situation. It feels wonderful to be standing up, to be away from Pucallpa, and to know that the Río Shesha awaits us. The fact that we don't know where we're going to sleep or where the sardines are (I'm hoping we won't find them) seems incidental.

In due time each item is discovered and Manuel sets off across the field to a house which has a kerosene stove he will use for cooking. The night is warm and humid, so when someone points out that we are in fact at a bar, we all put in an order for anything wet. The beer and soft drinks are warm but they will be our last luxury, and accordingly we act like gluttons. When Manuel brings back a huge pot of spaghetti, we dish it up eagerly and find places to sit down. The talk is full of good humor, and diminishes only a little when Angelo reveals the sleeping arrangements—he wants four volunteers to sleep here on the floor, surrounding the gear on all sides. The rest of us will perhaps get to sleep in some of the houses, though Manuel hasn't negotiated that yet. Angelo, who is known to be easily disturbed from sleep, nevertheless says he will be one of the four, and Manuel will be another. Pete, as low man on the LSU totem pole (as an M.A. student on his first expedition he has already been referred to several times as the "camp slave"), volunteers, and Tony, with some reluctance showing on his face, will be the fourth. Pete and Tony insist that Angelo sleep elsewhere, and Camilo volunteers to take his place.

The spaghetti is gone within fifteen minutes, and Manuel disappears into the darkness to find out where the rest of us can sleep. Meanwhile, we begin restacking all the trunks so there will be room on the floor around them to lay down four sleeping pads. It will be much too warm to get inside a sleeping bag, which means the mosquitoes are going to have a feast. Manuel comes back to say that fifty feet away there is an empty building with screened sides where we can spend the night. We won't have to pitch tents or lie on the floor of someone's house. Paul and Mara, Cecilia and Gabriel, Al Gentry, and myself grab our personal belongings and head off to investigate our good fortune. The building is nearly new, a modern structure that seems out of place here. As we go inside, we quickly realize it is a medical building. There are half a dozen rooms, one with a modern sink and some cupboards with empty medicine bottles in them. Paul and Mara pull together two rows of waiting room seats (an incredible anomaly here) and lay their pads down on them. Gabriel and Cecilia stake out a corner of the next room, and Al Gentry and myself each take individual rooms nearby. I open the door of my room to discover a hospital bed. It is stripped down to the bare springs, but with a foam pad on it (luckily O'Neill packed some extras or I would have none) it will certainly be very comfortable.

Paul shouts from the other room. He has found a wolf spider that is larger, he says, than the one we saw a little while ago on the wall of the bar—which itself was the size of my palm. The spider is nondescript and harmless. You can keep him, I tell Paul. The air is heavy, but a faint breeze comes in through the screen windows, and in a short while I've drifted off.

6

 During his first years in Peru, O'Neill quickly realized how little anyone knew about the country's birds. It became apparent that he could spend the rest of his life studying Peruvian avifauna. There are now seventeen hundred species of birds known in Peru, more species than in any other country (double the number that can be found in all of North America)—18 percent of the world's birds in a country that is less than 1 percent of the earth's land mass. Shaped a bit like California, though three times larger, Peru lies on the west coast of South America where the continent bulges into the Pacific, on the same longitude as the eastern United States. The country's northern border, just touching the equator, hugs Ecuador in the northwest and Colombia in the northeast. Brazil and Bolivia are its eastern neighbors, and thirteen hundred miles south of the equator, in a barren no-man's-land, Peru fades into Chile.

Although the Spanish conquistador Pizarro founded Lima in 1535 and started the search for the cities of gold, today Peru remains, zoologically, a lost world. The famous early naturalists whose names most readily come to mind—Baron von Humboldt, Charles Darwin, Charles Waterton, Henry Walter Bates, Alfred Russel Wallace—spent little if any time in Peru. Richard Spruce, a botanist, lived in South America for fifteen years and did explore the Peruvian Andes for his monograph on Andean flora, but at his death in 1892, when the first great wave of zoological exploration of South America had passed, little was yet known of Peru. Hiram Bingham's discovery of Machu Picchu in 1911 renewed interest in the country, but most subsequent studies were short-term and local, and the amateur collectors that U.S. museums paid to bring back specimens of plants and animals most often kept inadequate records of their work, failing to note exact localities where birds were collected, descriptions of the habitat, and so forth. Stay-at-home researchers pored over the specimens and drew questionable conclusions about the zoogeography of Peru.

What was known of the country was restricted to the coastal towns that were easily accessible by sea routes. To reach the interior one had a choice—from the west, climb across the precipitous Andes, which run the length of the country or, from the east, find a way across tens of thousands of square miles of unbroken jungle. As one of the poorest countries in South America, Peru had few roads and fewer still that were actually passable year-round, which is still essentially the case today. Modern transportation has had little effect on the country. Until recently, air travel was hard to come by. That the wilderness has remained largely undisturbed is one reason Peru's birdlife is still abundant, but the great variety of species is a result of two closely related factors: the country's geologic past, which encouraged intense speciation, and its present form, which contains a greater variety of habitats than an ecologist might be disposed to create if he was to design an ideal country from scratch.

About half of Peru is tropical rainforest where plentiful rain and constant warm air have created a perpetual spring and summer. For centuries plants have flowered throughout the year and animals have gone through their life cycles at an accelerated rate, making the rainforest, in one ecologist's words, a "powerhouse of evolution."[1] Tropical rainforests are the oldest continuous ecosystems on earth. Though over the centuries particular species and ecological communities have come and gone, the general makeup of the tropical rainforest has remained unchanged. We know from fossil evidence that there are rainforests in Southeast Asia that have existed in roughly their present form for seventy million to a hundred million years.[2] Thus, this basic stability and continuity allowed evolution to proceed undisturbed. At the same time there were enough "constructive disruptions" to foster fresh evolutionary changes.

Jurgen Haffer, a German zoogeographer, has been studying neotropical evolution and speciation for more than twenty years, and his theories on how avifauna evolved in South America are widely accepted.[3] The most notable constructive disruption in the neotropics was the glacial activity of the Ice Age, the most recent glaciation having occurred ten thousand years ago. As glaciers spread out from the polar ice caps, the climate of South America changed in two important ways: it became cooler, quite obviously, but also drier, since much of the planet's moisture was locked up as ice. The rainforests then became temperate, like our North American forests, and, what is more important, they shrank into isolated pockets—"forest-islands"—that were surrounded by grasslands too dry and cool to support mature woods. Haffer and others have relied on the work of palynologists to reconstruct these changes in climate and subsequent vegetation. Palynologists have meticulously counted and identified the species of pollen found in core samples of peat taken from South American swamps to determine the kind of vegetation that grew there at different times.

The forest-islands acted as refuges for woodland flora and fauna, or, in other words, genetic reservoirs of plant and animal species that would spread out and repopulate the tropical forest when the glaciers receded. In the meantime, however, the gene flow between individual communities of birds of the same species—trapped in different localities—was suspended. The birds in these forest-island communities responded to particular environmental stimuli and evolved traits best suited to their immediate surroundings. Thus, over a period of time, one species split into two or more distinct birds, which, when they came back into contact with one another, no longer interbred.

Add to this another factor: the Andes, which cover nearly 30 percent of Peru. In glacial times the whole tops of mountains became covered with ice and the temperate zone moved down the mountain, eventually cooling the tropical forests below, which in turn became subtropical or temperate. As the glaciers receded, the lowland forests spread back up the mountain, taking with them birds that were then adapted to temperate or subtropical habitats. Slowly the lowlands grew warmer until they were once again tropical, and the temperate and subtropical birds that had gone up the mountains found themselves isolated from each other on "mountain-islands" (any of the countless lower peaks of the Andes foothills), with unsuitable tropical habitat separating them. Thus new species evolved on many of these mountain-islands. The Cordillera Divisor is a model example of a potential mountain-island, and it falls within an area that Haffer has identified as a likely site for a refuge formed during the Ice Age.

The rainforest and Andes mountains are only the two most conspicuous features of Peru's geography. The country contains other vastly different habitats. Off the coast of Peru, the year-round cold waters of the Humboldt Current blow cool, dry air onto the land, where it warms up quickly and retains what little moisture it had in the first place. Since moist air from the east cannot make it over the high Andes, and there is little seasonal change in most of Peru, this weather pattern remains fairly constant along the coast. Consequently, much of the Peruvian coast is among the most arid spots on earth. The Atacama Desert, which lies mainly in northern Chile but also extends into southern Peru, in fact if not in name, is generally considered to be the driest desert in the world; in many places rainfall has never been recorded.

Moving inland, the west slope of the Andes, sparsely wooded and dry, is tropical at the base, subtropical at the lower altitudes, and temperate higher up. Canyons, rocky ridges, and forest give way to high valley grasslands and finally to icy, windswept peaks as high as twenty-three thousand feet. As the warm coastal air rises on reaching the Andes, it cools down. When it billows over the peaks, moves

43

eastward across the high mountain plains, and descends the warm eastern slope, the warm air from the east that rises to meet it releases its own moisture, creating a perpetual cloud-covered jungle—the "cloud forest" of which so much has been written. Humid and relatively warm throughout the year, the cloud forest is greenhouse-lush, more profuse with orchids, flowering bromeliads, mosses, and ferns than the lowland rainforest most tourists see. Below, at the eastern base of the Andes, is the lowland rainforest—part of the Amazon basin, that vast network of rivers as large as the continental United States. Warm, equatorial air passing over the abundant river water collects moisture, rises until it meets cooler air at higher altitudes, and releases rain in daily showers that total as much as 150 inches a year. The heavily forested lowlands—virtually endless tracts of vegetable matter divided only by rivers and spotted with oxbow lakes and small savannas, warm and damp year-round—are what we think of as "jungle."

The driest desert in the world, the highest mountains in the Western Hemisphere, and the wet, warm rainforests of Amazonia—Peru's geographical extremes breed extreme floral and faunal diversity. But even this description is greatly simplified. From west to east, and to a lesser extent from north to south, the habitats change in imperceptible increments that attract particular birds to these ecological niches, as if they were carefully zoned subdivisions.

Within the more general life zones, LSU ornithologist Ted Parker has identified twenty-three particular habitat types from the pelagic waters offshore to the Amazon lowlands.[4] In between are the coastal waters, beaches and mudflats, coastal marshes, desert, mangrove swamps, agricultural areas, riparian thickets in tropical and subtropical deserts, dry forests mainly of the western Andes, desert scrub, montane scrub, montane lakes and streams, puna (dry montane) grasslands, páramo (humid montane) grasslands, elfin forests, humid montane forests, oxbow lakes, tropical rivers, tropical savannas, and forest edge with second-growth vegetation. The lowland virgin rainforest is divided into dry terra firma forest and *varzea,* or seasonally flooded forest. The birds adapted to these habitats represent over half the birds known in South America, which itself contains one-third of the world's nine thousand species. Penguins to parakeets, condors to hummingbirds, parrots, trogons, and toucans, rheas and flamingos, ovenbirds, honeycreepers, cotingas, oilbirds, curassows, motmots, puffbirds, manakins, and potoos—even the names become increasingly diverse and unfamiliar. There are woodpeckers as small as some hummingbirds, hummingbirds as large as some woodpeckers. It is the greatest exhibit of birdlife in the world.

"The whole problem with Peru," O'Neill once told me, "is that although now [after more than twenty years of LSU expeditions] we would consider it one of the most well-known countries in South America, ornithologically speaking, you still could practically throw darts at a map of Peru, and wherever a dart hit there would be something interesting we don't know much about."

7

In the morning the sky is overcast and the air a bit cool. A wind has been rising and falling since the middle of the night, rustling the leaves of banana and palm trees in the *chacra* behind the building. The village has a sleepy pall over it, though a few children are up and about, and the dogs and chickens are nosing around. Like many Peruvian villages, Abujao is laid out around a soccer field. There are a dozen or so houses, most of them constructed in the old way, with materials taken directly from the surrounding jungle, though some include milled lumber in places. The roofs are made of thatched palm fronds, and though many of the structures have sides that extend from floor to roof, none have glass or screen windows; instead, square openings let the light in. Doorways are covered with cloth. There is, however, another modern building like the one we slept in—a schoolhouse complete with modern toilets, which cannot be used since they are not joined to any septic system. The houses are spaced evenly apart in a neat line, and it appears that down a path there are several more dwellings, set farther into the jungle, that are not part of the plan. In villages like Abujao, where the majority of Peru's twenty million

people live, electricity and running water are unheard of. Only one in
seven rural Peruvians have potable water—for most the river is both
their sewer system and source of drinking water—and only one in
forty-three have indoor plumbing.[1]

Manuel has already gone upriver to try to find more dugout canoes.
It seems there are fewer canoes and willing drivers available than he
and Angelo had been told just two days ago. It's a typical scenario.
Someone agrees to hire out his canoe to the gringos, but the next day
a friend says let's go hunting upriver, and they're both gone for who
knows how long. At the moment we have only three canoes to use; we
need at least two more, preferably three. Since Al Gentry has to be
back in the United States in just two weeks, he will leave this morning
regardless, taking only a light load in order to make good time. He'll
take a chainsaw that one of the villagers has agreed to lend and try to
clear some of the worst deadfall in the Shesha, so that when we follow
with the heavy stuff the going will be easier. Camilo and Magno will
go with Gentry. Their destination is an abandoned banana *chacra* on
the upper Shesha where the river draws within a few miles of the
mountains; we are now told that remnants of an old hunting trail lead
from the *chacra* toward the hills. There are a few men in the village
who have been up the Shesha. Some of them say it will take us two
days. Some say eight.

The first order of business this morning is to go through the
supplies and pull out what Gentry will need. Most of the supplies are
either in trunks or *costales,* large, fiber-reinforced plastic bags that are
used throughout Peru; but the master list of the items in the *costales*
is missing, so they all must be opened up and a new list made. One of
the trunks has ruptured, and a bag of sugar has split open as well. An
hour and a half later, at nine, Gentry, Camilo, and Magno, accompanied by a boatman and guide, settle into a canoe with a couple of bags
of supplies and the three liquid nitrogen tanks that Angelo has
brought to preserve tissue for his biochemical studies. They wave, and
within minutes are out of sight upriver. Since we are at least two
canoes short of what we need, Angelo has already decided that we

47

won't leave Abujao today. It will be best anyway to wait for O'Neill, who should show up this afternoon with Donna and Marta if everything went as planned. Manuel will go upriver to look for more dugouts to hire. Angelo, Pete, and Tony will sort out all the supplies, repack the damaged items, and make a new master list.

Late in the morning, Manuel returns. The news is not good. He has not found any more dugouts for hire, though one man, who is off somewhere now, may be willing to hire out his canoe when he returns this afternoon. Angelo is chagrined, and he questions Manuel for several minutes about other possibilities. Manuel explains slowly, taking into account Angelo's less than perfect Spanish, and then ends by saying he will try another group of families upriver. He takes a pocketful of crackers—his lunch—and is off again. The sky remains overcast, though not dark, and after lunch Pete, Cecilia, and Paul head out into the jungle looking for birds and herps. Tony, who says he did not sleep more than two or three minutes last night because of the mosquitoes, announces that he intends to take a long nap.

The birding crew returns in midafternoon with a pink-toed tarantula that Paul found while turning over deadfall. The spider is jet black except for the tips of its legs, which are indeed bright pink. A picture-taking session follows. Paul releases the spider onto a banana leaf, then tries to keep it there by poking him with a stick every time he gets to the edge of the leaf. After several minutes the tarantula gives up and stands still in the center of the leaf. Spiders, like all else in the tropics, are often larger than their North American cousins, and one genus, *Mygale,* is known to feed even on small birds trapped in its gargantuan web. Henry Walter Bates recalled seeing a group of Indian children "with one of these monsters secured by a cord round its waist, by which they were leading it about the house as they would a dog."[2]

By late afternoon there is still no sign of Manuel or O'Neill. Though I've seen very few birds near the village, I decide to walk around the edges of the forest again and have a look. I'm rewarded almost immediately when a group of Dusky-headed Parakeets swoop down into a *chacra* to pick at the maize. Parakeets generally remain high in the trees where they are virtually invisible among the greens of the jungle foliage, so this is a treat. I can see them clearly—they are only thirty feet away and they are ignoring me, giving me all the time in the world to look them over. They remain for twenty minutes, then burst into the sky, chattering, and are gone. There are other birds in the garden as well, another species of parakeet I cannot make out, then a pair of Black-tailed Tityras flitting about. A Silver-beaked Tanager zips through my field of vision and up into a nearby tree. As I watch him, I spot two Yellow-tufted Woodpeckers working their way up the trunk of the tree. They are the strangest-looking woodpeckers I have seen—mostly black, with a ruddy belly, striped sides, and a white rump. But it's the head that is startling. Below a small red cap is a yellow eye surrounded by a custard-yellow eye ring and covered by a bright yellow brow that extends to the back of the head. They circle the tree, woodpecker fashion, for fifteen minutes before moving on.

When Manuel returns, Angelo is quick to ask what the canoe situation is. A long conversation ensues in which Angelo becomes confused. Cecilia and Gabriel intervene and try to translate Manuel's explanation into English for Angelo, but their English is no better than Angelo's Spanish and Angelo is soon frustrated. This goes on for a full half hour, until finally we wake up Tony, whose Spanish is better than Angelo's. Ten minutes later we have it straightened out. In a nutshell, Manuel has not been able to locate any more canoes. We have only two, Gentry having taken one, and figure that we need at least two more dugouts. The conversation turns to how this situation should be handled. Should we wait around Abujao, hoping more canoes will show up, or send part of the expedition upriver, leaving some of us behind to wait for O'Neill? Or should we send all the supplies upriver in the canoes while we walk? Without O'Neill there is more indecision than there otherwise might be.

Angelo at first seems to prefer breaking the supplies into two groups, taking half now and then sending someone back to get the other half. If it takes four days to reach our destination (our best guess for the time being), that means four days back to get the remaining gear, then four more days to haul it upriver—nearly two weeks to get where we are going. Since the expedition is already more than a week behind schedule, this option is finally discarded. Angelo, as the official co-leader of the expedition, opts for packing all the supplies into the two canoes, sending them upriver with two people to watch them while the rest of us walk the distance, and coming back later for supplies that won't fit. Supposedly there is a trail that follows the river about halfway, though it is poorly kept up, and we will have to reopen it as we go. The good news is that the Shesha has enough water in it to use small motors on the canoes, so perhaps they can get everything to camp in good time and then come back and pick us up at about the halfway point where the trail stops.

There are too many variables in this plan to make it appealing, but it appears to be the best option. It's disappointing that we will be walking, not because it will be difficult (actually it may be more comfortable than sitting in a cramped canoe for ten hours each day), but because I've been looking forward to what we might see along the river. These new plans initiate a lot of talk about how much we can carry as we walk, what we will need, who is going with the canoes, and so forth. The need to make these decisions temporarily over-whelms the frustration everyone must feel. When there is no choice, any impulse to dwell on this bad luck is pointless. We focus our attention instead on what we must do to get ready. After supper I retire to my room and begin separating my personal gear, looking for things that I can do without. I want to put as much stuff as I can in the duffel bag that will go on one of the canoes so I will have a light load to carry. The essentials—camera, binoculars, notebooks—will be heavy enough by themselves. Paul and Mara join me and begin the same process with their stuff. They are both upset because they have not been able to find their tent since we left Pucallpa. At first they figured it had been put into a bag with other items, but no one came across it today when most of the supplies were reorganized. Now they wonder if it wasn't stolen along with my bag, or maybe just inadvertently left behind. A bag of supplies is missing as well, and Angelo thinks it may never have left Lima.

These problems with transportation and supplies are perhaps the reason O'Neill did not seem especially disappointed to have to stay behind in Pucallpa. (And since he did not show up here today, it looks very likely that we will start upriver tomorrow without him.) Getting fifteen people and a ton and a half of supplies up a small river in an isolated area is always a task laden with difficulties, small and large. In recent years O'Neill has occasionally left this work to some of the more experienced graduate students. No one questions this. O'Neill has paid his dues many times over. It's doubtful that there would be any such expedition to the Cordillera Divisor had O'Neill not been coming to Peru for the last twenty-seven years, roughing it in the jungle and smoothing the way diplomatically.

When O'Neill first began traveling in Peru, there were few commercial airplanes operating anywhere except between the major cities. On his first flight over the Andes in a DC-3 prop jet, a bell rang in the cabin to let passengers know they should begin breathing oxygen through the tubes provided for them. The cabin was not pressurized. To reach the isolated areas where he carried out his initial research, he was dependent on planes owned by the Summer Institute of Linguistics, an endeavor operated by missionaries at Yarinacocha, an oxbow lake near Pucallpa. During his third summer in Peru he made two trips southeast of Pucallpa to an Indian village known as Balta. Navigation aboard the plane that took him to Balta was accomplished strictly by compass and visual landmarks. From Pucallpa they flew south, following the Río Ucayali below them, the most distinguishable feature in an otherwise homogenous mass of rumpled green vegetation. The plane stopped to refuel at Chicosa, a river village where a missionary family kept a landing strip cleared and stored gas, and then headed on south again until the pilot spotted the Río Inuya, at which point he banked east and followed the smaller river. The idea was to follow the Río Inuya until it dwindled and finally disappeared, then fly by compass for about thirty minutes and look for more water, which should be the headwaters of the Río Purus, another small river. From there they headed northeast along the river and looked for signs of a settlement north of it. That was Balta. On one occasion the pilot disagreed with O'Neill about the water they sighted after leaving the Río Inuya, O'Neill claiming that it was the Río Purus and that they should follow it, the pilot saying no, he knew this area, it was not the Purus yet. O'Neill gave up the argument and settled uncomfortably into his seat. After another half an hour of nothing but trackless jungle below them, the plane's fuel supply diminishing, the pilot swallowed his pride and turned back.

On the
Río Shesha

8

 By six a.m. we are all up and eating a hurried breakfast of soda crackers and jam. It's Thursday, June 18. The sun is rising behind mottled clouds, and here and there a few jagged patches of blue sky hold the eye. Tony, Angelo, and Pete are already going over the supplies again, this time taking out food and other necessities to leave behind for O'Neill, Donna, and Marta, who never did show up yesterday. We cannot wait for them since we don't know how long the wait will be, and the canoes that are available today might not be tomorrow. It seems bad form to be setting out without O'Neill, but there's no choice. Manuel comes back into the village from one last attempt to find canoes and tells Angelo he has come up with a third dugout that has a double motor on it. With this good news there's a change in plans. Manuel and Pete will take as much gear as they can in this newest addition to our fleet and go on ahead of the rest of us. Since this dugout has more horsepower, they hope they might actually be able to reach our destination in one day and begin to set up a camp. This means the supplies need to be sorted into what they can take with them and what we will need on our way upriver. We're all happy that this will put us back on

the river. But as the supplies are carried out onto the soccer field and stacked in a long row, it seems clear that they will never all fit into three canoes, to say nothing of a dozen people going with them.

It takes two hours to get everything laid out this way, and another half an hour to divide it into three groups, one for each canoe. Meanwhile, Angelo writes a note that he will leave at the village for O'Neill, telling him what we've done and that Gentry's canoe will be back in a day or two and they should be able to hire it. There is a lot of talk again about what all of this will cost, and Angelo asks Paul and Mara how much money they can lend him if he needs it. At nine o'clock everything is hauled to the riverbank, placed again in three separate piles, and then slowly carried down and loaded into the dugouts. Steps have been carved into the mud, but they are slippery, and with one person at each end of the heavier trunks the slope is difficult to negotiate.

The first boat is loaded to the point of sinking. The dugouts are shallow and sit low in the water to begin with, but this one appears about to disappear entirely. These canoes are the main source of transportation in the lowlands. As the name implies, a tree trunk is dug out, its ends tapered, and its sides often reinforced with planks. Our dugouts are about sixteen feet long, two feet wide—rough-hewn and beat up, but sturdy. Dugouts are paddled or, if the water is shallow, poled. For those who can afford them, jerry-rigged motors provide the power. The motors that are much in use throughout Peru are lawnmower engines, which sit up well out of the water at the back of the canoe and are connected to a small propeller by a six-foot shaft. This makes it possible to raise the propeller out of the water quickly and to position it at sharp angles from the canoe to negotiate snags in the rivers. These motor-driven dugouts are called *peki-pekis,* after the noise made by the two-stroke engine. Our boatmen, then, are *peki-pekeros.*

The bulky LSU trunks have been placed into the canoe first, then *costales* and smaller bags positioned on top of them. As I watch this enterprise, our third dugout shows up, but like the others it has only a single motor, and the boatmen who are now loading the second dugout are shaking their heads at the amount of gear yet to be put on.

Angelo realizes our newest plans are not going to work. He huddles with Manuel and Tony to discuss the problem. We will be lucky just to get the gear into the three canoes. We are back to walking, says Angelo. Tony comes up to the top of the bank and stands off by himself looking disgusted. When I point out as delicately as I can that one of the tents which has just been loaded looks as if it will fall off into the river at the first sharp turn, he stares at the ground and says, "I know, but there's nothing more I can do." The two hours spent dividing the gear up this morning was for nothing. And everyone is tired of waiting. Paul and Mara are bickering over how to use one of the cameras. Angelo is trying to direct traffic, and Manuel and the boatmen are arguing over how to load the third canoe. As the boatmen grow aware of how much strain will be put on their dugouts, one of them suddenly volunteers that he knows where to get a fourth canoe. At the mouth of the Río Shesha there is a small village known as Nuevo México, and there, he says, he knows someone with a canoe. He feels sure the man will hire it out, though the canoe is not in good shape, we are warned, and its motor does not run smoothly.

It's ten o'clock. The rest of the supplies have been stacked precariously into the third canoe. Without any more discussion the *peki-pekeros* yank on the flywheels and all three motors sputter to life with the familiar high-pitched clattering I associate with summer weekends in the Midwest. They set off upriver. We grab our daypacks and without looking back at Abujao move out at a brisk pace toward Nuevo México. We follow a path that parallels the river and leads past several dwellings, reaching the mouth of the Shesha in forty-five minutes. There we are ferried across the Abujao to a big sandbar where we sit down to wait while Manuel goes off to see about the fourth canoe. Tony and Pete walk upriver along the sandbar to look at the birds we can hear rustling about in the tops of several big trees. The rest of us lie in the sand and absorb the late morning sun that is trying to burn through a slim layer of clouds. It takes forty minutes for Manuel to come back with the fourth boat.

A PARROT WITHOUT A NAME

Some of the gear from the first three canoes is placed in the fourth dugout, with room left between it for seats. One of the local men hacks up a small tree with his machete, chops it up into short pieces that he wedges into the canoe, and thereby fashions places for us to sit. We climb in, Angelo, Pete, Tony, Paul, Mara, and myself. Gabriel and Cecilia will go with another canoe, and Manuel with a third one. As predicted, the boatman cannot get our motor started for a good fifteen minutes, but when he does we all shove off quickly. At last we are on our way up the Río Shesha. There is a lot of shifting about as everyone tries to find a comfortable position. If I rest my hands along the sides of the canoe, gripping it, my fingers trail in the water—that's how low we are sitting—and if anyone shifts his weight too suddenly, we tip and water rushes in over the side. Though it's a bit precarious, this is an intimate means of travel.

Van Remsen, Curator of Birds at LSU, spent the better part of two summers in a small dugout for his study of Amazonian kingfishers. He reminisced one day in Baton Rouge about the pleasure of getting into the dugout each morning at dawn and entering the river. Remsen, who worked on the Amazon near Leticia, Colombia, recalled an experience that illustrated all too well the intimacy of travel by dugout. He was paddling slowly along one morning, the river quiet and peaceful.

"All of a sudden I felt these swells rocking the canoe," Remsen said.

Waves were making the dugout bob up and down as if a speedboat were passing by. Remsen looked around only to find an anaconda swimming parallel to him about fifteen feet away. The snake was perhaps half again as long as the canoe. Remsen was stunned by the size of the snake—anacondas can reach twenty-five feet and weigh two hundred pounds, with a girth more suited to a pig than a snake—and its calm, purposeful movement through the water. He knew the snake could easily capsize the canoe, and that if it attacked him there was little he could do to defend himself.

The anaconda is the largest snake in the world, and though reports of forty-foot anacondas by early naturalists are now scoffed at, the creature is large enough to swallow wild pigs, deer, dogs, and many other mammals, including man.[1] Many people consider it the most dangerous animal in South America, partly because it has a reputation for being aggressive. The snake is known to lie submerged near the banks of rivers, waiting for prey to come within striking distance. Apparently, the snake drowns its victim as often as it kills by constriction. When Remsen was working one year in Bolivia, a local man showed him a horseshoe-shaped scar on his side, which looked like the result of a shark bite. The man had gone down to the river one day to water his horse, and a large anaconda, coming from nowhere, seized him by the abdomen. The snake had gotten a good grip and began pulling the man into the water. The man clung to the reins of his horse and hollered for help from a companion, who arrived just in time and with a pistol fired several shots into the snake. The anaconda released its grip and swam away.

The Río Shesha is so shallow this time of year that an anaconda would have little luck drowning anything bigger than a mouse, so we have little to fear. Our problem at the moment is that we seem to be sinking—the boat is leaking steadily. Our guide inspects the problem, tears a chunk of material out of the shorts he is wearing, wads it up tightly, and with his machete stuffs it into the crack beneath his feet. Voilà!

There is already an inch of river water at our feet, so I put my daypack into a plastic bag and position it across the hull to keep it above the sloshing water. We're off again, and the canoes quickly spread out. Our guides, who have been chattering all morning, are suddenly completely attentive to their work. One man stands on the nose of the dugout watching for sandbars and snags while the boatman at the rear of the canoe stands bent over, one foot in the canoe, the other on the rear edge, his hand on the throttle. We speed around a bend and leave the last houses of Nuevo México behind us. During the first hour, we pass eight or ten dwellings where children stop and stare as we go by, probably the first gringos they've ever seen. The banks are lined with second-growth vegetation—grasses and new trees—the primary forest having been cut for building material and to make way for crops. The river, about seventy feet across here and rarely more than three feet deep, winds back and forth, so that we are often heading in any direction except northeast, our overall course. The sky is still overcast, which will save us from baking under the tropical sun, and our movement along the river stirs the air pleasantly. There are snags of half-submerged deadfall that we encounter every few minutes, one we hit with a thud that throws us forward, but in general our boatman swerves expertly around them.

By midafternoon we are far enough upriver so that the last houses are behind us. From now on we do not expect to see any more signs of human enterprise. We could, if we were inclined, continue eastward into Brazil (the border is only fifty miles away) and travel for a couple of weeks, maybe a month, before we would come upon a village. The same is true if we traveled north or south of here. Only to the west, where the Río Ucayali encourages habitation, are there signs of civilization. South America is the least explored continent on earth. Ecologist Norman Myers has noted in *The Primary Source* that several large tributaries of the Amazon were discovered only relatively recently and that entire mountain ranges have turned out to be hundreds of miles away from where cartographers drew them.[2] The jungle—more properly, rainforest—is still a mysterious, little-known place. Of the 2.4 billion acres of rainforest left in the world, 57 percent is in Latin America, and the great majority of that is here in these Amazonian lowlands.[3] Along the banks of the Shesha the trees rise to seventy-five feet, forming a nearly level canopy that is interrupted only now and then by an "emergent" tree that breaks through and steals some sunlight. The trees are wrapped in vines and covered with bromeliads and other epiphytes, so that it is difficult to distinguish one individual from another. The vines and lianas form such an intricate and pervasive network that on occasion a tree cut down at the base by foresters will remain standing, held up by the vines that connect it to the other trees around it. And no two trees look alike. In one acre of temperate woods there are usually four or five species of trees; in an acre of tropical rainforest there may be as many as eighty-six species. We have names for only 10 percent of them. "It has been said that we know more about some areas of the moon than we do about tropical rainforests," says Catherine Caufield in her excellent book *In the Rainforest.*[4]

We are now in the midst of virgin rainforest, and, accordingly, birds are plentiful. We frequently disturb kingfishers, who fly ahead of us a hundred feet only to be rousted again a moment later. Most often we see either the Amazon Kingfisher, the size of our Belted Kingfisher in the States, or the Green Kingfisher, only a little more than half that size. Flocks of parakeets shoot past overhead, their chattering audible above the engine noise, and once a small group of macaws flaps heavily across the sky, their long tails dragging behind them. There are also dozens of Swallow-winged Puffbirds darting out over the water and flitting past our heads—stout little black birds with white rumps, short wings, and stubby tails, as acrobatic as the North American swallows they remind me of. Oropendolas move across the river in groups. These crow-sized orioles make a hanging nest like our orioles, but they are social birds, so they nest together, and the trees they choose as nest sites look as if they are bearing some peculiar, hairy fruit. We also come across Roadside Hawks, which are usually sitting on an exposed limb above the river. They are the most common hawk in the neotropics and like our Red-tailed Hawk live around man as well as in wild places. The most handsome birds of prey we see, however, are a Slate-colored Hawk and a pair of Bat Falcons. The Bat Falcons are especially striking—finely barred black-and-white breasts, white throats, dark heads with yellow eye rings, coal-gray wings and back, and a ruddy belly and leg feathers. None of these birds quite compare, though, to my favorite bird of the day, a Capped Heron that we find sitting in a tree. It is a little larger than a Night Heron, though not as stocky. Its legs are gray, its coat white, almost beige, but what is startling about the bird is the small black cap that sits on its head like a beret, two long feathers sprouting from it and falling over the heron's back; and most wonderful of all—a pale blue face and blue-silver beak: a heron wearing a Mardi Gras mask.

Tony is happily identifying all the birds, noting their features and sometimes distinguishing them from something similar, most of this for the benefit of Pete, whose binoculars have not left his hands since we departed. Pete, in turn, is testing everything he knows of the birds from his lab work. Angelo tosses in bits and pieces of information, and Paul and Mara, without binoculars, use the telephoto lenses on their cameras to look at the birds. Paul, who told me yesterday that he has brought along a hundred rolls of film, is not wasting any time using it. The other dugouts are nowhere in sight, and I've lost track of which ones are ahead of us and which behind us. Late in the afternoon Pete shouts and points to a tree on the bank. A snake, five or six feet long, is hanging in the branches above the water. As it twists about, a lemon-yellow underside shows clearly. Paul is reeling off every picture he can get, though we are already fifty feet away and leaving the snake behind us. It's something in the genus *Chironius,* Paul tells us, but what species he can't say. Nonpoisonous.

The sun is dropping below the tree line behind us, and we are looking now for a place to camp this first night. At five o'clock we come around a bend and see Manuel's canoe pulled up to a sandbar. Within minutes all four dugouts have arrived and we are standing up to stretch our legs. The first thing to do is unload all the supplies and put them in four separate piles. Not only do we need to find the tents and tonight's dinner, but Angelo fears that if we leave the trunks in the canoes we may find them sitting on the bottom of the river in the morning.

Our guides say that we are now only three hours away from our destination and that we will be there before noon tomorrow, but no one believes this. If this is true, why haven't we passed Al Gentry's dugout on its way back to Abujao? The local people measure distances differently than we do. To begin with, they are accustomed to moving much faster than we are able to, so it's not wise to take their predictions at face value. This is particularly true when it comes to walking through the jungle. Something that is an hour away for them is two hours away for us. So now there's a lot of speculation about how far we actually have to go. Two days? Three? By the time the boats are unloaded, it is nearly dark. I set up my tent hurriedly while I can still see what I'm doing. Angelo, Paul, and Mara are putting up a large tent that they will share (Paul and Mara have given up on ever finding their own tent). Manuel and Pete meanwhile are once again trying to locate the spaghetti mix and noodles, and the headlamps as well. Oscar, our head guide, has started a fire and filled the big kettle with river water. Though the Shesha is mud brown, the water is probably free of most harmful bacteria since there are no people living upriver from here.

By seven, dinner has been served: tuna-fish spaghetti. Tuna fish is a staple on LSU expeditions and the main source of protein. We stand around the trunks, using them as tables. It is completely dark now and I've turned off my headlamp, as has nearly everyone else, in response to the sand flies that mob the light and dance around one's eyelashes. I cannot see the food in my bowl, but better this than to be eating several sandflies with each mouthful. Our guides are huddled about the fire eating their farina, talking and laughing, probably already spending the money they will make from this once-in-a-lifetime opportunity. After the series of false starts this morning, Angelo is happy that we are on our way. The day has gone quite well and there is nothing but primeval rainforest ahead of us. He would be even happier, I think, if O'Neill were here. Though Angelo has plenty of experience with expeditions, he clearly does not enjoy making all the miscellaneous decisions that must be made, especially for a group of this size.

An hour later everyone has retired to their tents. The camp has quieted down except for our guides, who are playing a radio they've brought with them. The static is clearer than the music. The jangle of songs drifts into the night like the thinning smoke from the campfire.

9

 At first light we begin breaking camp. Though it's overcast, the air is warm and humid, and within minutes everyone has worked up a sweat. In twenty minutes the canoes are ready, but we don't seem as eager to get in them as we were yesterday when we first set off. Then, there were arguments about who was to sit in the front; Paul and Pete both wanted the spot for their picture taking. This morning, that is easily resolved because Angelo has asked Pete to take a different dugout to watch over one of the young, inexperienced boatmen we had to hire. This kid sees the trip as great fun and easy money, and he smiled all day yesterday, even as he hit a sandbar and dumped a couple of bags into the water. Perhaps Pete's presence will subdue his enthusiasm. A second dugout also has two young boatmen who appear careless, so Gabriel has been assigned to them. Manuel takes number three as yesterday, and the rest of us get into number four in our same places. But now we sit and wait. The motor that was troublesome yesterday appears entirely lifeless today. A long fifteen minutes go by before it sputters to life. It's seven-thirty when we shove off, and it seems like midmorning already. The other three dugouts are ahead of us. The

jungle is quiet, the water smooth. Within two minutes we hit our first snag, a morass of dead branches, but Oscar spots a way through it and signals our boatman to proceed. Five minutes later we come up on Pete's boat, which is pulled over to the bank. The kid with the smile ran them up onto a submerged log and dumped half a dozen *costales* into the water. Pete already has them back in place and is looking over the damage. It was sheer carelessness, he tells us, exasperated that he has already had to chase bags downriver. Nothing appears to be damaged, however, so Pete climbs back into the canoe and the kid, as if to show us that this won't slow him down, guns the motor, throwing Pete off balance before he is fully seated. Pete throws up his hands as they speed off ahead of us.

This morning, the water appears lower than it did yesterday, even though we are farther upriver. Angelo has his compass out and a hand-drawn map of the Shesha that we were given in Abujao. He is looking for Quebrada Negra, the first main feeder stream that we should come across, and a short while later Oscar points to the left bank—there it is. This means that we are about halfway there, but because there is more deadfall to work our way around we are proceeding at perhaps half the speed we managed yesterday. There are fewer birds in this dull weather, but we catch sight of a Sunbittern onshore, a peculiar bird with an extraordinarily beautiful "sunburst" pattern on its flight feathers, which can be seen only when its wings are unfolded, a sight I was fortunate enough to witness on my first trip to Peru in 1985. The bird's display—spread wings, fanned tail, lowered head— puts a peacock to shame and invariably elicits oohs and aahs from even the most jaded ornithologists. Otherwise, though, the Sunbittern is an odd-looking bird. It's most often found tiptoeing solitarily along the edge of a shady stream, thrusting its long neck forward, then bringing its body up to meet it. The bird's shape is bizarre: the long, heavy body of a duck, its brown back barred with black and gray; the dainty posture, and unwebbed feet, of a rail; the head and neck of a heron (the platypus of the bird world). This is all strange enough to make it the only bird in its family (*Eurypygidae*). Paul tries over and over again to photograph him, hoping to catch the sunburst pattern as he unfolds his wings, startled into flight by the approach of the *peki-pekis*. The bird stays with us for twenty minutes or more, flying ahead each time we draw near before it finally gets wise and doubles back behind us. About midmorning we spot a fresh campsite on a small sandbar, which we assume is Gentry's first camp. If he made it this far the first day, then he must have taken two days for the entire trip. Since we are carrying more weight and generally moving slower, it seems unlikely that we can get there in only two days as well.

Everyone has found a way to get comfortable in the dugouts. Paul sits directly in front of me, camera around his neck, his vest pockets bulging like an inflated life jacket. They are stuffed with film, lenses, filters, and who knows what else. There are a couple of dozen pockets altogether, and, since Paul often forgets where he put something, he sometimes goes through half the pockets in search for the item. We all soon come to associate Paul with the sound of Velcro tearing apart. His beard and dark curly hair might have a sobering effect on anyone else's face, but Paul is too animated and energetic. Mara sits in front of him, her fair skin getting the worst of the intermittent sun. Tony and Angelo, at the front of the dugout, keep their eyes on the foliage and are usually the first to spot a bird. We sit, one after the other, in the long shell of this dugout canoe, very much like the proverbial peas in a pod.

At eleven o'clock we pass a major fork in the river and begin to see bits of rock deposits along the bank.

"We're getting near the mountains," Angelo hollers. A few minutes later we come across a cayman sunning himself (so to speak) on the bank, a small one no more than four feet long. The river has narrowed quite a bit. It is perhaps forty feet wide now, and we are having more trouble with scraping bottom on shallow stretches and running into tangles of deadwood that stretch from one bank to the other. Oscar has cut a staff of bamboo with which he pokes the river bottom ahead of us when we reach a bad spot, and then if we need some extra *oomph* he will dig it into the sand and push on it with all his weight while our boatman opens the throttle. He communicates with our boatman by hand signals, one moment holding his hand high above his head and slicing the air with it, at other times dropping his arm to his side and motioning like a football referee who is signaling a clipping penalty. Usually, the motion he makes with his hand indicates the direction the channel takes in the river. He will cut a graceful arc in the air to illustrate it—a long, slow curve to the left or a quick *S* followed by a straight line. Don Oscar—the villagers refer to him this way, a sign of respect—is as cheerful and knowledgeable a guide as we could ask for. His handsome face sports a Clark Gable mustache. He wears a brown cowboy hat complete with string drawn up under his chin. That it is a child's plastic-coated hat is less important than how well it sheds rain and keeps the sun off his head. And besides, he wears it at such a jaunty angle that he clearly enjoys how he looks in it. By midmorning he has usually stripped off his shirt and tucked it under the prow of the canoe, working in only an old bathing suit. He is lean and muscular, maybe in his midforties, and assumes his role as head guide with aplomb.

Late in the morning we are halted by a big tree that lies completely across the river. The top of it is no more than an inch below the surface and the front of our canoe is hung up on it. Oscar and our boatman go to work pushing and rocking the dugout, but it doesn't budge, and Angelo says we will all have to get out to lighten the load. Before he has time to say any more, Mara has gotten up and stepped over the side into what she expects to be a foot of water, judging by where Oscar is standing, but she hits a hollow in the river bottom. She sinks in to her chest, stumbles in the current, and nearly goes under completely. She comes up laughing, but Paul has the good sense not to joke about it. The rest of us take off our shoes, roll up our pants, and get out at the front of the canoe. Oscar rocks and heaves the dugout over the log. Then we stand in the water and wait for the other three canoes, all of them heavier, to see if they'll be able to make it. Meanwhile, Mara goes onshore, removes her drenched jeans, and ties around her waist the extra blouse she brought along this morning.

At the first sign of trouble yesterday, Manuel had to get into the water and quickly stripped down to his underwear, spending the rest of the day standing on the prow of the canoe in bright red briefs, which brought him whistles from the gringos.

It takes half an hour to get all the dugouts over the log. Fifteen minutes later, as we round a bend, we see several *costales* and small bags floating downriver toward us. Pete is in the water chasing them. We jump out quickly and slosh toward them, grabbing them as fast as we can, hoping to get them before they sink. The *costales* float, but smaller things—including someone's daypack—are filling with water. Paul and Mara's duffel bag is soaked on one side and water drains out of both of the small packs that I pick up. Pete is furious.

"He's just careless," he tells Angelo, looking at the kid with the smile. "He tried to fly through a snag and hit a log. The whole canoe nearly turned over. It's ridiculous!"

If this continues we risk damaging essential items and losing supplies entirely. We are all glaring at the young boatman, but Angelo says nothing to him. We put the bags back in the dugout and continue upriver.

At one o'clock we meet Al Gentry's boat coming back downriver. The boatmen have a note for us from Gentry, but our attention is drawn first to the tapir that is belly-up in the bottom of their canoe. They came across the animal in the river twenty minutes ago and killed it with a machete. The largest animal native to South America, the tapir is prized by hunters for the quality and quantity of its meat. It's a strange-looking hoofed animal that has been described as a cross between a pig and a hornless rhinoceros, and like the rhino, to which it is related, it has changed very little in the last twenty-five million years and certainly appears prehistoric. One man is gutting it, tossing the entrails into the river, which float away downstream like big white balloons. He takes out the heart and lays it on a seat, and then begins to butcher the tapir expertly with his machete. Within a few minutes the animal has been reduced to several hefty slabs of meat. Oscar is given the heart, which he wraps in a cloth and stows under his seat. He will smoke the heart over tonight's campfire. Onshore, Mara has just found the skull of a capybara, another big mammal that likes the water. A member of the rodent family, the capybara looks more like a prairie dog than a mouse, albeit a big prairie dog, since the capybara often weighs over a hundred pounds.

Angelo and Tony, meanwhile, are reading Gentry's note. It says that he reached the abandoned banana *chacra* in two days, though the second day was rough going. He cut as many big snags with the chainsaw as he could, the note says, but since he was anxious to make good time he left many more behind him. It's imperative that we get the chainsaw from this boat and bring it with us or we'll never make it. Also, we are to pay his boatmen. Both items are bad news. Angelo wasn't expecting to have to pay these people and is not happy with Gentry for leaving it to us, but worse is the fact that they no longer have the chainsaw with them. They've lent it to someone else who took it off farther upriver. Manuel questions Gentry's guides about the condition of the river ahead of us, then confers with Oscar. We have an ax and several machetes. If there are any big trees across the river and our heavier dugouts cannot cross them, we'll have to unload the canoes and portage. We came across a mammoth tree this morning that Gentry had cut through, and we'll have to assume he did the same with any others like it.

Gentry's crew say they left camp at eight this morning, but they were going downriver with nothing in their boat. It's clear that we won't make it to the final camp tonight, but we should make it tomorrow if the ax is enough to get us through. Angelo now writes a note for these men to give to O'Neill, who should be in Abujao when they get there. We've spent nearly an hour at this stop, and while all four canoes are in one place Tony searches for his backpack, which he thought was on Pete's boat but now is nowhere to be seen. He worries aloud that it was dumped overboard with the *costales* and swept beneath the water before anyone could notice it. He gets into his place in the boat and falls into a glum silence.

The river continues to grow narrower, though there are stretches where it widens again. For half an hour we pass through a particularly pretty area where the banks are solid rock covered with green mosses. There are several small waterfalls, and with the trees arcing out over the river, which here is only twenty-five feet across, the place is enchanting. It looks nothing like a lowland river. The mountains feel nearby. A few moments later I catch sight of something high in the trees to our left. I get my binoculars on the spot and for five or six seconds am too enraptured to speak. Tony has spotted the bird also and, pointing upward, is now shouting at the boatman to stop the boat.

"Harpy Eagle!" he says. "No, maybe it's a Crested Eagle. Look at it. Do you see it?"

We are already past the tree and the bird has begun to move. Then, unfolding his wings, he lifts off and flies away from us, and is almost immediately out of sight behind the trees. No one else has gotten a good look at the eagle, and Tony is frustrated because our guides did not understand that we wanted them to stop. The Harpy Eagle and Crested Eagle are both large raptors, the size of our Bald Eagle, and both are rarely seen. The Harpy especially is a prized sight among birdwatchers and ornithologists, and for many has become a symbol of the South American wilderness, much as the grizzly bear is in North America. (It is one of the two animals I most hoped to see on this trip; the other is the jaguar.) The Harpy is among the first animals to disappear from an area that man moves into, and its numbers have diminished considerably in the last two decades as people have been encouraged to open up the jungle and settle new land. Ornithologists, usually restrained in their prose about birds, lose their objectivity when it comes to the Harpy. In *The Birds of Venezeula,* Meyer de Schauensee pronounces the Harpy "one of the greatest and mightiest eagles in the world," feeding on "monkeys, sloths, other arboreal animals, and large birds which it pursues through the branches with great agility."[1] Tony declares that he's not sure whether it was a Harpy or Crested Eagle. One major distinction is the black collar of feathers about the Harpy's neck. Later, when I study illustrations of both birds, I will swear that I saw this collar, but I'm also afraid that my memory may be fogged by wishful thinking.

As it turns out, this will be the highlight of the day. For the remainder of the afternoon the hours pass slowly. We come upon snags and shallow water every fifteen or twenty minutes. Oscar spends a lot of time walking ahead of us searching for the Shesha's main channel, which has become imperceptible. Often where the water is deepest there is an unmovable logjam, so we must try to scoot across the shallowest part of the river. We wind from one bank to the other looking for any advantage we can find; an inch of water makes a difference. At other moments Oscar stands in the middle of the Shesha and debates with our boatman over which course to take, gesturing at one spot, then another, while we sit and wait. Angelo and Tony get out to push if it's especially rough going, and though the rest of us are willing — we're already wet — we are told to stay put, especially by Oscar, who feels he is not doing his job if we all must get out. An hour before sunset we are faced with a pile of debris that extends from bank to bank. The water level in the river seems lower than ever, less than six inches deep in many places. Oscar stands on a tree trunk and goes to work with the ax. As we sit and wait, Pete's canoe catches up with us and Pete is fuming again — they have dumped more bags in the river and the boat almost tipped over entirely once. Canoe number two, with the other young crew, comes in and Gabriel has the same story to tell. Nearly half the gear in these two dugouts is now wet.

Though we all feel the same anger, no one seems sure what to do with it. The language barrier complicates the matter, but it also seems to me that Angelo, who is the official expedition leader since O'Neill is not here, is reluctant to confront the Peruvians. He may be thinking that if a serious rift develops these young villagers can easily dump our supplies on the nearest sandbar and go back to Abujao. We might end up in a serious predicament, and we will need just as many canoes to get us out of the jungle two months from now. Consequently, our complaints remain in English for the time being. Oscar, meanwhile, continues working his way through the log, the ax splashing into the water with each swing. When the deadfall is finally cleared away, Gabriel's dugout goes through first. The boatman lifts the motor out of the water as the canoe goes over a submerged log and then forgets what he's doing and nearly loses the motor to a big branch sticking up out of the river. In Pete's boat the kid with the smile maneuevers past us, makes a sharp turn, and then lifts his whirring propeller out and, without looking, swings it across our canoe. Paul yells, and we all duck as the propeller flies by our heads.

We are the last ones to leave and the last ones to arrive at camp a half hour later. We unload the supplies in the oncoming darkness, and there is a chorus of complaints as we discover how many of the bags are wet. I have found Tony's missing backpack, but as I carry it over to him, water runs out of it freely.

"Goddammit, goddammit," he says through his teeth. His face is tense and he looks as if he's about to explode. All of his books are in this backpack. He takes out his copy of *The Birds of Colombia*, a recently published book that is now the closest thing there is to a guide to Peruvian birds. It is completely waterlogged.

Mara and Paul are hauling their gear across the sand and Mara is cursing also: "Oh shit! Now I don't have any dry clothes to change into. Everything is wet."

Pete and Manuel are inspecting the damage to the main supplies. There is water draining out of two trunks, one of which contains rolls of cotton for stuffing specimens, but Angelo says to forget about opening them up. What difference will it make? "We'll find out how bad it is soon enough," he says. It is dark before we have time to get our tents up, so we all stumble about, sand flies forming clouds in the light from our headlamps. By the time we get around to eating we've all regained a little of our composure, but one wonders what tomorrow will bring. The river is bound to get shallower, and if Gentry was right there will be more logjams to break up.

10

 The news this morning is that Manuel has chastised the young boatmen for their recklessness. Books, clothes, binoculars, shoes, food, and all kinds of equipment have gotten drenched. The canoes are loaded up and we file into place. Today, both Tony and Pete will accompany the trouble-makers. We set off, the quiet river quickly filling with the sound of the *peki-pekis*. Within ten minutes we come upon a barely submerged tree extending from one bank to the other and too big to cut through with an ax. Three days ago, when Gentry passed through here, the water must have been high enough to cross over this tree without a problem. Oscar walks ashore and disappears into the jungle, hacking at the undergrowth with his machete as he goes. At first I'm afraid this means he thinks we will have to unload all the canoes and portage around this spot. The other dugouts pull up behind us and we all wait for Oscar to return, though no one has any idea what he's doing. Several minutes later he comes back carrying three hunks of bark from a cecropia tree. The inside of the bark is orange and fibrous like a pumpkin. Oscar signals for us to get out of the canoe, and then he reveals his intentions. He wedges the bark, pulpy side up, between the

log and the canoe. With a heave from all of us the dugout slides over the log. On the inside, the bark, known locally as *setico,* is as slippery as grease. All four dugouts go over this way. Oscar puts the pieces of *setico* beneath his seat and we climb back aboard.

Expecting the worst today, Pete and Cecilia have started out wearing shorts, and Mara is in her bathing suit (possibly the only dry thing she has to wear). This morning it is brighter than it has been, the sun pushing at the edges of white clouds and big jagged pieces of blue sky turning about like colored glass in a kaleidoscope. The foliage of the jungle, accordingly, is brighter and all the myriad variations of green come forth. But around the next bend—we've only been under way for thirty minutes—is trouble. We come up on Tony and Pete chasing supplies downriver. We jump out to help, and this time it's a frantic few minutes of charging through the water after loose items since almost one-third of the dugout's gear has gone overboard. The canoe itself is sinking with all the water it has taken on, and the two Peruvian boatmen are lugging it to shore and bailing water furiously. They manage to get the boat onto the sandy beach, where it won't sink, but it takes a good twenty minutes to bail it out. Everyone is standing onshore shaking water out of bags and mentally cataloguing what was in this dugout. It's hard to tell if something has been lost downriver, but it seems unlikely if only because the water is so shallow.

Tony is stalking up and down in the sand. Then he turns, points his finger at the kid with the smile, and explodes.

"This asshole ran full speed into a log."

The Peruvians, of course, do not understand a word of Tony's English, but Tony's pointing finger and tone of voice need no translation. He immediately apologizes, but does so under his breath. The young boatman stands ten feet away with a sheepish expression on his face. All the guides are standing next to their canoes. Angelo has remained calm. Tony turns and speaks to him.

"This is just ridiculous. There's no reason for any of it."

Manuel, who has been unusually silent, now comes over and enters the conversation with Angelo and Tony, and then Oscar ventures to say something. Tony's anger flashes again, this time in Spanish. Paul and Mara are looking at their bags, which have been dumped in the water for the third time, and I notice that my duffel bag has gone in again as well. Manuel and Angelo continue talking with Oscar. Eventually the situation seems to be diffused simply because there is nothing concrete that can be done about it. The canoe is loaded up again. The trunks that were sitting in the bottom are leaking water from all four corners.

For the next three hours we get out of the canoe often to push it over sand or through masses of deadwood. We are able to proceed unobstructed for no more than ten minutes at a time. Several times as we approach a tree fallen across the river Oscar signals that we will slip under it; to do so we must all lean back as far as we can, lying down into the lap of the person behind us, and still we come close to scraping our noses. We also approach some of the snags at full speed, when Oscar thinks we can shoot through them, which means we must guard against the branches whipping by our faces. In one shallow area Oscar digs his bamboo pole deep into the river bottom and nearly lifts himself off the canoe pushing on the pole as our driver guns the motor. When we break free and spurt forward, Oscar cannot draw the pole back out of the sand and, because I'm looking elsewhere when I shouldn't be, it springs back and swipes the side of my head.

The upper Shesha here is a grand obstacle course. The local hunters who venture upriver generally do so when the water is higher. Our progress is half the speed of what it was yesterday, which was half the speed of the day before. On the good side, for the first time since we left Abujao the sun has broken out, and by noon it is blazing above us. With it have come all varieties of butterflies, including several superb swallowtails that circle us before going on about their business. They sweep across the water and line up in the mudflats along the bank. The colors and markings of these butterflies do not correspond to anything I've seen before. Some of them are positively gaudy. During the last hour we have also seen the tracks of peccary, capybara, and cayman, all an indication of how far we are from man's influence. Better yet, Pete's boat spotted the tracks of a jaguar, and I wonder how many of these animals we might have seen had we been poling upriver rather than sputtering noisily along by way of these lawnmower engines. As we pass a *quebrada,* Angelo tells us that this is the last one on his map before camp. We must be getting close. We hit another snag, push the canoe through it, and then wait for the others to catch up.

Standing on the bank, we eat peanuts and dried apples for lunch. Paul chases a brilliant orange butterfly about, trying to snap a picture as it opens its wings, and I am searching through the stones on the shoreline for fossils. The stones, like the rocky banks we passed yesterday, are another sign of the Cordillera Divisor being nearby. The sun feels wonderful, or is it just the blue sky above us that has so quickly changed the mood of the day? This morning's anger seems to have dissolved. We are told we'll have to walk along the bank a couple of hundred feet while Oscar gets the empty dugout through a second snag, and as we do my toes sink into the dark mud, then my feet disappear up to my ankles, and finally with surprising quickness my whole leg sinks in up to my knee. The cool mud feels so good on the chigger bites I got in Abujao that I hardly want to move; in fact, I hardly can move.

Back in the boat, black flies have begun to pester us (the sun has brought them out as well). Their bites are quick and sharp, and the spot of blood they draw to the surface often swells considerably. Mara, who is fair-skinned, is already covered with dozens of large welts from the past couple of days. Greater Yellow-headed Vultures are wheeling above us and we hear the chatter of parakeets occasionally. The river has narrowed, and is now thirty to thirty-five feet across; with the rainforest rising a hundred feet on each side of us, it gives me the sensation of being absorbed by our surroundings, as if we are some tiny microbes in the planet's bloodstream. By one o'clock the afternoon already seems endless. Paul passes out some hard candy he bought in Pucallpa and I suck on the sugar with passion. For another hour we get in and out of the dugout, pushing it over sandbars, sliding it through a labyrinth of branches, and rocking it back and forth when it gets hung up on a big treefall. We are lucky it is not any worse than this. At two o'clock we round the thousandth bend in the river and see Pete's boat stopped at the shore.

"This is it!" he shouts.

The left bank rises sharply about twenty feet, and atop it we can see a thatched-palm roof that comes almost to the ground, a small shelter that is the only remaining structure of the abandoned banana *chacra.* A clearing has been cut around it, and there is an old firepit next to it. Oscar pulls our dugout up alongside Pete's and jumps ashore, sinking to his ankles in the mud. Immediately he grabs pieces of deadwood and begins laying them down to form a little walkway for us. We stand up in the canoe, all smiles, looking over our home for the next two months. We've made it here in a bit less than three days, which suddenly does not seem like very much time at all.

There are a good four hours of daylight left, so this is no time to be admiring the scenery. Since the sun is bright and hot, we might be able to get some of our wet belongings dried out before nightfall, and with that in mind we begin unloading the dugouts immediately. I carry only the lighter bags so as to avoid aggravating a recent back injury, and then stand aside and watch, feeling a bit foolish, as everyone else struggles up the steep embankment. There are only a few footholds, half eroded before we began, but no one stops to improve them. The trunks that appear relatively dry (nothing seems to be completely dry) are taken directly into the shelter and stacked along both sides. Angelo and Tony begin to open wet trunks and pull out the items that most need to be dried. Pete, who has been hustling up and down the bank, groaning and sweating, suddenly stops and sits down saying he can do no more. From the first day he has taken all the hard work as a challenge and an obligation, quickly volunteering to handle the heaviest trunks. Now that the end is in sight, his will has given out momentarily. He sits down for ten minutes. Meanwhile, Cecilia and Gabriel are stringing up clothesline on the bank wherever there is an anchor for it. Oscar and Manuel have already begun clearing the undergrowth for tent sites. In two hours the initial work is completed and we rest for a few minutes as Angelo confers with Manuel and Oscar about payment for the dugouts, three of which will begin the return trip right away. He needs 6,000 intis (about $275), and borrows some from Paul and Mara, worrying over how little money is left. When all is said and done, the Peruvians, except Oscar and his boatman, get into their canoes and take off. We wave halfheartedly and return to our work.

Next to the shelter is a small, crudely built table. Pete lays out an assortment of small food items that have gotten damp and soon is stacking one thing on top of another. The riverbank is covered with squares of ceiling tile that will be used as pinning boards for specimens. They have soaked up a lot of water and it will probably take several days to get them dried out. Mist nets are set out along a fallen tree, and clothes are hung on the clothesline and every branch that will support them. Pete, Mara, and I sit down along the edge of the bank and begin drying two hundred batteries one by one. Tony, who is opening *costales* in the shelter, suddenly shouts. He has found Paul and Mara's tent. It had been repacked in the bottom of an unlabeled *costal.* Paul and Mara are ecstatic.

The river here runs north-south. We are on the west bank, so by four-thirty the sun has sunk below the tree line behind us, and in another hour it will be dusk. So far there has been little sign of Gentry having been here, and Manuel is upset because Magno was not here waiting for us as he was supposed to be. Gentry made a beeline for the mountains to set up a small camp there with Camilo, but he was to have left a few things behind, in particular the three liquid nitrogen tanks, which he was to have hidden somewhere nearby. The talk turns to how far away the mountains are. The plan is to establish a base camp here at the river and then set up one or two satellite camps in the mountains.

In the last hour of light everyone attends to personal matters, putting up tents and individual clotheslines, and sorting out the wet from the dry. It's a pleasure to have set up a tent knowing that it won't have to be taken down again in the morning. Feeling settled and at ease, I cannot resist the desire to be clean as well, so I search my gear for soap and towel and walk down to the river. A fallen tree that toppled when the bank eroded extends into the river. The roots at its upended base look like severed tentacles, the mass of them making a clump of mud and fiber that is eight feet high. I sit on the smooth, branchless trunk and undress, then slip off into the river. Kernels of trapped air percolate between my toes and rise up my legs. The water does not come even to my waist, so I must sit down to get completely wet. The bottom is sandy and cool. When I've finished washing, I remain still for several long minutes, feeling cool and refreshed and wonderfully pleased at the sensation of standing naked in the waters of an unknown river where just now a black-and-white swallow is doing loops and long glides around me in the graying light.

By nightfall Manuel has a good fire going and has made another batch of tuna-fish spaghetti. We eat standing up and talk about the day's events. There is more speculation about the mountains, and Angelo decides that he and Manuel will leave first thing tomorrow morning to see how far away they really are. There appears to be a trail that leads northwest from camp and we assume it is the path Gentry took. Everyone else will stay in camp and continue drying out the clothes and equipment. Magno has not showed up yet, and we must assume he is with Gentry. My guess is that he did not like the idea of staying here alone. He's young and shy, and like most Peruvians has never been in the jungle.

This is the first cloudless night since we left Abujao. The nearest ground lights would be Pucallpa, and they are probably too dim to attract a moth. Above us, the sky is deep black. We talk as we eat our dinner, guessing at O'Neill's present whereabouts, discussing the work to be done tomorrow, exclaiming our pleasure that at last we're here. I glance up every few minutes. The heavens are filling up with a bucketful of stars I've never seen before, ancient shapes appearing above my head—Scorpius, Corona Australis, Capricornus. When the Southern Cross finally appears, I know that I'm in the land of Darwin and Bates.

11

 The sun is shining brightly, slanting into camp from across the river and lighting up the trees as it pours into them. In the upper branches on the opposite bank a Chestnut-eared Aracari sits quietly in plain view. The aracari, a crow-sized toucan with a red band across its yellow underparts, is common in *varzea* forest and forest borders, such as the one created here by the river. A painting of this aracari by Louis Agassiz Fuertes, my favorite natural-history artist, shows the bird leaning forward on a branch, about to take flight, displaying more life than this drowsy individual sunning himself above the Río Shesha.

Tony and Pete have already disappeared into the jungle to get their first look at the birds in the area, but the rest of us are occupied with organizing our belongings and generally getting settled in, a process that will keep us busy for the next two or three days. Breakfast is pancakes with marmalade. O'Neill expeditions are known for their attention to culinary matters, and it is rumored that O'Neill makes an excellent no-bake cheesecake that boosts spirits after a few weeks of tuna-fish spaghetti. Angelo, Manuel, Gabriel, and Oscar have set out for the Cordillera Divisor, hoping to run into Magno along the way.

The trail that Gentry left behind should not be too hard to follow, as Gentry is very handy with a machete, an essential skill for a botanist in the tropics. Nevertheless, Angelo takes a compass reading and has a notebook with him to record major landmarks on their hike. It's easy to get lost in the jungle if you're not paying attention to what's around you, not so much because the vegetation is dense but because there is no apparent order to it. One does not walk through a stand of oak trees for a mile or two and then enter a beech-maple forest. In fact, it's difficult to find two trees of the same species within close proximity of one another, and the interconnecting network of vines and lianas obscures where one tree ends and another begins. In addition, most of the leaf shapes are not even remotely familiar to the North American eye. Walking is not unduly difficult, though you have to be careful what you rub up against or where you put your hand. Many plants are protected by biting insects and many others are guarded by spines.

By midmorning, feeling satisfied from his predawn walk in the forest, Tony is going through every item we brought with us, cataloguing and checking for water damage. The riverbank is covered with things laid out to dry and the trunks in the shelter are open, their contents lined up beside them or neatly repacked. He goes about this chore with a steady concentration and patience. In O'Neill's absence, Tony has taken on the responsibility of co-leader, something he is certainly accustomed to from the birding tours he conducts. We have all joked with him once or twice about his status as the camp doctor, and he's happily accepted being called "El Médico." ("El Doctor" was already in use—Manuel has called O'Neill this for years.)

The morning goes by slowly. The afternoon, as expected, is hot and humid. The river, about thirty feet across here, creates an opening in the forest, so from midmorning to midafternoon the sun hits the camp square on. The abandoned shelter from the banana *chacra,* which has become the center of activity, is only four feet from the edge of the high bank, and everything we do around it is directly in the sun. Inside the shelter it's considerably cooler. Its steeply sloped roof, seven feet high at the center beam, is covered with a thick layer of palm fronds that shed the rain and hold out some of the heat. A shelf has been constructed along each side about a foot off the ground, which no doubt was where the bananas were laid out and now makes a handy place to keep our supplies. Next to the shelter there is a long, skinny table big enough to hold our pots and pans, tins of coffee and cocoa, one tin of sugar, drink mix, and a few other food items we will use daily. It's surprising how little it takes to make the place feel civilized—adequate shelter and a sense of order.

When Angelo comes back with the others in midafternoon, he reports that it was a steady two-hour walk to reach a ridge from which they could see the Cordillera Divisor across a valley. They did not go any farther because the trail was rough at that point and they thought it might take several hours to cross the valley. Magno is with them and he gets a round of greetings, which he takes with a shy smile. He stayed last night at Gentry's camp, having taken some supplies to him. Gentry and Camilo, oddly enough, were not there and Magno doesn't know where they might have spent the night. With Gentry it's hard to tell. He's known to be carefree in the jungle, focused on his work and nothing else. (A story is told of a time when Gentry, climbing a tree, reached above his head into the foliage and felt a sharp prick on his hand. Taking this to be nothing more than a spine he had brushed against, Gentry reached again for the same spot. This time, when the same thing happened, he looked and saw the source of the problem: he'd been bitten by a snake—twice—and moreover it was a fer-de-lance. Fortunately, the bites turned out to be minor and Gentry did not suffer serious consequences.) Manuel and Oscar are working their way back more slowly, improving the trail as they go along. There are places where they lost it on the way out, though in general it was not too hard to follow. It rises and falls over a few hills just outside of camp, Angelo tells us, then hits a couple of steep ravines nearer the final ridge. A few little streams cross it and one larger one, four to six feet wide. The latter is nearest the mountains and holds large table rocks and pebbles. This gets the attention of Paul, who says there will surely be some interesting herps in a stream like that—a clear, fresh-water "mountain stream" in the lowlands.

Angelo took compass readings along the way and now wants to figure out where we are exactly. It's the first basic fact that must be established before any birds can be collected. Most of the maps, however, are with O'Neill. Furthermore, Angelo forgot to set his altimeter at sea level in Lima, so when he got to Pucallpa he had to make a guess at the right setting. This can be corrected later on, but it will mean some extra work for someone. For now, he judges that we are about two hundred meters above sea level. We do have one large satellite photograph of the area. Angelo spreads this out on the ground and tries to follow the Shesha, which is barely visible on the map, to a point where it is near the mountains. The Cordillera Divisor is divided into two clusters and for a while it's not clear which group is closer. I've brought a map with me that O'Neill lent me several months ago and though it's a projected land use map, it shows the Shesha and the Cordillera Divisor clearly enough; using the two maps Angelo eventually works out our position—"65 kilometers east-northeast of Pucallpa." This will be recorded in the camp log and will be the official location given for all the birds we collect.

As Angelo folds the maps back up, brushing dirt off them, I'm struck by how fantastic it is that we've just consulted a photograph taken from a satellite to tell us exactly where we are after three days in *peki-pekis* on the Río Shesha. I can scarcely imagine that the faint, squiggly, silver line in the photograph *is* the sunlit river forty feet to my right. The two perspectives do not jibe. It makes me feel far away, and small, as if I were a speck in this photograph that was taken from outer space. For me, this whole endeavor has the feel of something otherworldly about it, something incredible.

What we've come here for (in part at least)—to study the taxonomy of Peruvian avifauna—would appear to be quite mundane, certainly esoteric, were we not in the middle of the jungle. Taxonomy (also called systematics), the science of classifying organisms, is a word with no glitter to it, and Angelo, I expect, must often be met with a pained smile when someone asks him what he does and he answers that he is a biochemical systematist. O'Neill once wrote that not long ago "ornithologists with little foreign experience [i.e., field experience outside of the United States] began to think of the areas of systematics and taxonomy as being the fields in which a few 'old-time' museum people still dabbled."[1] At the moment we are far from a museum, and whatever we are doing here in the jungle, it could not be described as "dabbling." This work is charged with adventure of high seriousness. We are in an immense wilderness where scientists have never been before, and there's a chance, however slight, that we may find a new species of bird before we leave. Because the focus is on species, the stakes are high. Species is the one unit in nature that biologists consider to have a basis in fact. Genus, family, order, and so forth are categories that biologists have devised to indicate general degrees of similarity. Degrees of similarity are, of course, subjective. In 1960 Alexander Wetmore placed birds in twenty-seven orders, whereas European ornithologists, led by Erwin Stresemann, used fifty-one orders for birds. It's all a matter of "lumpers" (those who look for key traits that suggest birds belong in the same category) and "splitters" (those who find that small differences are reason enough to separate birds into different categories). The goal of all classification is to reconstruct the phylogenetic relationship of birds—that is, to establish which birds are most closely related by virtue of having evolved from the same ancestor. One problem for ornithologists is that birds apparently attained their basic forms in a relatively short period of time after their origin in the Jurassic period (135 million to 180 million years ago). Consequently, the family tree of birds is more like an unpruned bush. The lines of descent are difficult to follow, and ornithologists freely admit that no one really knows which family of birds is the oldest.

Unlike the broader categories of family and order, species is not open to so much conjecture. It is thought of as a fundamental, "natural" unit, but this concept is relatively new. As recently as 1957, Harvard Museum's Ernst Mayr felt it necessary to defend the concept of species, noting that "there is even a modern textbook of evolution in which the authors attempt to interpret evolution without mentioning species."[2] Darwin himself said, "I look at the term species as one arbitrarily given for the sake of convenience to a set of individuals closely resembling each other."[3] And Mayr has pointed out that even today the matter is confused by mineralogists who speak of a "species of mineral" and physicists who discuss "nuclear species." In other words, *species* in this sense means "type," and is no different from the way we think of family and order as categories, or types. On the contrary, the current widely accepted definition of *species* is "a living population in nature made up of birds (or other organisms) that have about the same structure, size, color, behavior, and habitat, and breed with each other rather than with members of similar groups."[4] The last criterion—that the birds interbreed—is considered to be the crucial one. Robins breed only with other robins and produce birds that have the same basic traits as all other members of the species. This, in theory at least, makes the matter objective—the birds either breed with each other or they don't. This criterion is based on fact rather than opinion. But the issue is more complex.

It's easy if two "different" birds that "have *about* [my italics] the same structure, size, color, behavior, and habitat" live in the same place, in which case whether or not they interbreed is immediately evident. In South America, however, so many unexplored areas remain that ornithologists are finding that birds which they thought did not live in the same area in fact do. This is precisely why Field Museum ornithologist John Fitzpatrick made the case for reclassifying a little-known antshrike (*Cymbilaimus lineatus sanctaemarae,* now known as the Bamboo Antshrike) as a distinct species.[5] When I visited Fitzpatrick at the Field Museum, he could not resist poking fun at Ted Parker of LSU, something he felt comfortable doing because he and Parker are friends as well as colleagues in neotropical ornithology. For a long time, Fitzpatrick told me, the bird he had just reclassified as a new species was considered to be a local race of another species, the Fasciated Antshrike. Fitzpatrick explained: "This is something"—and here he stopped to chuckle—"that Ted Parker used to tell me about. The Fasciated Antshrike had two different calls, Parker told me. And Ted [who is renowned for his memory of bird songs] would whistle these two different calls. Then a year or two later I was in Peru and heard this other race of the Fasciated Antshrike and saw it. I collected several of them and realized it wasn't the same as the Fasciated Antshrike. It was a new species." A smile came across Fitzpatrick's face. "Ted has always been embarrassed about that," he added.

The Fasciated Antshrike, a small bird of the forest that is barred black and white from head to tail and looks at the world with bright red eyes, was known to occur widely in South America, its features varying slightly from one region to another. This variation alone, relatively minor, did not make biologists think there were several different species of antshrikes, any more than different speech dialects in New York and Georgia would lead sociologists to declare that New Yorkers and Georgians speak different languages. Variety within a species is common. As long as there is the potential for continuous gene flow through interbreeding, then two or more different populations may still be considered the same species (they may be designated as subspecies or geographical races, however). In this case the "Bolivian race" of the Fasciated Antshrike was a bit different from its nearest relative, the "Amazonian lowland race." What Fitzpatrick found, however, was that both birds occurred in southeastern Peru (there were several recent observations and specimens to support this), and when he saw the "Bolivian race" there for himself in 1981 and heard its song, he realized it was not a subspecies at all. He found three sites where both the "Amazonian lowland" Fasciated Antshrike and the "Bolivian" Fasciated Antshrike occurred together. Since the two birds showed some differences—the "Bolivian race" was smaller, and had a more developed crest and a distinctly different song—the two, by definition, had to be different species. If they were the same species, they would be interbreeding and their traits merging until there was one bird with the same song, same crest of head feathers, and so forth. Consequently, Fitzpatrick described what had before been known as the "Bolivian race" as a new species: the Bamboo Antshrike. (Several months later, when I saw Parker and he showed me a new species of flycatcher he had just discovered, I remembered that flycatchers are Fitzpatrick's specialty, so I asked him if Fitzpatrick knew about this new species, assuming Parker had probably already needled him about it. A grin came over Parker's face. "No," he said. "We're not going to tell him for a while.")

But what if two populations of birds that look and act pretty much alike do not live in the same area? Are they two different species? Or are they really only one species, meaning that the two populations would interbreed if they came together? This is the question regarding two tanagers, the Burnished-buff Tanager (*Tangara cayana*) and the newly described Green-capped Tanager (*Tangara meyerdeschauenseei*). The Burnished-buff Tanager is known to occur throughout South America, but no records exist of its presence in extreme southeastern Peru, where in the fall of 1980 LSU ornithologist Tom Schulenberg collected two tanagers that generally resembled the Burnished-buff Tanager. The tanagers he collected were larger than the Burnished-buff Tanager and had green head feathers rather than an orange-buff cap. There were several other differences in coloration as well. Since the two tanagers' ranges did not overlap, Schulenberg could only speculate whether or not they would interbreed if they came together. After detailed analysis of the two populations of tanagers, with regard to appearance, behavior, song, et cetera, he decided they would not, and therefore described the two birds he'd collected as a new species.[6] In a similar situation, with two other birds, an ornithologist might make just the opposite decision. In the end, such decisions are matters of opinion simply because all the facts have not yet been uncovered. No one has argued with Schulenberg over his judgment, but he's been harassed for having named the bird after the late Rodolphe Meyer de Schauensee, whose book *The Species of Birds of South America and Their Distribution* has been invaluable to ornithologists working in the neotropics. Meyer de Schauensee is greatly respected, but *meyer-deschauenseei* is a mouthful.

A PARROT WITHOUT A NAME

Such speculation about a bird's status as species is only as valuable as the ornithologist who makes it is knowledgeable and wise. (And it is not restricted to searching for "new" birds in the wilderness. Many taxonomists spend their hours in museums looking at already known birds in an attempt to split one species into two or lump two or more together based on new data or reinterpretation of old data. There are many examples in the United States: the Yellow-shafted and Red-shafted Flickers were recently lumped together as the Common Flicker, two races of one species.) When new species are described from recently acquired specimens, ornithologists scrutinize the research. François Vuilleumier of the American Museum of Natural History co-authors a periodic, annotated list of new species with Ernst Mayr, who started the project in 1941. The most recent list contains quite a few "new" species that Vuilleumier scoffs at in print, noting that many of the official descriptions proclaiming new species were published in small, obscure journals because no reputable journal would have them: "The authors deplore the practice of some ornithologists to describe allegedly new species of birds without reference to a type specimen [the printer's plate for the ten-thousand-dollar bill in one of the various museum collections]. Far too often, the 'description' of a new species of birds is published in very obscure journals, at times even in privately printed 'journals'.... This sort of shoddy work is inadmissable in systematic ornithology."[7] When I spoke with Vuilleumier in New York City one afternoon, he was quick to assert that everyone he knew had the greatest respect for the work being done by LSU ornithologists. Their integrity was unquestionable.

Toward the end of the afternoon a young Peruvian I have not seen before walks into camp with a gun over his shoulder and a large black bird in one hand. He is wearing only a pair of shorts, no shoes, no shirt. Magno and Oscar greet him—he is one of the local guides that Gentry brought upriver with him, who has remained here to help with camp chores—and immediately half the camp rushes over to see the bird he has shot.

"Razor-billed Curassow," Tony says.

"Oh, wow—look at this thing," Angelo calls to Pete, admiring the bird, a big black fowl with a bizarre red bony growth atop its bill. Angelo has an envious gleam in his eye. Though nothing is set up yet to begin preparing specimens, this curassow would make a spectacular first entry in the expedition's log. Vladimiro, the young Peruvian, has other ideas, of course, and before Angelo has finished admiring the bird, Vladimiro begins plucking its feathers and tossing them over the bank. The bird is quickly becoming tonight's dinner: curassow soup.

The next morning Manuel and his crew set to clearing a big area for the work tent. They use their machetes for everything—scythe, ax, hoe, and rake—slashing through the vines and slim understory plants, hauling them away first, then attacking the few trees remaining. When all the vegetation is removed from the area, which is about twenty by forty feet, they loosen the dirt and chop up hidden roots. Oscar goes off in search of three trees that will make the end posts and center beam over which a plastic tarp can be draped. The trees are selected and stripped of their branches. One end of each is sharpened to a point. Manuel picks the spot for the first end post, raises the first pole, and holds it vertical. He lifts it a few inches, then drops it gently. It sinks two or three inches into the loose soil. Repeating this half a dozen times gives him a well-shaped starter hole as a target. Now he spreads his legs farther apart, squats just a little, raises the wobbling pole as he stands up, then heaves it downward, letting go at the last second. The pole stands by itself; already it is a good eight inches into the ground. Loosening it, he goes through the same motions. The pole sinks in two inches deeper. Like a human piston, he goes on hurling the pole into the earth and pulling it up again until both he and Oscar are needed to withdraw it. In fifteen minutes the post is sunk two feet deep and Manuel stands beside it sweating, sizing up his work. It stands perfectly straight.

Oscar places the second pole in the same manner, and then it's Magno's turn. Since he is the smallest of the three men, he shins up the first post and ties the center beam into a natural notch they have left for that purpose. At the second end post he must do the same. Manuel and Oscar hoist the other end of the beam up to him and he goes to work, but the procedure takes much longer since there is no notch to place the beam into, and Magno begins to laugh when he loses his grip and starts sliding down the tree. He gets back in position, fifteen feet off the ground, and finishes tying the center beam in place with the vines they cut down earlier.

When this is completed, they have something that resembles one of the goalposts on the soccer field back in Abujao. The plastic tarp is draped over it, and then it's back to selecting a dozen smaller posts that will be stuck in the ground along two sides. The tarp is tied to these supports and, suddenly, we have a roof above our heads. Now, Manuel gets out the work tent that will be erected here, a newly purchased Eureka tent with screen sides. He pulls all the poles out of the box, takes a glance at the instructions in English, and discusses with Oscar how they should put the poles together. An illustration with the instructions gives them some clues, but Manuel pays more attention to a photo of the tent on the side of the box. With this image in his head he applies his native intelligence to the task and, a few arguments notwithstanding, he and Oscar have the tent erected in twenty minutes. Angelo and Pete, who've been going through the ammunition and cleaning the guns, come over and make a ceremony of unzipping the doorway and being the first to enter the work tent.

"Perfecto, Manuel. Muy bueno," Angelo says, and Manuel's long serious face erupts into a smile. The tent is rectangular, eight by twelve feet, seven feet high at the center. It looks comfortable, but Pete has already gone to get the folding aluminum tables, and as soon as they're set up in the center, like all tents this one quickly feels crowded. When the canvas folding chairs are added and one of the liquid nitrogen tanks is placed in a corner (Angelo found them yesterday where Gentry had hidden them), it's apparent that the structure is really too small for all of us.

"Yeah, I know," Angelo says to me, "but we'll manage. Paul and Mara will only be here for a couple of weeks, and you'll be going after that. And eventually some of us will be working in the mountains, so it'll be okay."

Paul and Mara have both taken time off from their jobs in Houston, and two weeks in camp is all the time they can afford. My plans are to spend four weeks here, then leave so that I can get back to the States in time to have a couple of weeks to work on my notes before I go back to my teaching duties. Having to postpone the expedition a week when the equipment was held up by customs has shortened the overall time in the field for everyone. It is already June 22; late August is as long as anyone can stay.

Tony, having put in a long day of housecleaning yesterday, headed off into the jungle early this morning and just now he has returned. He looks tired but is flushed with excitement.

"There's a Hawk-eagle out there," he tells Angelo. "I've been watching it for an hour. It's still there."

Tony has taped the bird's call and has been playing it back to lure the bird out of the high branches. The Hawk-eagle is not far from camp, having followed Tony, so Angelo wonders if they should go out and try to collect it. The guns are cleaned and ready, the work tent is up—why not? A few times the bird came down within range when Tony was playing the tape, so he and Angelo decide to give it a try. The Hawk-eagle, however, refuses to come within range of the rifle once Tony and Angelo take up their positions. Tony plays the taped song repeatedly and the bird circles somewhere above the canopy out of sight, calling back to a ghost of himself, and once or twice lighting in the branches a hundred feet above us. Angelo can see him, but never clearly, so he does not fire a shot. Neither Angelo nor Tony seems particularly disappointed. First thing tomorrow Manuel will put up several mist nets, so soon enough there will be plenty of birds to deal with.

During the afternoon, Angelo inspects the items that were left to dry on the riverbank. Most things appear to be in good shape. Half an hour before dusk Vladimiro returns to camp from another hunting excursion. From the bag he has over his shoulder, he pulls out today's kill: a red howler monkey. He lays the creature on the ground, its long tail curling half around its body, the thick, red-brown hair glistening in the sun. While we all stare at the monkey, Vladimiro reaches into the bag again and pulls out a baby that whines loudly and immediately clings to its dead mother. Vladimiro pokes the baby once or twice, saying something to Oscar, and the monkey squeals again. It appears that the young howler has been wounded and the Peruvians try to examine it, but the baby snaps at them, then curls its head into its mother's fur. This is too much for Paul. The monkey's whine sounds unbearably human. Paul walks away, muttering. Vladimiro and Oscar appear unaffected. They soon ignore the creature and go about their business. An hour later, as dinner is prepared, the baby is still clinging to its dead mother. No one can stand to be near the scene, so we all carry our beans and rice to the work tent, where Tony has lit a kerosene lantern.

12

In the morning, as we collect near the fire to claim our pancakes, the infant howler monkey is still lying against its mother, but half an hour later I notice Oscar taking both monkeys down to the river, where, I assume, he will drown the baby. We are certainly in no position to judge our Peruvian guides. This is their country, after all, and we are the visitors—gringos who are accustomed to buying our dinners wrapped in cellophane and who now, with the righteous manifest of science tucked in our back pockets, have come into the jungle to collect a thousand or more birds, most of which we hope to take back to our American museums. I recall that the morning after we arrived Paul checked on a toad he'd caught the night before, discovering that the container he'd put it in had lain in the sun for a couple of hours and the toad was nearly dead. He splashed it with cold water and talked the toad back to life, wanting to keep it alive and healthy for photographs and observations. Then he would kill it—for the sake of science—or, as he said, "nuke 'im." No one thought twice about Paul's attitude. A toad doesn't elicit much emotion. It seems that we tend to feel increasingly sympathetic toward an animal the more it resembles us,

and the monkey, of course, is a primate, as we are. I doubt that I will ever forget how human the young howler monkey's cry was.

And now, this morning, Pete has come back from his predawn hike with the expedition's first bird, which he shot just minutes ago—a Buff-throated Foliage-gleaner, a dull brown bird in the ovenbird family. He is already preparing the specimen when I enter the work tent. Most bird-watchers would find this scene unpleasant, and even a few ornithologists question the necessity of collecting birds. Alexander Skutch, an ornithologist who has worked for many years in Central America and written a number of highly regarded books, has chosen not to collect birds. But among ornithologists Skutch's feelings are unusual. (O'Neill pointed out to me one of the problems with Skutch's method: Skutch often studied a bird for years, writing a detailed life history of it, without ever knowing what bird he was looking at. This was before some of the recently published field guides that might have helped Skutch, but even with them some birds are difficult to distinguish from one another without a close examination.) Naturalists have been collecting birds for centuries. Audubon himself first shot most of the birds he painted. And if you look carefully in the Harvard Museum's bird skin collection you'll come across several specimens prepared by one of the university's most illustrious graduates—Henry David Thoreau.

O'Neill is sensitive to the average birdwatcher's feelings, but he feels most people do not understand the importance of collecting specimens, and he has complained in print of our illogical view of the matter: "Ornithologists . . . have problems in getting adequate samples because birds are 'pretty' and 'popular,' and thus governments are not often willing to permit the collection of enough material. A permit to collect a series of 30–40 mice or frogs is usually granted without hesitation, but a request to collect 30 birds of a common species is usually considered excessive!"[1] Given the abundance of birds in South America it is unlikely that collecting birds has any effect whatsoever on the overall populations of individual species. Even if O'Neill were unwittingly to collect twenty specimens of a species on the verge of extinction, it could be argued that if the population of the species is as low as thirty or forty birds it is doomed to extinction any-way. This, however, is almost certain not to happen. Thus, neotropical ornithologists collect whatever birds come their way, knowing that more good specimens are needed of almost every species and that the negative effect of their collecting is virtually nil.

Ornithologists need a series of specimens to examine for taxo-nomic work. The differences between two related species of South American birds are often minute, and even someone with O'Neill's experience often has to have the bird in his hand to make a positive identification. In fact, it is sometimes hard to tell one neotropical bird from another even in the museum. One of the birds that Mildred Larsen handed O'Neill in 1963 along with the new Orange-throated Tanager was a cacique, a neotropical blackbird. Caciques are predominantly all black, sometimes with yellow or red on the rump and occasionally yellow in the tail and wings. This cacique was black with a yellow rump and traces of yellow in its wings, and O'Neill and Lowery quickly were able to identify it as *Cacicus leucorhamphus,* the Mountain Cacique.

Two years later, in 1965, a graduate student at LSU named Burt Monroe was looking over a collection of Bolivian birds that the museum had just acquired. The collection contained a series of Mountain Caciques, and as Monroe was placing these specimens in the collec-tion next to O'Neill's Mountain Cacique, he immediately felt that something was wrong. O'Neill's cacique was much smaller than the others, more the size of a Golden-winged Cacique (*C. chrysopterus*). When Monroe looked more closely, however, he noticed that the bill was slightly broader and less rounded than that of a Golden-winged. He called this to O'Neill's attention, and the two of them came across other differences as well. O'Neill's specimen had slightly larger feet, a more graduated tail, and showed a bit more yellow in the rump, which, now that they compared it with other specimens, seemed more orangeish. O'Neill got out his calipers and began making measure-ments. The Bolivian Golden-winged specimens measured between 99.4 and 106.4 millimeters at the chord of the wing; his specimen measured 109.5 millimeters. This might be considered an insignificant difference, reflecting nothing more than the traits of one particularly healthy individual. But earlier that year O'Neill had collected a second specimen of "his" cacique from the same area as the first, and it measured 109.0 millimeters. The two birds' middle toes were also a couple of millimeters larger, and this variation of a few millimeters showed up in all the other measurements.

When O'Neill and Lowery had initially identified the cacique, they based their decision on detailed descriptions of caciques in the available literature. Now, direct comparison with a series of other specimens made it clear that they'd made a mistake. In the end, O'Neill's cacique was described as a new species, the Selva Cacique. If LSU had not purchased the collection of Bolivian specimens, the Selva Cacique might still be unknown.

It might be argued that since the American Museum of Natural History already has a series of specimens of most South American birds, it is no longer necessary to collect any more. All one needs to do is look at those specimens. Besides the purely practical problem of traveling to and from the American Museum several times a year (the museum will loan out specimens through the mail, but with some rare birds it will only lend one specimen at a time), there is another important consideration. In the past many birds from South America were obtained by amateur collectors who kept poor records, if any, of exactly where the birds were collected, what the area was like, and so forth, all vital information for many different kinds of studies. In an article in *The Auk,* an ornithology journal, O'Neill explained the new approach: "A specimen collected today is often accompanied by tape recordings for vocal analysis, detailed notes on foraging activities, exact locality data, extensive notes on the ecology of the area where it was collected, careful documentation of its reproductive condition, and a whole host of other valuable data. . . . The days of the nonbiologist, professional collector are essentially gone. Now, the people who are describing populations of birds are the same ones who are collecting specimens."[2]

Without collections of specimens, ornithology would still be in the dark ages. Every branch of ornithology—ecology, behavior, evolution—

depends on having specimens to examine in detail. Furthermore, as ecologist Norman Myers points out, "Before we can gain a concise under-standing of the scale of the challenge to save species, we need to learn the dimensions of the problem. We must establish just how many species exist, where they are located, how far they are threatened, and so forth."[3]

This leads to a more fundamental question: What does it matter if ornithology is in the dark ages? Who cares if we had never learned the difference between a Mountain Cacique and a Selva Cacique? One answer is that the quest to understand evolution is a quest to under-stand life, and the study of neotropical birds—the relationship of one species to another—has taught biologists a great deal about the prin-ciples of evolution. The effect of climate and changing land forms on evolving species is illustrated dramatically in the tropics (which, after all, is where Darwin was inspired to study the finches on the Galápagos Islands). Forty to fifty percent of all plants and animals live in tropical rainforests, though rainforests cover less than 2 percent of the planet.[4] Moreover, understanding how evolution occurs affects the research of scientists who are studying the medicinal value of tropical plants. The importance of tropical plants to medicine is nothing less than astounding. Today, such operations as tonsillectomies and most abdomi-nal surgery would be out of the question had nineteenth-century naturalists not discovered that the substance South American Indians used to create their poison-tipped arrows was effective as an anesthetic. Curare, made from the bark of a liana and lethal on the tip of an arrow, kills by immobilizing the body's muscles; thus, the victim stops breathing. In 1814 the English naturalist Charles Waterton took some curare back to London, where he injected it into a donkey. The animal promptly keeled over, but a minute later Waterton revived the donkey by inserting bellows into its windpipe and giving it artificial respiration.[5] If an animal or person could be kept breathing, the drug would be an effective anesthetic. This, in fact, is the case today. Organic com-pounds derived from curare are used as anesthetics and muscle relaxants.

Such discoveries continue today. The odds are one in four that a prescription drug we take is directly or indirectly derived from a rainforest plant, and 70 percent of the three thousand plants identified by the United States Cancer Institute as having anticancer properties are from the rainforest.[6] Chemicals taken from a plant known as the rosy periwinkle are one spectacular example. Eli Lilly and Company researched and developed the natural chemicals after seeing the plant used by local tribal herbalists in Madagascar. As a result, a child with lymphocytic leukemia now has better than an 80 percent chance of remission as compared with a 20 percent chance in 1960 before the drug was developed.[7] Rainforest products affect nearly every American, albeit in somewhat less significant ways: coffee, artificial sweeteners, and bananas sit on our breakfast table; our cars would go nowhere without rubber tires; and a steroid known as diosgenin, made from a tropical plant, is an essential element in birth control pills.

If we accept that the rainforests of South America need to be preserved as reservoirs of valuable plant species (less than 1 percent of tropical rainforest species have been examined for their possible use to mankind), then we must know which areas of the rainforests are most valuable ecologically. Where should parks be established? How large should they be? Certainly areas that appear to be particularly rich in plant and animal diversity should be at the top of the list. But how will we know where these areas are if we don't know which animals live where and how they are related to each other? There is no way to know this without surveying unknown areas, as O'Neill has been doing all these years, and while one could capture some birds in mist nets and then release them, many birds will walk around or fly above mist nets.

Since plants seem to have the most potential as sources of lifesaving drugs, one might wonder what birds have to do with this; but to think this way is to forget the crucial interdependency of plants and animals. It may be that a particularly useful plant cannot survive in the wild without the help of a bird that eats its seeds, which remain undigested and are dispersed to produce new plants when they pass through the bird's system. Examining the stomach contents of birds, as LSU fieldworkers routinely do, reveals these kinds of relationships. And it would be a mistake to think that once we have identified a plant as useful we can propagate it indefinitely in greenhouses. Botanists and agriculturalists have learned many times over that cultivated plants often need infusions of genes from wild plants to remain vital. (The world coffee crop was very nearly lost to disease in the 1970s but was saved by locating resistant strains of wild coffee plants in Ethiopia.[8])

This rationale, which seems entirely acceptable to me, presents itself now with its rude details--Pete, having removed the skin of the Foliage-gleaner, is now turning it inside out in order to clean it. This bird was shot, but birds that are caught in the mist nets are "dispatched" by squeezing them, one's thumb pressed firmly against the bird's chest until its heart stops. (If the bird is too large for this, a lethal injection of sodium pentobarbital can be administered.) The biologists are accustomed to this, and apparently it is painless for the bird. But there will be times during the coming days when my heart and head are not in accord on this matter. When a beautiful Yellow-ridged Toucan is brought in from the mist nets, Angelo puts on a glove and holds him for photographs, but the bird is indignant, stabbing at Angelo with his six-inch bill. I joke with Angelo that he should let me hold the toucan, "just for a few seconds," but Angelo sees the look in my eye and is probably even less sure than I am myself what I will do if I have the opportunity to let the toucan slip from my grasp.

By afternoon, the work tent is in high gear, Cecilia, Angelo, Pete, and Gabriel all preparing specimens brought in from the nets. These include a White-throated Woodpecker, Ochre-bellied Flycatcher, Blue-crowned Manakin, and Buff-throated Woodcreeper, all relatively common birds of the Peruvian rainforest. This work continues through dinnertime and into the evening. It's been a full week now since we left Pucallpa, and since we last saw O'Neill. There is no way to know where he is at the moment or when he'll get here. Angelo has been frustrated several times in the last couple of days with all the problems on this trip, and now the O'Neill expedition is *sans* O'Neill. As a matter of fact, it also seems to be without Al Gentry.

Over dinner there was talk about Gentry's whereabouts. Vladimiro had gone to Gentry's camp in the mountains, as he had yesterday, but there was still no sign of him. Gentry was supposed to be there to get the supplies Vladimiro was bringing him. The camp has been undisturbed for three full days and Vladimiro says that Gentry did not take enough collecting supplies with him three mornings ago to last him all this time. He must be lost. Camilo is with him, and though he's Peruvian, he has less experience in the jungle than Gentry, who, like Ted Parker, can never seem to get enough of the rainforest, and, again like Parker, is sometimes a bit too at ease in the jungle for his own good. Angelo talked over the situation with Manuel, and it became clear that we should send out a search party even if it seems hard to believe that someone has gotten lost during what is only our first week here.

The next morning at dawn a search party—Manuel, Oscar, Magno, and Vladimiro—is getting ready to leave camp. They have enough supplies to stay in the jungle overnight and each person carries a whistle to attract Gentry's attention or call for help. As Manuel is shouldering his pack, we hear a shout from Cecilia, who left camp moments ago to walk upriver. A few seconds later she comes into camp with Gentry and Camilo, who both are haggard and disheveled. Gentry's hand shakes as he takes a cup of hot chocolate. His dark hair and thin, scraggly beard are more tangled than usual (Gentry, as far as I can tell, has been wearing the same, mud-caked blue jeans since we left Pucallpa) and his face is pale, greasy with sweat. They have indeed been lost for over three days, though last night they finally came upon the Shesha and camped along the bank less than a mile from here. Gentry talks rapidly between gulps of hot chocolate and mouthfuls of pancake. Camilo sits slumped in a chair. They had gone up into the mountains four mornings ago to collect plants and decided to hike back down to their camp by a different route. In the process, they followed what turned out to be the wrong stream, which they didn't realize until dusk. Neither of them had any food with them, no compass, no machete, no matches, nothing more than a miniature flashlight. One day they collected nuts to eat (something only a botanist could do), another day snails, and on the third day Gentry cut down a palm tree with his jackknife to get to the palm heart. Although the evening temperatures were in the high sixties, they were wet to the bone from several rainfalls and thus spent the nights shivering. Gentry danced and sang college fraternity songs to keep warm. They continued to follow the original stream, knowing that eventually it would lead to the Shesha, but it meandered and took them by a circuitous route through the jungle. Now, Gentry is a little wild-eyed, but seems under control, surprisingly so. His blue jeans hang a bit looser on him, but he was thin to begin with, a man who seems so focused on his work that food is an afterthought anyway. He has been lost a couple of times before, he says, but only for short periods. Camilo, meanwhile, has hardly spoken.

Within forty-five minutes, Gentry, having eaten two pancakes and drunk two cups of hot chocolate, rises from his chair and announces that since he plans to leave here altogether in two days, he must get back to the mountains and break camp. He can't leave his equipment and collections behind. The mountains are beautiful, he tells us, full of waterfalls and pretty streams.

"Anyone want to go have a look with me?" he asks without a hint of irony.

He is met by stares. "You expect us to go with a man who's just been lost out there for three days?" comes the reply.

Gentry chuckles lightly, but is too intent on getting back to his gear to dwell on this. He sets off alone. "I'll be back by this afternoon," he says.

Camilo gets up, crawls into an empty tent, and sleeps the rest of the day.

An hour later camp has returned to normal. Angelo and Tony are in the work tent studying a bird that was collected yesterday and discussing its markings. It more or less matches the description of a White-chinned Jacamar, but the white patch on the chin seems much too pale, and the bird has never been found south of the Amazon.

Jacamars, which look a bit like kingfishers, are not the kind of bird one would normally have trouble identifying.

"Well, I guess we've got our new species already," Tony jokes. "We have our *ridgleyi.*"

Tony has been joking all along about naming a new species after Bob Ridgley just to spite Ted Parker for not coming on the expedition. Ridgely, who works with the Philadelphia Academy of Natural Sciences, is the only ornithologist whose field experience with neotropical birds rivals Parker's (O'Neill's *field* work, though extensive, has not kept pace with Parker's in recent years).

"Ridgely's Jacamar," as Tony is now referring to it, just isn't quite right to be a White-chinned Jacamar, but neither he nor Angelo really thinks it is a new species. More likely they are overlooking something. That Tony can stand with the bird in one hand and a field guide in the other, make detailed observations, and still not be certain what bird he is looking at is an indication of how complex and subtle is the variation in species of Peruvian avifauna. It also points out the lack of an adequate guide to Peruvian birds.

Ted Parker's
House

13

During the 1960s, as word of O'Neill's fieldwork got around, LSU's ornithology department began attracting considerable attention. O'Neill went to Peru every year but one from 1961 to 1974, by which time he had earned a Ph.D. at LSU. In 1969 Ted Parker came across O'Neill's description of the Elusive Antpitta in *The Auk.* The Elusive Antpitta was the fourth new species O'Neill had discovered since 1963. Parker, a sixteen-year-old high school student in Lancaster, Pennsylvania, was thrilled at the glimpse of *terra incognita* when he saw O'Neill's painting of the antpitta and the introductory notes about "the vast lowlands of eastern Peru [where] prolonged fieldwork, even in a small section of humid forest, often results in the repeated discoveries of species of birds not previously encountered there."[1] O'Neill's painting shows the antpitta in the shadows of the forest understory, a moss-covered branch at its feet, around it a few skinny plants searching out the light. The bird is not brightly colored but it is beautiful nonetheless. Except for a large beak and the wild glint in its cinnamon eye, its general appearance suggests a farmyard chick. Its head, upper back, and wings are a subtle blend of colors that O'Neill described as

metal-bronze and tawny-olive. The bird's breast and lower back, a cream-buff, are covered with bold veins of black-brown.

"The Elusive Antpitta was a classic," Parker said one evening in Baton Rouge on my first visit there in 1984. "I must have read it a hundred times."

Parker was reminiscing about his first awareness of LSU's South America expeditions. He and O'Neill had gotten together this particular evening to talk with Mort and Phyllis Isler, a Virginia couple who were in the final stages of a book about tanagers. The Islers had come to Baton Rouge to confer with Parker and O'Neill about the complexities of neotropical tanagers. They had been driving from one museum to another in a motor home that they had converted to an office on wheels, which O'Neill, with characteristic hospitality, insisted they park in his driveway. We climbed into their cramped headquarters. O'Neill sat down at the table and Parker slumped into a chair in the corner. The two ornithologists could hardly be less alike, and one doubts that they would ever have anything to say to each other if they didn't share an obsession with birds.

O'Neill was in high school during the Eisenhower administration, Parker during the turbulent sixties. The forty-two-year-old O'Neill is neatly groomed and unfailingly polite. Parker, thirty-one, is tall with long hair and a bushy beard that hides a boyish face. He harbors a general dissatisfaction with the civilized world, and though politics and philosophy interest him, a resigned shrug of the shoulders is often his last comment in a conversation that has dead-ended on the dubious ways of mankind. At such moments a disconsolate, pained expression passes over him. Sometimes, even in discussions about birds, he will give in to the impulse to make pessimistic, universal proclamations: "No one knows anything about how birds live. We just invent these little formulas and pretend we understand something." O'Neill refers to such statements as "Tedisms." Fortunately, Parker has a sense of humor that extends to his own foibles:

"Ted, when are you going to have that paper done so we can use the data in our book?" Mort Isler asked.

Parker: "A week."

Isler: "Which week?"

Parker, aware of his tendency to procrastinate, was the first to laugh, his cheeks reddening and his laugh rising almost to a cackle. To change the subject, Parker picked up one of the Islers' notebooks, which contained a transcript of some of Parker's tape-recorded observations of tanagers in Peru. He read aloud from the abbreviated notes:

"At Machu Picchu, uttering a loud *cheet* note, going from flower to flower in *Brachyotum*. Seen piercing flower only once. Apparently knows which flowers have nectar by looking."

Parker interrupted himself. "Oh yeah—that's interesting. Why is that?"

"You sure it's not seeing which flowers already have holes in them from another bird?" O'Neill asked.

"You couldn't tell, but it was doing something. I saw it pierce one, but the others it just glanced at and moved on." Parker turned to Phyllis Isler. "How about *Hemispingus* [a genus of tanager]—did you get any useful information on it?"

The conversation moved in this way from one bird to another. One could mention almost any bird known from Peru and Parker would have a question about some aspect of its behavior. Whenever they were together, he and O'Neill would toss these questions back and forth for hours.

Parker and O'Neill both showed an interest in birds at an early age. Phyllis Isler asked O'Neill if he had ever been discouraged from pursuing such an impractical interest.

"Not from my parents," O'Neill said. "But I do remember one thing that really made me mad. I was, eleven, I think. My parents had company over one evening. It was about eight o'clock and I was painting a Green Jay, and this man looked at me with no smile and said, 'Why aren't you doing your homework or something *important?*' So I painted a *better* Green Jay."

The Green Jay that the eleven-year-old O'Neill was painting he had seen for the first time earlier that year when he went on a birding jaunt to south Texas with the local Houston bird club. It was his first experience with tropical birds.

"It really got me going," he said. "I started reading things like Sutton's *Mexican Birds* and of course I was very much aware of Peterson because of the field guides. He had come to Houston and given some of the Audubon lectures. But as far as people doing things in the tropics, Sutton was the first one I knew of. In Sutton's book he mentions Lowery."

Two years later O'Neill's junior high school biology teacher invited O'Neill to accompany her on a trip to visit her mother in Baton Rouge, where she would take O'Neill to meet this Dr. Lowery. O'Neill, thirteen years old, had just gotten his hands on Lowery's newly published *Louisiana Birds,* so he jumped at the chance. However, four years later, when he applied for college, his interest in painting led him to the University of Oklahoma rather than LSU. He wanted to be near "Doc" Sutton, considered one of the finest bird painters in the country.

Parker's early interest in wildlife was just as single-minded as O'Neill's. As a ten-year-old he would take a ruler, pen, and stack of index cards with him on father-son fishing trips so that he could properly record each species of fish he caught before throwing it back in the lake. He also began hanging out on the campus of Franklin and Marshall College, where each spring freshman botany students were required to identify a hundred different trees on campus. Parker would stand next to the chestnut tree, the first tree on the list, and when a student showed up he'd say, "So, you want to know where the ginkgo tree is?" For this service he charged a dollar. About this time Parker met a man named Harold Morrin, who took a fatherly interest in him and began inviting him on birding trips around the East. Morrin showed the young Parker his first tropical birds in the Florida Keys. Hearing through the grapevine that a Caribbean bird had strayed into the keys, Morrin would get off work early on a Friday, pick up Parker, and drive nonstop to southern Florida. There they would spend Saturday afternoon searching out the bird, get back in the car Saturday evening, and head back, reaching home Sunday—an adventure they repeated several times.

Parker's parents were supportive, sometimes to the point of embarrassment: "I used to caddy for my father, not during spring or fall migration, but in the summer, and we would be out there on the golf course, and all my father's friends were doctors and lawyers, and their kids, many of whom went to school with me, were planning to go to med school or law school, and my father would say, 'Oh, Teddy, tell them what you told me the other day about that bird nest you found,' and I'd be just mortified."

In 1971, while still in his last year of high school, Parker set out to see as many birds in North America as he could in one year, a major form of competition for serious birders. His father, an attorney in Lancaster, had given Parker a credit card to use for gas when he started college at the University of Arizona (chosen in part for its proximity to Mexican birds). When the bills came in from the birding trips all over the Southwest, his father was aghast, but at the same time Parker announced to the American Birding Association his total for the year—626 species (of a possible 700 or so)—a new national record and the first time anyone had gone over the 600 mark. Birdwatchers still talk about this feat, and it is all the more impressive because Parker accomplished it without the aid of private jets and "birding hotlines," which are now standard equipment in the game for wealthy birders in pursuit of new records. (Parker's record has since been broken, but he later set and still holds the World Big Day record: 331 species, all seen in a twenty-four-hour period. Parker and another ornithologist, Scott Robinson, set this record in Manu National Park in Peru. Parker and Robinson share the record because birding rules stipulate that two people must identify each species, though in 1971 Parker's companions changed from one trip to the next over the course of the year.)

Not surprisingly, Parker's general studies at the University of Arizona suffered somewhat. But in the biology department he quickly made himself known. The ornithologist there, Steve Russell, had studied under George Lowery at LSU and knew a gifted birdwatcher when he saw one.

"Did you get the same treatment from Russell that I got from Sutton when I was a freshman at Oklahoma, that you got included with the grad students?" O'Neill asked.

"Yeah. I started to hang around the grad students who were doing work in the tropics, and when I started going to Mexico all the time Russell realized I was really serious. I remember being in the museum and listening to these guys bragging about the things they'd done in South America, and I'd listen and then go back to my dorm room and scheme and plot. I finally decided to just quit school and go to South America on my own."

"When did Lowery first get in touch with you?" O'Neill asked.

"I was in the museum one day when Russell came in and said, 'Ted, you have a phone call,' and I thought, Oh my God, someone must have died. I went in and picked up the phone and it was Lowery. That's the first time I'd ever heard him. In that real deep southern voice he said, 'I don't know if you've ever heard of me, but I'm George Lowery, the director of the museum at LSU.'

"And I said, 'Yes sir, yes sir.'

"Lowery said, 'I want to get right to the point. We're going to have an expedition leaving for South America in three weeks and I was just wondering if you might be able to go along. . . . '

"And my heart was pounding so hard I said, 'Ahh, ahhhhh well, I'll have to think about it, can you call me back tomorrow?' And I hung up the phone and nearly fainted."

O'Neill, who by now was leading LSU's expeditions to South America had heard about "this kid Ted Parker who had already memorized the book and was doing better fieldnotes than most graduate students." "The book" was Meyer de Schauensee's *Birds of South America.* Russell, hearing that Parker was planning on quitting school, had gotten in touch with O'Neill and Lowery at LSU. O'Neill, perhaps remembering his own first trip to Peru after his freshman year at college, had suggested to Lowery that they ask Parker to go with them.

Parker, hair down to his shoulders in the style of the day (it was 1974), was excited and eager to impress Dr. Lowery, "a good southern gentlemen." Russell told Parker that Lowery demanded that all his students be neatly groomed. When he flew back to Lancaster to talk with his parents about the trip, Parker made a visit to his childhood barber.

"All through high school I'd walk by the barbershop, and my old barber would come out on the porch and say, 'Teddy boy, come here.' It was a ritual. So I went to him and said, 'Just cut off all my hair. I'm going to South America and I don't care anymore.'"

A week later Parker showed up at the Baton Rouge airport to meet the expedition members:

"Here were all these graduate students with long hair and beards—they looked at me and thought, Oh who is this character?"

"Who were you with that first year?" Phyllis Isler asked.

"Gary Lester and Dan Tallman. The three of us went to Peru first, and John came later. In the first two weeks there, we were arrested as spies," Parker said. "What happened was we went to southwest Peru to the coast, went out one morning to collect seabirds, and when we came back in the afternoon we set up camp on what we thought was this unused airstrip. We had all the birds out and were skinning them, and suddenly we heard this roar that got louder and louder, and this jet was coming from the south right along the beach, and it came right over us. It was so low it almost forced us to our knees. And when it passed we saw these two big red stars out on the end of the wings. It was a Chilean fighter jet. We didn't think much of it until about an hour later we looked out on the highway and saw this big caravan of military vehicles coming along. We thought, 'Oh, wonder where they're going?' And they turned into the entrance to where we were. Thirty guys with machine guns got out and told us to get up against the truck. They found our guns, and Gary Lester was wearing a U.S. army jacket, and we had what looked like a shortwave radio."

Parker and the two graduate students were arrested. Though they were released from jail later the same day, the police would not return their "weapons" right away, which meant they had no guns to collect specimens with.

A couple of days later, in the high mountains a few miles inland, oblivious to the altitude sickness that plagued his companions, Parker noticed a small bird in the roadside brush—something that didn't match any species he knew about. The next day, convinced the bird he'd seen was something special, Parker insisted they go back and try to collect it.

"We had nets, but it was windy and real rugged terrain, so we went into the kitchen of the hotel restaurant and whispered to one of the waiters, 'Do you know anyone who has a shotgun?' And the guy said, 'No but I have a friend whose brother's uncle has a shotgun.' The next day we met this guy and he had an eleven-gauge shotgun with two hammers that you pulled back. It was huge, like a blunderbuss. We had some ammunition we had salvaged, so we headed back to the mountains the next morning.

"It was real cold. By first light we were at eleven thousand feet, and we came around this bend and there's a tinamou on the side of the road. Our friend with the shotgun got all excited and said, 'I'll get it, I'll get it,' and he put the gun across my lap inside the truck and fired out the window. Kaboom! Feathers flew everywhere. I saw stars.

"Finally we found the bird I'd seen before. There were two of them in a bush about three feet tall. We were so close that I can remember Tallman saying he'd better back up a little. He raised the gun and kaboom! again—the bush just disintegrated. We had to wait for the smoke to clear. About fifteen feet back in another little bush is the bird. You should have seen the shape it was in. We got three of them. What an experience." The little bird Parker had spotted turned out to be the first Peruvian specimen on record of the newly discovered Tamarugo Conebill, a bird known only from one locality in Chile. It was an auspicious introduction to Peru.

In the fall, when the LSU graduate students headed back to the States to resume classes, Parker refused to leave; he stayed on for a full year. Helen Koenig, a Minnesota woman who married a Peruvian (Dr. Arturo Koenig, the orthodontist O'Neill called in Lima), told me that she remembers Parker coming to their house for a rest from his travels and to look at the mail that had been piling up there for him. He was gangly, his clothes didn't fit him, and with his hayseed haircut, which still had not grown out, he looked worse than a Minnesota farmboy. He spilled into a chair and began going through the mail. When he came to his bank statement and found out he was far overdrawn, he slouched a bit more, and then moaned and sank further into the chair when he came to his grades from school.

There are some who still feel it's a minor miracle that Parker ever finished college. And with only a B.A.—all serious ornithologists are expected to earn a Ph.D.—it was difficult for him to find a place in the hierarchy of the professional ornithological community. His notoriety as a birder elicited both mistrust and envy. For years he was treated like a second-class citizen, his fieldwork used in papers by others with little or no acknowledgment. This embittered Parker toward the ornithological establishment, and though he still complains (Parker loves to complain) that he can't get a paper clip from the museum office without being questioned, in fact he is now widely thought of as the leading authority on the birds of Peru, if not all of South America—John O'Neill and Bob Ridgely notwithstanding. If some still see him as a bit of a maverick, it's a role he is not unhappy with. Roger Tory Peterson says simply, "In the neotropics, Parker is supreme."

O'Neill knows this better than anyone: "When it comes to birds, Ted is incredibly smart. If something will help him understand birds, he'll pursue it to the ultimate. It's almost frightening."

His personal priorities are less predictable. While O'Neill is always responsible, Parker can occasionally be maddeningly self-absorbed. In 1986 Parker was to meet LSU colleague Tom Schulenberg and me in Lima for a two-week excursion into the mountains in northern Peru; but, tired out from an expedition to Bolivia, he never showed up in Lima, leaving Schulenberg to tell me the news when I got to the Lima hotel where I was to meet him and Parker. Parker had decided to spend the time resting at the Explorer's Inn. What was more important, he was to have participated in the Cordillera Divisor expedition, but a couple of months before we were to leave he complained about how much time it would take just to get to the study site. He was busy with VENT birding tours and he wondered if it wouldn't be possible for him to come in by helicopter after a camp had already been established. Later, O'Neill laughed this off: "Yeah, Ted wants to be flown in like a movie star."

That evening in the Islers' motor home, however, a sense of comradeship prevailed and the talk was spirited and warm. O'Neill began talking again about his childhood, noting that he had kept hundreds of birds in the backyard and had even stored bird bodies in the refrigerator.

"I had cages all over the place," O'Neill said. "I'm talking about pheasants and chickens and ducks and geese. Things came and went. I must have raised twenty barn owls. Some I just released, or we would . . . " O'Neill paused momentarily to clear his throat.

"Eat them?" Parker interjected, laughing hard. "John's incredible. I can honestly say that John has eaten more birds in Peru than most people will ever see."

At this, I remembered that earlier in the afternoon, while looking at the museum's bird skin collection, we came across a tinamou, a partridgelike bird, and O'Neill whispered, "Delicious white meat."

O'Neill, who had finally stopped laughing, responded.

"I'll eat anything once, but I'll tell you that Greater Yellow-headed Vultures are low on my list."

"I can't believe you ate one," Parker said.

"I had to get it on my taste test."

"The worst thing is when you're with these damn mammologists," Parker added. "For some reason they always have to throw a bat body or two into the stew. It ruins everything. You get this real musky, terrible taste."

Looking back, O'Neill once jokingly described himself as "a vicious little kid with a BB gun." Most birdwatchers shudder at the grisly prospect of ornithologists turning birds into "specimens," and O'Neill and Parker are very sensitive about the issue. How one child's interest in birds is limited to reverent observation and another's extends to dissecting the very bird he has watched with joy a moment before is something of a mystery. It has to do perhaps with the difference between avocation and vocation, fascination and obsession—a distinction made clear when Mort Isler asked Parker about his experiences with O'Neill's first discovery, the Orange-throated Tanager.

"That was incredible," Parker replied.

In 1978, in northern Peru, Parker knew he was not far from the habitat of the Orange-throated Tanager. Fourteen years had gone by since O'Neill and Farrand first saw the bird; no one else had seen it since. With that in mind, Parker got up one morning and left camp with a hunting party of Aguaruna Indians who had promised to take him into the mountains where the Orange-throated Tanager lived.

"The Aguaruna are like Apaches," Parker said. "They still have a lot of pride and aren't intimidated much, not at all meek and subordinate like the few Indians I had been around. You're there on their terms." Parker remembered the air feeling a bit cooler than normal that morning, but he thought nothing of it. One of the Indians, he was told, spoke some Spanish, so he'd be able to communicate with his guides. In two canoes Parker and the four Aguaruna men poled upriver. At lunchtime Parker remarked that he was getting hungry and wouldn't it be a good idea to stop for lunch, but the man who was supposed to speak Spanish just smiled and said nothing. Parker's heart sank. Perhaps this man didn't speak Spanish after all. At the end of the first day they arrived at an Aguaruna village.

"I was almost like a prisoner. They just took me by the arm and led me to this longhouse. Everything was very ritualized. There was an elderly man in the middle of the room sitting on a log with his blowgun. And they just pushed me forward and a woman brought me a bowl of masato, which is this beer made out of manioc. We drank that and the old guy said something and then they took me and put me over on the side of the room. They all got together and started talking and laughing and eating. And this went on for hours, and I just sat there. I had no idea what was happening." Genaro, the man who spoke Spanish (he did, it turned out, have a handle on some rudimentary Spanish), took Parker to his father's house where they ate manioc and banana gruel. Genaro's family were traditional Aguaruna with painted faces and highly formalized customs. Parker remembered the eerie feeling of sitting across from them around a flickering fire, red paint on their cheeks, half of their teeth missing, "people like no other people you've ever been around before," he said.

After a night on a cane mat, Parker was up at dawn for a second day's journey into the mountains by river and foot. They reached a crest of nineteen hundred feet at five p.m. and pitched camp in a thundershower. When the rain broke, a dozen Aguaruna hunters, camped over the ridge, came bursting into camp with barking dogs and squealing pigs. Parker thought that he had reached a pristine garden of Eden from which he'd set out the next day and see the Orange-throated Tanager, and his spirits sank again at the ruckus and noise. Dinner was the same as lunch on the previous two days: tuna fish and cold *yuca.*

He fell asleep in the early darkness amidst the commotion of the celebrating hunters. Sometime in the middle of the night he woke. A three-quarters moon was shining brightly and the silence seemed profound. To the west an Ocellated Poorwill called. Then, from farther away, a deep, low humming—four notes—like the night wind blowing over the lip of a bottle: the Nocturnal Curassow, one of the least understood birds in South America, whose mysterious call was virtually all that was known of the bird. Parker felt that he should get up and go out, but instead lay there transfixed by the curassow and eventually fell back asleep. When he woke again at dawn it was raining, and the cold air that Parker had noticed on the day he'd left was now clearly the beginning of a rare cold front that had made it across the equator. There was nothing to do but go back.

The way down the mountain was a trial of nerves and spirit. The river was swollen with rainwater and ripped by waves which thoroughly drenched everything in the canoe and nearly capsized it. With no dry clothes to change into and his sleeping bag soaked, Parker lay shivering all night on a cane mat, a pair of wet pants wrapped around his feet and a towel around his head. The temperature dropped into the midforties. He woke once in predawn light to the haunting, melancholy music of a flute. Later in the day he found the source of the music: one of the villagers was playing an instrument made from the barrel of a shotgun.

Two days later, Parker stumbled back into the LSU camp, ate lunch, and took a long nap. There were no stories of the Orange-throated Tanager to tell.

"No birds sang the whole time we were up there. I didn't see a thing," Parker said. "I still dream about that trip though."

Telling this, Parker smiled at his own misfortune. The ill-fated search for O'Neill's Orange-throated Tanager had been an adventure he would never forget, and coming up empty-handed seemed almost incidental. One set off on such journeys because the search itself was important. Science, after all, is a search, a method, not a set of rules. But few people anymore seem to have the mental and physical where-withal to do what Parker did, what he and O'Neill continue to do year after year. The spirit of adventure and a disciplined scientific mind are seldom found in the same person. Parker could afford to laugh at his failure because since that day six years earlier, he has not only been successful on another attempt to see the Orange-throated Tanager but has also seen 95 percent of Peru's birds (over 1,650 of the 1,700 or so species), more than anyone else past or present. That he is ten years younger than O'Neill and stealing some of his glory is only occasionally an awkward subject around LSU. In fact, Parker has become the perfect accomplice in O'Neill's dream project—a comprehensive book on the birds of Peru. O'Neill is painting many of the plates (he has given up on trying to do them all; artist Larry McQueen is now doing the majority of them), and Parker is writing the text, nearly all of it from firsthand experience, something unheard of in monographs on neotropical birds. The book, slowly moving forward, is already being spoken of as the finest work ever done on birds of the New World tropics.

14

In June 1983, at the edge of a flooded section of rainforest in northern Peru, Ted Parker heard a sound he didn't recognize. He stopped and leaned an ear toward the bird call that was coming from somewhere amidst the green profusion of vines and foliage; one note didn't sound right. Puzzled, Parker listened again and then decided to tape the call and play it back to lure the bird into the open, a trick every birdwatcher knows. But this time it didn't work.

Parker was with his wife-to-be, Carol Walton, and they had been walking since dawn along the *varzea.* They were not on an expedition. In fact, though Parker was as intent as ever in his daily routine of observations and notetaking, the time he was spending at this study site a hundred miles northeast of Iquitos was something of a retreat too. He was busy much of the year leading nature tours, and when he was home in Baton Rouge with Carol he was forever trying to catch up with himself and a handful of projects for which he had more notes and ideas than he knew what to do with. Carol, a student in veterinary medicine, was equally absorbed in her studies. So, there on the Sucusari River, north of Iquitos, they were alone together for a few weeks.

Still, the bird was calling and Parker didn't know what it was. There was one unusual twittering note in the bird's call, and "you don't just walk by a sound you don't recognize when you know most of the sounds," he said later. He put the tape recorder down on the trail and stepped into the wet undergrowth, his hightop Converse basketball shoes sinking into the muck. The mystery bird was twenty feet up in dense vine tangles. Craning his neck, Parker caught a glimpse of a small olive-yellow flycatcher. Finally he got a good look at the bird.

"I can remember seeing that it had a real pale iris, and I knew it had to be a flycatcher in the genus *Tolmomyias,*" he recalled, "but the voice was so different I thought, Well, this just can't be."

There are three species of the drab *Tolmomyias* flycatchers in the Sucusari area. Like our North American flycatchers of the genus *Empidonax,* they are virtually indistinguishable by sight. These South American *Tolmomyias* flycatchers, in a habitat infinitely more complex and disruptive to the eye, are guaranteed an anonymity to all but a few ornithologists. Which was it? Why was its voice different? Parker, without a collecting gun at hand, could do nothing more than make a few notes and go on down the trail that June morning in Amazonia.

In the late fall of 1983, after Parker had returned to Baton Rouge, he listened again to the tapes he'd made and compared them with recordings of known flycatchers in the Sucusari area. His *Tolmomyias* didn't sound quite like anything else. Parker tried to think of other birds that might make a similar call but came up with nothing. For anyone else this wouldn't mean much, but Parker is famous for his ability to recall bird vocalizations. It's unlikely that any other ornithologist would have noticed that the flycatcher's call sounded different from other *Tolmomyias* flycatchers.

O'Neill had discovered his first new bird twenty years earlier, and by 1983 he'd been involved in the discovery of ten new species. Several other people at LSU had authored or co-authored descriptions of new birds, as had John Fitzpatrick and E. R. Blake at the Field Museum. Even a missionary in Peru, Peter Hocking, had co-authored one of the

Field Museum discoveries. Today, Parker freely admits how badly he wanted to find a new bird.

"The frustrating thing is that over the years each time I found a bird that I didn't know, down deep I'd feel, Oh my God, this is it. And that happened a lot the first years. I found all sorts of new species and then I'd get back to camp and I'd look through the book and . . . " His voice trails off, registering the inevitable disappointment. "So one by one all my new species dissolved. So I gave up. I realized there was no way you can guess when you're going to find something. And most of the people at LSU who have found things have just stumbled on them—had no idea what they were. A number of them were identified really when they were brought back to the museum."

So Parker filed his tape recordings away, mentioned the unusual flycatcher to O'Neill and Van Remsen, then forgot about it for a while, pressed by more immediate concerns and reasoning that he shouldn't get his hopes up again.

Six months later, not having heard or seen the bird again, he'd put it out of his mind even though he was once again in northern Peru, this time leading a nature tour. His group had just spent a few days at a lodge about fifty miles south of the Sucusari camp where he had first heard the unknown flycatcher. The group was getting settled into a boat that would take them back to Iquitos when photographer John Dunning approached Parker with a small bird in his hand. Dunning had been photographing the birds of South America for years by catching them in mist nets, taking a picture, then letting them go again, and many times he had sent pictures to Parker, who helped him identify a bird he was unfamiliar with. Dunning handed the bird to Parker, asking him what it was. Parker remembers:

"Everyone was standing around us, and I looked and it just didn't quite register. We were in a hurry and it was obvious I couldn't just squeeze this bird in front of everyone, so I said, 'Well, I'm almost sure it's an immature Gray-crowned Flycatcher.' And I gave it back to him and we left."

The Gray-crowned Flycatcher (*Tolmomyias poliocephalus*) has an olive-green back, gray cap as the name suggests, a pale yellow to olive breast, and a dark eye with an eye ring. But the bird's range extends from as far north as Venezuela south to Bolivia and from Ecuador east along the Amazon to eastern Brazil. Within this range its features vary, adding to the difficulty of making a quick, certain identification. The bird Parker was looking at had a "pale buff wash across the breast" and a "distinctive facial pattern with pale cheeks and an orange eye," not quite right for the Gray-crowned Flycatcher, but these are the kinds of differences that one might note in an immature bird. An hour later, though, on the river, Parker was stricken with a pang of recognition: he had seen that orange eye once before—on that June morning a year earlier. He was seized with grief at the thought that he had possibly just held a new species in his hand and let it go—he might never see it again. At that point there was nothing to do. He was leading a tour and could hardly justify turning the boat around in the name of science. Besides, Dunning had probably released the bird by then.

A month later, back in Baton Rouge, Parker asked Dunning to send him the picture he'd taken of the bird at Yanamono. As soon as he had the photograph he began showing it to everyone at the museum. Angelo Capparella, a new Ph.D. candidate at that time, was heading for the Iquitos area in a few months, and Parker told him to keep an eye out for the bird and try to collect it if possible.

When Angelo returned at the end of the summer, Parker sought him out and asked about the flycatcher. Angelo confessed he'd forgotten all about the bird and didn't remember seeing anything like it. Consequently, Parker didn't look at the specimens Angelo had brought back until a few days later, but when he did open up the specimen drawers he instinctively went to the flycatchers. The first *Tolmomyias* flycatcher he looked at had a "bright orange" eye, according to the data tag! The tag on the bird read:

"Shot in *varzea* undergrowth; N. bank Río Amazonas, 85km NE Iquitos; 30 July 1984; A. P. Capparella."

After "species" was a question mark in pencil. Angelo had shot the bird, taken a quick look at it, and mentally catalogued it as "one of those little flycatchers that all look alike."

"It was a fluke," Parker says.

"It's the only true *discovery* of a new bird that I know of," Van Remsen told me. In 1985, two years after Parker's initial observation of the *Tolmomyias* flycatcher, Remsen and I were on our way to Sucusari. Parker was waiting for us at the camp where he'd first seen the bird.

"Ted's in a league all by himself. There's no one like him, no one who knows as much about neotropical birds." That's why, Remsen went on to explain, Parker may be the only ornithologist alive who has actually discovered a new bird in the wild rather than after the bird has been collected.

Discovery is the word I used many times when talking with the LSU people about the new species being found in Peru. Early on, O'Neill corrected me, pointing out that he had "described" several new birds, not really discovered them. First of all, in many cases local people were very familiar with the bird that the western scientists were all excited about, and *discovery* implies an immediate recognition of something new, which has been the case only a few times, and then only when the bird was "in the hand." But Parker knew enough when he first heard the new *Tolmomyias* flycatcher to realize it might be an undescribed species. Remsen says that there are several ornithologists and birders who think they know the neotropics as well as Parker, but who have never collected birds or done enough detailed taxonomic work to realize how often they might be wrong when they point to something flitting about a hundred feet above their heads and identify it.

"They've never had the humbling experience," he says, "of shooting a bird out of the canopy only to discover that not only is it not the species you thought it was, but it's not even in the same family. You can't learn the neotropical birds by just watching them."

Poring over specimens in the lab gives ornithologists a healthy respect for the diversity of neotropical birds and also implants a concrete, schematic image in their minds by which they can gauge their reactions in the field. Birdwatching in the neotropics without this kind of museum study is akin to an Illinois farmer driving into New York City without a map. Parker and Remsen, however, do not watch birds so much as they listen to them. Despite their often brilliant colors, South American birds are difficult to see amidst the shadowy, tangled latticework of vegetation, and those birds that are secretive by nature are virtually impossible to find, except by ear.

In 1972 Parker took a borrowed cassette tape recorder with him to Mexico.

"After a few earlier trips I realized it was going to be real tough to see undergrowth birds without a tape recorder. You'll be walking along a trail and these birds will be close to the path and singing, but as soon as you get close enough to see what they are, they stop singing and disappear."

With the recorder Parker could tape the song, play it back as he would for the *Tolmomyias* flycatcher, and entice the bird to make another appearance as it looked for the source of the new song. Today, Parker takes two or three recorders with him to South America, just in case something goes wrong with his pride and joy—a Nagra reel-to-reel recorder he has used since 1979. The Nagra is exceptionally durable and weather resistant. Though he handles it like a baby, Parker admits he has dropped the recorder a couple of times; he refuses, however, to let it be packed on a mule in case the animal stumbles and falls on the machine. Instead, Parker lugs it everywhere he goes on a well-padded strap slung over his shoulder. A bit bulkier than a stereo amplifier, the Nagra weighs a wearying twenty-five pounds. Including the special shock-mounted microphone Parker uses, the equipment is worth seven thousand dollars. Parker has it on permanent loan from John S. McIlhenny, whose grandfather created Tabasco sauce and is himself godson of Teddy Roosevelt. A somewhat eccentric southern gentleman, McIlhenny has been a patron of LSU for over twenty-five years.

Parker made somewhere between six thousand and seven thousand recordings between 1972 and 1985. If he had hung on to them himself, he would have the third largest collection in North America after the Cornell Library of Natural Sounds and the Ohio State Museum. In fact, he donates his recordings to Cornell, which loans them out to scientists worldwide for a wide variety of research projects. James Gulledge, the director of the Cornell collection, considers Parker to be the library's finest contributor. Of the five thousand species represented in Cornell's collection nearly two thousand are Parker's. Roger Tory Peterson, whose keen ear has long been the standard against which others are judged, states unequivocally that Parker has "one of the best ears I've ever known . . . one in a million. Ted would have probably made a great musician."

Parker may have been born with exceptional hearing, but he has also worked hard to develop it. As he played some recordings for me one day at his home in Baton Rouge, he momentarily advanced the tape at fast-forward and then casually identified the bird songs that were whizzing past as rapid squeaks and slurred notes.

"That's how many times I've heard this stuff," he said, laughing.

The Sucusari camp, where Parker and Carol Walton were staying, was a two-day river trip from Iquitos, a city of more than 100,000 in north-eastern Peru. Iquitos has been a major port on the Amazon since the nineteenth century when it was generally the final destination of ocean-going vessels that had made their way up the Amazon. Today it is the farthest point upriver where big ships can still turn around. Though the city seems quite active, it can be reached only by river or air. To get from Iquitos to Sucusari, Remsen and I had taken a boat operated by Explorama, S.A., which has several well-run tourist lodges on the Amazon and Napo rivers. We made good time going down the Amazon the first day, but slowed down when we turned up the Rio Napo, which we followed until we came to the mouth of the much smaller Sucusari River. The camp, known by the name of the river, is only a few miles upriver on the banks of the Río Sucusari. The area immediately around the camp was virgin rainforest with a few trails kept open for the small groups of tourists that arrived now and then. Two big open-air, thatched-roof structures were connected by a covered walkway, all of it on stilts four feet above the ground. A few hammocks and some crudely constructed tables and chairs made the place inviting; sleeping quarters consisted of a white tent of mosquito netting suspended from the rafters and tucked in beneath a thin mattress. There were also two sunshowers and even an old icebox where soft drinks were kept cool as long as the ice held out. Isolated, but civilized—it was exactly what Parker wanted in a study site. When Remsen and I arrived, the young Peruvian guide made a grand gesture and said, "Welcome to Ted Parker's house."

During dinner the first evening, Remsen said that now he knew why Parker had spent so much time here during the last few years rather than going on expeditions. Parker was getting soft, Remsen said. Parker, in fact, had not collected a bird in over two years, preferring to concentrate on observing bird behavior. As Curator of Birds at the museum, and thus responsible for building the collection of specimens, Remsen was somewhat concerned about this trend. When Parker tried to defend himself, Remsen reached into his shirt pocket and pulled out a piece of paper which he handed to Parker. Parker leaned back on his bench and laughed. On the paper was the catalogue number of the last specimen Parker had collected, something he would need to know if he did any collecting while he was at Sucusari.

A discussion followed about the merits of spending one's time collecting (and subsequently spending hours each night involved in the tedious process of preparing the specimens) versus observing. Parker protested that if he collected birds at Sucusari he would be killing the very birds he wanted to observe, and besides it was behavioral data he needed most for the birds of Peru book he and O'Neill were working on. In addition, there were too many tourists coming and going who would be horrified by gunshots and dead birds falling out of the trees. Remsen countered that Parker already had enough data on most of the birds, that fifty good observations were as theoretically sound as a hundred.

"You're getting soft," Remsen repeated.

Carol jumped into the conversation at this point, defending herself against an unspoken accusation that since she and Ted had been together he had lost his stomach for shooting birds. Carol is notorious in Baton Rouge for her affection for baby animals. She is teased by the hard-nosed biologists for this weakness, which she takes good-naturedly. But now she protested that she had not influenced Parker at all.

"I know that's what people think," she said, "but it's not true."

Parker's first years in Peru, when he was in his early twenties, proved him to be anything but soft. He often stayed in Peru on his own long after an expedition was over and, as he did when looking for the Orange-throated Tanager, he sometimes broke away from camp to go off in search of a rare bird. He was especially interested in birds that were endemic to *Polylepis* woodlands.

Tree line in the Andes is generally around twelve thousand feet. Above that grow only grasses and a few low shrubs. Snow is common during the wet months, and the higher peaks, up to twenty-three thousand feet, are snowcapped year-round. The nearness of the equatorial sun and the clear skies make the days seem warmer than they are— an average in the midforties. Without trees, which provide shelter, food, nesting material, and safety from predators, birdlife is sparse. But here and there, clinging to the thin, rocky soil, are miniature woodlands of gnarled, reddish, scaly-barked trees known generically as *Polylepis.* Stunted, usually no more than fifteen feet tall, *Polylepis* grow at higher altitudes than any other tree in the world, as high as fifteen thousand feet. As one might expect, the *Polylepis* woods, like the forest-islands created by the glaciers, are home to many species of montane birds found nowhere else.

In March 1932 a tall, sinewy New Englander named M. A. Carriker was tramping about in one such *Polylepis* woods above the village of Yánac in central Peru. Carriker had been traversing the Andes south from Venezuela for several years, working alone, collecting birds and mammals which he shipped back to the Academy of Natural Sciences of Philadelphia. He was not so much interested in birds as he was in bird lice.

"He probably knew more about bird lice than anyone else then or since," Parker told me once, laughing.

Certain kinds of lice appear on only one genus of bird; consequently, one can learn something about the relationships of birds by studying their parasites. Carriker was just the kind of man, it appears, to be interested in something as specialized and peculiar as this.

Iconoclastic, unappreciated, a bit of a loner, Carriker is one of Parker's heroes. He first came across Carriker's name on the specimen tags at the Philadelphia Academy, which he visited from Lancaster, but no one knew much about the man. Later, Parker learned that Carriker had collected over forty thousand specimens during his sojourns in South America. In Lima, on his own first trip to Peru, Parker was introduced to Manuel Plenge, a businessman and self-educated ornithologist, who graciously offered Parker the use of his library, said to be the finest private library on neotropical ornithology anywhere. When Parker began questioning Plenge on Peruvian birds, Plenge told him he should read all of Carriker's papers. Today, in his cluttered office, Parker keeps a photograph of Carriker on the wall. Carriker stands squarely between two Peruvian field assistants, his arms over the shoulders of the shorter men. A moment after Parker showed me the picture I noticed a photograph among the papers on his desk, showing him in exactly the same pose with two of LSU's Peruvian assistants. Parker blushed and insisted that his picture had been taken before he'd come across the one of Carriker.

From the *Polylepis* woods above Yánac, Carriker sent three new species of birds back to Philadelphia. One of them, the White-cheeked Cotinga, was, like O'Neill's cacique, misidentified. Twenty years later, in 1953, Maria Koepcke, Peru's leading ornithologist, "discovered" the White-cheeked Cotinga in a woodland in the western Andes seventy miles from Lima. Shortly thereafter she presented her find at an international meeting of ornithologists—a great discovery and one of the few of its day.

"When ornithologists from the Philadelphia museum saw this bird," Parker relates, "they said, 'Oh my God, we have one of those!'"

The two other birds Carriker collected—the Tawny Tit-spinetail, and a small flycatcher he named the Ash-breasted Tit-tyrant—were even more problematic. The Ash-breasted Tit-tyrant was described from only a single specimen Carriker got at Yánac, though two years later he collected two more specimens of the bird in Bolivia, in vastly different habitat, a fact odd enough to suggest the possibility of some bad recordkeeping. Another spinetail was also found in Bolivia. From that time until 1974, when Parker sat in Plenge's library reading about Carriker's discoveries, no one had seen either bird again. Carriker had never been back to either location in Bolivia or near Yánac. Maria Koepcke had made a special trip to Yánac in 1966 to see "her bird," the cotinga, in this very different habitat, and to look for the spinetail and tit-tyrant, but though she found the cotinga to be abundant, there was no sign of the other two birds, and Koepcke, publishing the results of her trip, concluded that the *Polylepis* woods that had harbored Carriker's birds had been destroyed for firewood by the people of Yánac. The spinetail and tit-tyrant, she feared, had been lost forever, an odd case of two birds seen only by the man who discovered them.

In May 1975 the twenty-one-year-old Parker left an LSU expedition and set off alone for Huánuco, the home of Reyes Rivera, a Peruvian who had helped on LSU expeditions in previous years. Huánuco is a mountain town at six thousand feet in the Marañón River valley of the central Andes, about 120 miles as the crow flies from Yánac. But across Peruvian roads through the middle of the mountains, it is twice that distance and not a trip to be taken lightly. Parker intended to talk Reyes into going with him to Yánac.

"I knew that Koepcke had gone to Yánac and not been able to find the birds, so it was an interesting puzzle. Was the habitat still there? Hadn't she been able to find the spot Carriker had been to? Nobody knew. So I went."

Parker says all of this matter-of-factly now, which does not reveal the emotions he must have felt as he waited in Huánuco for Reyes, who was off to a neighboring village at a festival. After sitting around for a couple of days while the battered truck he was driving was repaired by a mechanic (the muffler had fallen off for the second time and the engine was threatening to do the same), Parker decided to go on by himself, which, as he wrote in his notebook that day, "may or may not be a good idea."

The crumbling highway that runs between Huánuco and Yánac is tiresome and back-wrenching at best; at worst it becomes treacherous or impassable from rain or rockslides. Small wooden crosses appear frequently along the edge of the road, marking the places travelers have plunged to their deaths. Often at the sharpest turns or narrowest passes there are conspicuous clusters of these crosses and one would think they'd make an effective and sobering road sign, but apparently not. Peruvians routinely drive with complete abandon.

On the morning of May 20, Parker ate a big breakfast, took a quick last look around Huánuco, and said farewell to the children who had been following him about since he'd arrived. The evening before, he had indulged himself and stayed in the Turistas Hotel rather than sleep again in the cab of the truck. His notes refer repeatedly to how apprehensive he was about going on to Yánac by himself. But he set out regardless, making careful observations about the birds along the way and drawing maps to guide future expeditions.

By noon he had gone only thirty miles and run into a stretch of particularly muddy road with deep ruts that he was barely able to guide the truck through. A few minutes later he came on a crowd of people picking up potatoes strewn over the road and mountainside. A truck had just gone over the edge, dropping two hundred feet and landing upside down. Parker put his head down and tried to maneuver through the crowd but was stopped by a civil guard who asked him to take one of the injured men back to the nearest village. The man slumped against the door on the passenger side, apparently in shock, his arm broken. With every bump, he moaned. Parker tried to keep his eyes on the road.

An hour later, back on his way, he had to stop repeatedly to dig mounds of mud and rocks out of the center of the deeply rutted road so the truck could clear it. In the next several hours, crawling along in a light rain, he proceeded only six miles. But by nightfall he'd crossed the Río Marañón and made it to La Unión, where he found a hotel with small, dark rooms, and went to the local cinema, a shed the size of a two-car garage. A Faye Dunaway movie was playing. In the last words of that day's notes, he recalls: "Faye Dunaway was a big hit to the natives (most drunk) here. Everytime her boyfriend touched her the hall echoed with laughter and cheers. What a way to end such a miserable day."

When he reached Huaráz three days later, the truck went back in the shop with a badly bent tie rod, but his forced delay was fortuitous. At the hotel Parker met two fellow Americans who were using Huaráz as a base camp to survey the flora and fauna of the Cordillera Blanca, the central Andes mountain range they were in the midst of. Sponsored by the Peruvian government on the long-term project, they had settled comfortably into the mountain town. The three biologists compared notes and personal experiences they'd had with the famed "white mountains" and, in the tradition of all travelers who meet unexpectedly far from home, planned a future trip together. On his last evening in Huaráz, Parker was treated to rum-and-Cokes and the music of Bob Dylan from his new friends' record collection. The next day, refreshed by companionship and talk, Parker pressed on to Yánac.

At the end of the month, late in the afternoon, Parker drove into Yánac, a small village of a couple of hundred residents holding fast to the mountainside at eight thousand feet. Ten days had passed since he had left Huánuco. The journey had been agonizingly slow—averaging less than twenty-five miles a day—and the possibility of rewards was highly dubious. Would he find the tit-tyrant or tit-spinetail? Would he even see Koepcke's cotinga? Aware that not many strangers showed up in Yánac, fewer still with shotguns in tow, Parker went directly to the civil guard office, announced his intentions, and brought out his government permits. With the light fading fast, he asked if there was somewhere he might stay for a few nights. At the end of the road there was a family who took in boarders, he was told. A few moments later he parked his truck on the edge of the road, but before he could get out a face appeared at the side window. A little man no more than five feet tall, his head just poking above the door frame, stared in at Parker. Parker judged him to be in his sixties. The man introduced himself as Felix, proprietor of the "hotel."

The following morning Felix accompanied Parker on a short hike into the mountains. When Felix noticed Parker's collection of bird skins, he told him that once another American had come to Yánac and stayed at his house—his father before him had taken in travelers too—and that this American also had collected birds. "But that was before the world war," he told Parker, "so you wouldn't know about it." The man, Felix continued, was unusually old for this sort of thing, hiking up and across the puna, staying there by himself and skinning birds in privacy. Though he was friendly to the townspeople, he refused to show anyone the birds he was collecting. But one day the man came back very excited with a bird "unknown even to the wilds of Africa." By this point in Felix's story Parker was nearly hyperventilating with excitement. In the next moment Felix described the bird the man brought back, his words so precise and accurate that Parker felt as though he could see the bird materializing in Felix's hand again these forty years later. It was the Tawny Tit-spinetail. By some amazing grace Parker was standing in Carriker's footsteps.

Beside himself, Parker asked Felix to show him everywhere Carriker had gone. Felix agreed, but with his own work to get done he was reluctant to go far afield and led Parker to several areas, not so far away, where he thought Parker would find what he was after. Nothing turned up. Frustrated, with time running out, Parker had to leave Yánac. No White-cheeked Cotinga. No Tawny Tit-spinetail. No Ash-breasted Tit-tyrant. Felix admitted there were other places farther away that he had not shown Parker. Unable to do much else, Parker sent off a batch of postcards that would bear a Yánac postmark, trying to salvage a bit of the dream in this small symbol. Then he left town.

A year later, in May 1976, Parker returned to Yánac, this time with Reyes. He had told Felix he would be back about the same time the next year, and now Felix was waiting for them, the gear assembled, just as if Parker had phoned him the week before and said he'd be arriving on flight 509 at 2:40 p.m. Felix quickly hired a pair of mules and an extra hand to watch the animals. And then they were off, Parker leaving an hour before dawn, well ahead of the rest so that along the way he could record bird songs undisturbed. By late morning the crew had caught up with him and gone on ahead through the grasslands at eleven thousand feet, still ascending. The year before, he and Felix had tramped through the *Polylepis* woods just above Yánac, never going much higher than this. As the air got thinner, Parker could feel the onset of *soroche*—altitude sickness—and he began to slow down. The bulky tape recorder, twenty-five pounds, was still slung over his shoulder. He wondered if he could continue, but the others were far ahead of him now, hollering to let him know where they were, still climbing toward the ridge. By late afternoon, after ten hours of walking, Parker realized they had not gone nearly far enough the year before, but he was too sick to think any more about the possibility of finding Carriker's birds. Had it been possible, he would have quit. His head was pounding. But he couldn't just plop down where he was. As he reached the ridge, above fifteen thousand feet, he heard Felix's voice down below shouting, "Hurry, hurry."

A heavy fog was rolling up out of the canyon as the cool air of dusk passed over the warm rocks, and within minutes Parker could see little beyond his own feet, which were struggling for solid ground. Later he learned that the canyon was so steep they had backed the mules down most of the way. Sometime after dark he caught up with the three Peruvians. They had stopped a thousand feet below the ridge, where Felix had shown them a cave he used on hunting trips. Oblivious to everything but how sick he felt, and unable to see where he was, Parker crawled to the rear of the cave and curled up to sleep. Felix and Reyes lit a fire at the mouth of the cave and the smoke drifted back to Parker, increasing his discomfort. He fell asleep to the sound of the men's voices and an awful spinning in his head.

The next morning Parker raised his head slowly. The *soroche* had dissipated. He crawled to the front of the cave and looked out into the high mountain sunlight. It was a beautiful, clear morning. To the south were the towering snow-covered peaks of the Pico de Champará. Below was an alpine valley with a stream running through it, known locally as Quebrada Tútapac. The valley was narrow, no more than two hundred yards across, but several miles long. In many places sheer cliffs fell several hundred feet down the mountainsides to the floor of the valley. What Parker's eyes came to rest on, though, were the *Polylepis* woodlands that were nestled in this isolated valley, where, he suddenly knew, he would find Carriker's birds. The first birdsong he heard was certainly a good omen: the peculiar frog-like trill of Koepcke's White-cheeked Cotinga, the loudest bird of these high, mysterious woodlands.

When Parker hiked back down the mountain eight days later, his pack contained new specimens of all three of the birds Carriker discovered in 1932. Now, the Tawny Tit-spinetail, Ash-breasted Tit-tyrant, and White-cheeked Cotinga are also known from this second set of specimens in the LSU museum, tagged with the note:

Collected by T. Parker. Yánac. 1976.

133

15

Parker's routine at Sucusari was to get up shortly before dawn, hoist the Nagra recorder over his shoulder, and head off down one of the trails. Since birds are most vocal during the first hour or two of daylight, Parker wanted to be well on his way by sunrise. Depending on what kind of luck he had, he might return to camp for breakfast around nine or, if he got involved with a flock of birds, not come back until noon. (I once heard him argue with an ornithologist friend that her breakfast, a granola bar, was only a psychological need, and that carrying a jug of water on the trail was just a nuisance. The important thing, he said, was to get going as quickly as possible in the morning.) In the afternoon his schedule was more varied. He might go back out on the trails again or make a trip to one of the river islands in the Río Napo to work on the inventory of river-island birds for a project he and Remsen were involved in. By five o'clock it was already dusk (we were less than three degrees south of the equator), which meant it was time to take a shower or work on notes. Dinner was usually at six-thirty, followed by a couple of hours of talk ranging from bird behavior to LSU basketball.

On the trails Parker walked at the pace of someone lost in pleasant thought. In a T-shirt and army fatigues, a towel usually draped around his neck, he leaned slightly forward, his back straight, his legs a little stiff, his feet not rising far off the ground. It was a peculiar gait, one, Remsen speculated, that was partly the result of hundreds of hours of lugging the Nagra recorder over one shoulder, the extra weight realigning his vertebrae as surely as if he were in traction. Parker rarely hurried, not only because a slow walk was best for spotting birds, but also because he was at any given moment just where he wanted to be. He had no obligations, nowhere else he must be, and there would be no phone calls to interrupt his work.

One morning we walked for three hours without hearing or seeing a thing until Parker stopped suddenly and motioned to a ruckus in the trees fifty feet ahead of us: a group of saddle-back tamarins (marmosets) whipping through the high branches like a volley of coconuts fired from a giant slingshot. In a few seconds the tamarins were out of sight, and we continued down the trail. If Parker heard a bird, he would stop, lean his body slightly toward the bird call, and raise his hand next to his ear, his index finger pointed toward the noise. At such moments he said nothing. Two or three minutes might pass while he was frozen in this motion, and then if the bird called again, Parker would slowly move one hand toward the controls of the tape recorder and with the other hand angle the microphone toward the bird. Taping the call, playing it back to lure the bird closer, taping the call again . . . at such times half an hour could go by in slow motion.

Coming across a mixed species flock is the prize for one's patience in the jungle. Naturalists at least as far back as Bates noticed this phenomenon: "One may pass several days without seeing many birds; but now and then the surrounding bushes and trees appear suddenly to swarm with them. There are scores, probably hundreds of birds, all moving about with the greatest activity."[1] Bates also noticed that these flocks seemed to remain in a given territory and that once he knew the limits of their territory he could find the flock at will. The dynamics of these mixed species flocks is something that Parker finds particularly interesting. There are two distinct types of flocks—understory and canopy—which do not intermingle, though there are times when a canopy flock may occupy the upper branches of a group of trees while an understory flock forages beneath them. Birds in the tropics have adopted highly specialized feeding habits, so that a few acres of forest can accommodate a great variety of species, some birds feeding on the fruit in the high branches, others hawking insects out of the air in the middle story, and still others searching the leaf litter on the ground for insects. This explanation is, in fact, greatly simplified, a point proven by the existence of the mixed species flocks in which many species occupy the same area at the same time but use slightly different techniques to capture prey and search different parts of the trees.

Theories as to why the flocks form run along two lines, both of which probably hold some truth. Birds foraging in large groups may find food more easily for several reasons, one of which is that prey is flushed by the great commotion the birds create as they move from branch to branch. Some antshrikes and shrike-tanagers actually spend almost half their time pursuing insects that have escaped from other birds. In addition, Parker and others theorize that one species may learn a new foraging technique by watching others in the flock. According to one documented case, a Paruline Warbler (*Myioborus miniatus*), a bird that normally hawks insects out of midair, changes its behavior when it joins a flock, gleaning insects from the surface of leaves as other species in the flock do.[2] The second advantage to flock activity is that it reduces the danger from predators. A hawk may find it difficult to attack a large flock of birds by surprise because flock leaders act as sentinels, uttering alarm calls to alert the species that flush their prey; moreover, if the hawk does attack, it may also become confused by the fact that so many birds are scattering in different directions.[3]

The most surprising thing about mixed species flocks is that they are permanent units. Many birds spend their entire lives foraging with the same flock. In some canopy flocks a single mated pair of White-winged Shrike-Tanagers will lead the other birds from tree to tree, and some ornithologists have observed a unique vocalization the shrike-tanagers use to notify the flock that it is time to move on. In Manu National Park in southern Peru, the shrike-tanager leads flocks that include other core species represented by a mated pair: the Chestnut-shouldered Antwren, Yellow-margined Flycatcher, Yellow-crested Tanager, White-shouldered Tanager, and Dusky-capped Greenlet.[4] These birds compose the core of the flock, which is then joined by other birds when it moves into their individual territories. At times there are as many as seventy different species of birds and over a hundred individuals rustling about in the branches a hundred feet overhead. In the mosaic of leaves the tiny birds are difficult to see, but at such moments Parker would stand beneath a tree, his binoculars trained on the birds, and talk softly into the microcassette tape recorder cradled in the palm of his left hand, his thumb and forefinger operating the recorder, the other fingers steadying the binoculars that he held firmly with his right hand.

"Black-spotted Barbet pulling an insect off a hanging dead leaf . . . Lemon-throated Barbet . . . Paradise Tanager. . . . " Parker's voice was barely audible.

He would stand this way for an hour, moving only a few steps down the trail as the flock passed overhead. (My neck was painfully stiff in five minutes.) When the birds eventually left him behind, Parker would pause for a few minutes.

"This is pretty much what I do here," he said quietly on the first day I accompanied him. He let his binoculars hang from his neck again and walked on.

Understory flocks are often composed mainly of antbirds. One day Parker came running back into camp and shouted at Carol and me.

"There's an ant swarm out there. Antbirds everywhere. It's been incredible. Van and I have been watching them all morning."

Parker whisked past me and grabbed a handful of tapes out of his duffel bag.

"Come on. We've got to hurry," he said.

Carol grabbed her binoculars and we caught up with Parker at the dining tables, where he'd stopped for a moment to rewind one tape on the Nagra recorder and simultaneously search for the right bird song on another tape he inserted into the smaller cassette recorder. He was operating both machines at once and at the same time rattling off the birds he'd seen. Then, without another word, he slung the Nagra over his left shoulder, the cassette recorder over his right, picked up a loose tape, and was off. Carol and I charged after him down the trail. Parker was walking at Olympic racing speed, leaning forward and holding the recorders close to his side, ducking vines and branches. Carol was five feet behind him, myself another five feet back, watching for branches springing loose at my face and looking for safe places to step among the slippery vines on the ground. Parker never looked back. Carol stumbled once, nearly to her knees, and I slipped off balance several times, but Parker was absolutely gliding down the trail. It was all we could do to keep up with him.

After twenty minutes of this mad dash, Parker stopped suddenly. His left hand went to the controls of the Nagra recorder, his right hand to his binoculars. Neither Carol nor I dared speak at this point. In a moment I saw the column of army ants crossing the trail about twenty feet ahead of us. Parker slowly walked into the underbrush, signaling for us to follow him. Again he stopped, still intent on the bird call he heard somewhere ahead of us. As I looked about, trying to see what Parker might be after, I noticed that we were standing in the middle of the ants. They were marching in parallel columns that made a highway about twenty feet across. Carol's feet were overrun, so she backed up carefully in between columns and Parker, in the same situation, moved a step forward. Two birds ducked in and out of view amidst the foliage—a Yellow-browed Antbird and Hairy-crested Antbird—but this did not satisfy Parker.

"The flock has spread out," he said. "An hour ago there were antbirds everywhere."

Parker lowered his binoculars and made his way back to the trail, where we came across Remsen sitting on a log, his brow glistening with sweat, a look on his face as if he'd just climbed a mountain and seen the gates to heaven. For the moment, he could not look at another bird. Parker, about to sit down also, became attentive again. He heard the call of a Ringed Antpipit on the other side of the trail, a bird he had not gotten a good recording of in this locality, so off he went, this time telling us to stay put. He didn't want to risk losing an opportunity to tape this bird. But twenty minutes later he returned, unsuccessful. Remsen sat placidly, drinking from his canteen, smiling.

"What a morning," he said.

Returning to camp, Parker sat down with a big sigh and tired shrug. At such moments he appeared beleaguered, on his face the kind of expression that suggested an exhaustion not so much physical as metaphysical: we're all tired travelers on this planet and there's just too much to do, too many birds to see before we die. He would complain about how little he really knew about neotropical birds, and he, after all, knew more than anyone else. Then, aware of his reputation for complaining too much, he would look away momentarily, a barely concealed grin rising from behind his beard into his cheeks. He looked almost shy, hiding behind his bushy beard. His continual tiredness, so much a part of his countenance, must partially be a result of a biological clock that is hopelessly out of whack. During January and February he leads tours throughout Peru and Venezuela, getting up each morning at five, avid birders on his heels all day. In March he is home in Baton Rouge, where his daily routine is reversed. He often sleeps late, works around the house in the mornings and early afternoons, does errands, then goes to the museum to work late at night, when there is no one there to interrupt him. He stays in Baton Rouge from March through May except for an annual trip to Cornell each April, during which he keeps long hours in editing sessions at the Library of Natural Sounds. There is also a Big Day (a twenty-four-hour birding marathon) planned each April with Victor Emanuel and Roger Tory Peterson. In June it's back to Peru for a month to work on his own, then he conducts tours from July through August that will cover the guano islands offshore, the coastal desert, the Andean cloud forest, temperate scrubland near Machu Picchu, puna grasslands of the high mountains, and of course the lowland rainforest. During a four-week tour he and a co-leader will show a group of fourteen birders over seven hundred species of Peruvian birds, which is sometimes twice the number that would be seen on a tour conducted by some other organization. By the end of August Parker is back in Baton Rouge again, this time for five weeks, then it's off to Brazil for a month, another Victor Emanuel Nature Tour, five hundred species this time, then back to Louisiana for Thanksgiving and Christmas before the cycle begins again.

Parker has led tours for VENT nearly from the organization's inception. He met Victor Emanuel by coincidence on a trip to Texas when he was sixteen, and Emanuel immediately recognized Parker's exceptional knowledge of birds. His position with VENT is his main source of income, since without an advanced academic degree, LSU will not offer him a paying position at the museum, something Remsen is concerned about. Remsen would like to get some money endowed to the university so a special chair can be established for Parker. Otherwise, he's afraid that eventually someone else will do this and lure Parker away from LSU. As it is now, Parker is a research associate, a nonpaying position, though one of LSU's patrons occasionally donates money to give Parker a modest monthly stipend.

16

 One day Parker decided to spend a morning on one of the river islands, taking a census of the bird population there. We were delayed at first by three hours of steady rain that began just as we were about to get into the boat, but when it stopped the sky brightened and the sun burned promisingly behind a thin veil of clouds. We set out quickly and crossed the Río Napo in twenty minutes. Roger, a local man who was the camp guide, sidled the boat up to the island. The bank was dark mud that rose vertically about five feet, but Roger quickly took a paddle out of the boat and with the blade carved several neat steps into the mud. We stepped up and stood at the foot of a trail that Roger had cut yesterday afternoon. Parker asked him to take the boat and swing around to the other end of the island where the trail stopped, and extend the trail a bit through a small swamp if he could. We would meet him there in a couple of hours.

Parker had his small cassette tape recorder with him, rather than the Nagra, and a tape with the songs of some birds he expected to find on the island. He planned to walk slowly along, playing the songs to attract the attention of the permanent residents, who would come out to defend their territories. The river-island forest was only around seventy feet tall and not very dense, a younger forest, since the island was a relatively recent landform, probably fifty to a hundred years old. Parker and Remsen wanted to know how this different habitat affected the size of a bird's territory, so they planned to compare several species that lived on both the island and the nearby mainland, where Parker's ample notes gave them a basis for their study. The question was whether or not the study would ever be published. Parker spends nearly all of his free time in the field and little time publishing what he knows. His house is filled with piles of tapes that have never been transcribed. Nearly every ornithologist I spoke with who was working in South America said he and Parker were engaged in a joint project. Remsen sometimes thinks of himself as Parker's manager, not entirely without Parker's consent. He tries to get Parker to focus on one or two concerns and publish his findings.

"O'Neill is interested mainly in finding new species," Remsen said, "but Ted is interested in *everything.*" Remsen was exaggerating (Was this a "Vanism"? In these close quarters at Sucusari, perhaps Parker's penchant for hyperbole was rubbing off on Remsen), but he had touched on a central difference between Parker and O'Neill. O'Neill's interests are perhaps more limited than Parker's, but he is highly organized. He gathers his ideas together and publishes scientific articles regularly. The younger Parker, with boundless enthusiasm and curiosity, is forever treading water in a sea of observations and theories.

When Parker attracted a bird with the taped songs, it would follow him to the edge of its territory and then stop as if it had reached a well-marked barrier—which, of course, it had. As he went along, Parker would note the approximate size of the territory as well as list all the birds he heard or saw. For two hours we walked along the trail, backtracking frequently to get another look at a bird or double-check where his territory began and ended. The sun continued to play in and out of the clouds, the birds were very active and vocal, and Parker was in high spirits, taking time to give me his tour-guide lesson on each bird. The birds were easy to see not only because the forest was relatively sparse but also because the birds popped up and perched in the open to get a look at the source of the rival song. Parker toyed with them, working the recorder like a musical instrument. If he did not have a particular song on tape, he would pester the bird with other bird calls until it complained vocally and then play the bird's own song back to him. Parker let out a song as if he were casting a line. The bird would hop out of a thicket, agitated and alert, jerking its head around in search of the trouble. The taped song would end and Parker would reel it back in, then let it out again. The bird would fly to a new branch to try another angle on this mystery. After a few more minutes of this teasing, the bird would simply fly back into hiding. Parker would take three or four steps toward a new bird, turn the recorder toward him, and start again. In this way we walked the half-mile trail, from threshold to threshold, from Ash-breasted Antbird to Yellow-rumped Cacique, from Swallow-winged Puffbird to Silver-beaked Tanager.

At the end of the trail we found ourselves in a small clearing where a local family had planted some crops and a few fruit trees. Near the riverbank of the island a flowering *Inga* tree had attracted humming-birds. A Black-throated Mango was chasing a much smaller Blue-chinned Sapphire out of the tree, and a third hummer rested on a far branch. The sapphire returned to the tree's flowers every couple of minutes and the mango dive-bombed it repeatedly.

The sun was straight overhead, and as the hummingbirds twirled and hovered, their tiny, finely scaled feathers caught the light and vibrated with iridescent color. The black of the mango's throat spilled down his chest to the abdomen and was edged by a blue-green that darkened to olive-green on the back and wings. The underside of its tail was a surprising purple. In addition to their iridescence and dazzling speed, tropical hummingbirds may have long curved bills, outlandish frilly head crests, or dangling tail feathers that are twice the length of their body. Parker had found twenty species between Sucusari and Yanamono; over a hundred live in Amazonia. Faced with this diversity and wealth of beauty, taxonomists as far back as

Linnaeus apparently have lost their heads. The scientific names they assigned to hummingbirds remain classical and proper—*Phaethornis, Heliangelus, Lophornos*—but the common names for many taxa of hummingbirds are appropriately extravagant. There are five species known as Sapphires, sixteen species of Emeralds, and eight Brilliants. There are also Woodnymphs, Hermits, Fairies, Woodstars, Sabrewings, Lancebills, Pufflegs, Racket-tails, Metaltails, Sunbeams, Sunangels, Comets, and—why not?—Coquettes.

At the other edge of the clearing Roger had cut a swatch through a swampy section of the island, extending the trail another half mile. Parker marveled at Roger's work with the machete. To cut this trail straight through the forest, he had to bend over from the waist and whip the machete low along the ground like a scythe, stopping every few feet to slice up a bush or chop down a tree. In T-shirt, old gym shorts, and tennis shoes he sweated his way through the island's swamp, where he gave a generation of mosquitoes their first taste of human blood. Now we would follow him down the new trail. The swamp was only a few inches of standing water since this was the dry season, but the undergrowth was dense, and within minutes we were in a thicket of sturdy grasses and bamboo. There was less bird activity, but Parker suddenly tuned into a distant sound.

"Crakes," he announced, excitedly. "Black-banded Crakes! Only four or five people have ever seen this bird." (Parker, of course, was one of them.)

Parker was fiddling with the recorder as he talked.

"I'm going to try to call them in. We'll have to be very still and quiet."

Crakes, like all rails, are ground-dwelling birds with the posture and walk of a small, plump chicken. They rarely come out into the open from the swamp grasses where they live. Parker held the microphone out from his body and turned the machine on. The crake called once, and immediately Parker rewound the tape and played the call back. A moment later the bird called again, and it seemed closer, maybe a hundred feet off the trail.

"Okay, let's get down and stay very quiet," Parker said. "Don't move at all."

The three of us knelt on the path and I positioned one hand near my face, as I'd learned to do over the years, so I could wriggle a finger and keep the mosquitoes off my eyes. Slowly the crakes came closer. Roger slapped a mosquito and Parker admonished him.

"Don't move," he whispered. "They might cross the trail."

In ten minutes the crakes had approached to within twenty feet and Parker was pointing a finger. He could see them through the screen of grasses, though I hadn't spotted them yet. Three or four more minutes passed. The crakes were still coming nearly straight at us, and then I caught some movement about fifteen feet into the thicket. The birds veered away slightly but were creeping toward the trail. Parker's face was bursting with excitement, but he had frozen solid now, his hand dangling next to the recorder. I turned my head as slowly as I could to the point where I thought the birds might emerge onto the trail. And then they stepped out into the open, no more than eight feet away, both birds close together, still looking around for the rival call. They kept walking as they stared at us. They appeared to be startled by our presence, confused, but they continued at the same pace across the opening and into the undergrowth on the opposite side. In the fifteen seconds it had taken them to cross before us, we had gotten an eyeful. They were so close they seemed touchable. As they faded into the swamp, Parker let out a big breath and a high-pitched laugh of delight. We stood up and shook off the cloud of mosquitoes that had settled on us.

"Incredible," Parker exclaimed. "That was just incredible."

There are many other birds in Peru that only a few people have ever seen, and invariably Parker is one of those people. Consequently, hanging out with Parker for a few days in Peru is every birdwatcher's dream, and this presents a problem for Parker. The Explorer's Inn, one of the best study sites in South America, has a well-maintained system of trails, comfortable lodging, and a variety of habitat in which to work. In fact, the area immediately surrounding the Explorer's Inn, the Tambopata Wildlife Reserve, may be, biologically speaking, the richest area on earth. Since 1976, 545 species of birds have been recorded in Tambopata, more than 1,100 species of butterflies, and 102 species of dragonflies, more than anywhere else in the world. Much of this, of course, has to do with the fact that Parker and other biologists have spent considerable time surveying Tambopata. But now, though Parker conducts several VENT tours at Explorer's Inn, he has begun to avoid the place during his free time because he's never left alone when he's there. Birdwatchers who have come there on their own or even with another tour discover that Parker is staying there and begin dogging him on the trails. Parker cannot bring himself to be rude enough to dissuade them, so for the last few years he has been coming to Sucusari instead.

Many of the days Remsen and I spent at Sucusari with Parker were overcast, and consequently there was less bird activity than usual. When the sun peeked out one afternoon, Remsen suggested a trip to one of the larger river islands. At three-thirty we settled into the boat (Carol had come along too) and Roger yanked on the outboard motor, which kicked into action. The noise of the motor was no more than a stone thrown into a lake of silence. The black-brown water of the Sucusari held a dull reflection of the sky, and the shadows of the trees along the bank looked like oil ballooning out from the river edge and sinking slowly into the water. On the east bank Roger's wife was squatting on a short plank of wood that rode on the surface of the river. She was scooping water out of the river with one hand and washing her two girls, who were sitting back-to-back, on their knees, naked, their heads bowed. The kiss of skin along their bony spines was as pure as sculpture. They neither looked up nor turned away.

When we reached the Napo, there was an explosion of blue sky and water. There was distance again for the eye to measure. Here the Napo flowed east-southeast. Parker directed Roger toward a big island directly across from us. It was perhaps three miles long, half a mile wide. By the time we reached it, the current had carried us to its midpoint. Roger pulled up close to shore and cut the motor. The sun felt wonderful on my back. The air was warm and humid but freshened by a child's breath of a breeze coming off the river. Puffy white clouds hung just above the horizon and a few strays were crossing the sky.

A kiskadee (a tropical relative of the kingbird) sat on an exposed limb above the bank, his lemon-yellow breast catching the sun. A moment later a troop of Russet-backed Oropendolas flapped heavily through the high branches of a stand of lacy mimosa trees, looking very much like giant blackbirds, which in fact they are. They're roughly twice the size of their North American cousins, their name aptly describing their color, which is contrasted only by yellow tail feathers and blue eyes. And then a dozen anis flew out of the island forest, and several groups of parakeets chattered loudly in the canopy, though I couldn't see them; parakeets with their greens and yellows are as perfectly camouflaged among the tropical treetops as any bird is anywhere. I've had my binoculars zeroed in on a spot only 150 feet away where I *knew* there were a dozen or more parakeets and yet couldn't see them until they suddenly stormed out of the branches and swept across the sky. It was more than enough, of course, to see them streaking overhead like a piece of green from a rainbow gone wild. The birdlife that had remained elusive during the previous two days of rain was now showing itself.

As we drifted past the end of the island, Roger started the motor again and headed for the next island a half mile away. Then we drifted awhile, passing a dwelling where two whiteface cattle stared at us blankly. But there were fewer birds, so we turned around and headed back upriver. At the first island, we angled south to get a look at the backside. Immediately there were more birds. Mocking thrushes perched on small bushes in the marshy deadwater along this bank. More anis crossed the river, and then, suddenly, we were in shade, the late afternoon sun having dropped below the island's tree line.

The sky overhead was completely clear now, though there was still a ring of clouds hugging the horizon. We moved slowly upriver, the motor chortling softly. There was a second island on our left, to the east, and this stretch of water we were exploring was only a couple of hundred yards wide, a quiet, hidden channel. As we moved into the middle of the channel, we crossed into sunlight again, broad clear air falling on the island to the east, sharpening the edges of palm leaves and the waxy rosettes of bromeliads trailing their streamers of vines and lianas. Parker suddenly stood up in the boat, excited. He heard an Umbrellabird somewhere ahead of us. He scanned the island but saw nothing. Short-tailed Parrots were crossing the sky, one group after another, and a lone Yellow-billed Tern repeatedly swooped down to the river to drink. High in a tree, the sunlight hitting him full on, sat a troupial, a large oriole with the Crayola-orange and black of our North American orioles. A hundred feet farther on, on another high exposed perch, was a Plum-throated Cotinga, brilliant blue with a ripe red-purple throat.

"Oh look!" Parker stood up again. "The Umbrellabird!" he shouted.

The bird was flying low across the river, directly in front of us. It cruised into the undergrowth and found a perch a hundred feet into the interior of the island. There, in broken sunlight, the bird, black as a crow, was not much more than a silhouette, but I could make out the funny, extravagant crest of feathers that fell over its face like a veil even though this bird was a female and the crest was not well developed. It was a hairdo for the eighties. Parker was still animated, as excited as he had been when he saw the crakes. The Amazonian Umbrellabird is a secretive, solitary bird that is rarely seen. If this individual stayed around, Parker would score a coup by showing it to a tour he would be leading in this area in a few months.

We were drifting downriver again, still watching the Umbrellabird as we passed it. A moment after it was out of sight, a pair of toucans fluttered about in plain view, and then, working its way up a tree trunk, a big Lineated Woodpecker, which is very much like our Pileated Woodpecker, though its head is nearly all red. The sun now was just catching the tops of the island's trees. We were back in shade again. Warm air. Cool river water. In fifteen minutes the sun would be down. Parker signaled and Roger started us up the channel again so we could round the head of the big island and get back into the main waters of the Napo. In this last hour of daylight most of the birds on the islands were calling or moving about. Parker and Remsen shifted their attention to noting what was present and speculating again on which island to explore further.

As we reached the end of the big island, emerging from the now dark waters of the channel, the Napo's greatness was again startling. Our boat was hardly more significant than the countless clumps of vegetation that were floating downriver. And as soon as we were into the current, Roger cut the motor again. We were a mile or more above the Sucusari, and though the sun was going down blazing behind a wide funnel of clouds and the water and sky were a notch darker, no one was in a hurry to return to camp. Parker and Remsen were both standing up, their binoculars trained on the shoreline trees, where more and more birds were settling down with the last light of day. They whispered to each other and into their recorders. The water was hammered bronze. The boat was turning slowly around in the current, a ballet on river water which was itself moving across the continent on a planet that was revolving in the deep blue-black of space. In five minutes it was too dark to see the birds on the island, but many were crossing above us. A sickle of a moon grew sharper. We drifted past a starkly beautiful graveyard of deadwood caught on a sandbar. Daylight had edged into early night. There were no artificial lights visible anywhere. (I imagined, though, that the lanterns were being lit now back at camp.) Behind me Roger sat peacefully, one hand resting on the outboard motor, staring off across the water. He was wearing his camp uniform—a white T-shirt with "The Amazon" printed on it in an unnatural orange that contrasted weirdly with the muted colors surrounding us. His Amazon baseball cap was black and orange as well. We drifted.

Parker and Remsen were still talking when Roger started the motor and gunned it. We cut across the Napo, angling toward a barely visible opening in the opposite bank, which I would not have noticed if we hadn't been heading straight for it. Just before we reached the Sucusari River, three fishing bats, big as nighthawks, swept past us, dipping to the water repeatedly as if trying to stitch the sky to the river. Another group could be seen in the distance. Then more. All were crossing from the island to the mainland.

"I wonder where they are going." Parker said. "Maybe to still water? Then why do they roost over on the island?"

No one answered, and Parker gave up, sighing. "Ahh. . . . Too many questions."

17

When we first arrived at Sucusari, Parker had pointed to a nest hanging from a tree at the edge of the camp and said, "Well, there it is. They started building it a few days ago. I couldn't believe it—right next to the dock."

It was too easy. Both Remsen and I had expected to spend several days in the rainforest with Parker searching for the *Tolmomyias* flycatcher that he'd first seen here in 1983. Considering how elusive the bird had been until Angelo finally collected one, we thought we'd be lucky just to get a glimpse of the bird, and here it had built a nest less than fifty feet from where we would sleep. As if to make us feel better, Parker said that he was worried that the birds would abandon the nest. When they began building it, there was plenty of standing water beneath it, but now the ground was barely damp. The seasonally flooded forest at the edge of the river was getting drier day by day, and if this particular flycatcher was in the habit of seeking added safety from predators by nesting over water, it would probably soon move on, leaving this nest unfinished.

As it turned out, several days went by before the flycatcher made an appearance at the nest. At seven a.m. on a gray, rainy morning, Remsen stopped in midsentence during a breakfast-table conversation.

"Is that the *Tolmomyias?*"

A second later there was another faint, high-pitched call, two notes. Parker stood up immediately.

"That's it."

We moved slowly toward the dock, listening for a repeat of the call. Parker leaned forward and took exaggerated steps, pretending to be the great white hunter. Then he signaled for us to stop as he heard the bird call again.

"Okay, this may be the big moment. . . . "

Parker raised his eyebrows for effect.

"Oh, there he is!"

Instantly, Parker's mock drama became real drama. He and Remsen raised their binoculars toward a movement in the top of the tree. The bird fluttered down to perch on an exposed limb where it sat for several minutes. The orange eye, for which this flycatcher will be named, was plainly evident. Remsen and Parker oohed and aahed in whispers, and Remsen quickly ran through a verbal description of the bird, trying to commit it to memory. The flycatcher flitted about the nest for twenty minutes, then disappeared. At seven-thirty a.m. the day seemed complete.

It had been almost exactly a century since the last *Tolmomyias* flycatcher was described. The genus contains four other species: *sulphurescens* (Yellow-olive Flycatcher), *flaviventris* (Yellow-breasted Flycatcher), *assimilis* (Yellow-margined Flycatcher), and *poliocephalus* (Gray-crowned Flycatcher). There are, in addition, a host of subspecies that seem to get reorganized with every new paper on flycatchers that is published. Some of their names—*confusus, obscuriceps, neglectus*—attest to the difficulty of distinguishing one *Tolmomyias* flycatcher from another. *Tolmomyias* is a particularly difficult genus in the most complex and varied of all New World families: *Tyrannidae,* the Tyrant Flycatchers.

"Flycatchers," O'Neill once said to me, "do everything from walk on the ground to ride a bicycle upside down." That is, unlike most families of birds consisting of species that generally look alike, act alike, and prefer like habitat, flycatchers vary considerably in all these respects. There are 374 species of Tyrant Flycatchers in the world; 316 occur in South America, where they represent one in every ten birds, or, what is more instructive, nearly one in five passerines (perching birds), the order of birds with which flycatchers naturally compete for territory and food. Moreover, as John Fitzpatrick of Chicago's Field Museum points out, they dominate every conceiveable habitat in the neotropics, "from sea level to snowline, and from the mountains of Venezuela south to the frigid grasslands of Tierra del Fuego."[1]

Fitzpatrick's recently published survey of Tyrant Flycatchers notes the great variety of methods flycatchers use to obtain food. Some species capture flying insects in midair, which is known as "aerial hawking." Others fly down to the ground from a perch to pursue their prey, while other ground feeders run about along the ground or flit from spot to spot. One terrestrial flycatcher—the Ringed Antpipit, the bird Parker tried to record a few days earlier—even walks along the ground looking *up* for prey on the undersides of leaves rather than compete with all the other terrestrial birds that routinely turn over leaves beneath their feet. Many flycatchers sally forth from a perch to glean insects from leaves, some hovering in midair as they grab their prey. There are also species that, from their perch, simply pick at what is around them. Most surprising, a few species are fruit eaters.

The shape of a flycatcher's bill corresponds directly to these various feeding techniques. Early ornithologists used bill shape as a major characteristic to classify flycatchers. Flycatchers that glean insects from the bottom of leaves generally have short, spoon-shaped bills to scoop up their prey. One group of related genera with particularly short, broad bills is commonly known as flatbills. Flatbills belong to a subfamily of flycatchers that is the least morphologically varied, most of them looking like the typical "little green flycatcher." The genus *Tolmomyias* is one of the flatbills.

There are two pages of color plates in Meyer de Schauensee's *Birds of Venezuela* devoted to the subfamily that contains the flatbills. Sixty-three species are illustrated, thirteen tightly packed rows of little green birds. For months I kept the book on my desk, propped open to these pages. The display is bewildering. If I stood back, perhaps ten feet away, the birds blurred together like a tree full of leaves. Parker once saw three different species of *Tolmomyias* flycatchers in the same tree at the same time. I tried to imagine that scene, in which the birds would be neither as still nor as composed as on the page in front of me, and where one could not hope to get as close as ten feet. I sympathized with Baron Johannes von Spix who, in 1825, looked at what is now known as *Tolmomyias sulphurescens,* the first *Tolmomyias* to be described, and decided it belonged to the genus *Platyrhynchus.* 2

Spix might not have found *sulphurescens* at all had it not been for a royal marriage that linked Austria with Portuguese Brazil. Among the first of several important Austrian and German naturalists-explorers, von Spix and fellow Bavarian Karl von Martius, a botanist, decided in 1815 that they must go to South America. Their original plans called for them to travel from Argentina through the far western portion of the continent north of Ecuador, an area nearly all of which lies outside of what is now known to be the range of *sulphurescens.* However, they changed their plans when, after two years of trying unsuccessfully to secure passage to South America, they quickly accepted an invitation to accompany the royal entourage of the emperor's daughter, who was to marry a Portuguese prince in Brazil. In 1817 they sailed for the neotropics. They reached Rio de Janeiro in July and spent the first four months exploring the region. Later they would traverse much of southeastern Brazil, sail for Belém near the mouth of the Amazon, and travel up the great river as far as the Peruvian border before returning to Vienna in 1820 with a collection of 350 species of birds, 85 mammals, 2,700 insects, and 6,500 plants. 3 But it was sometime during their first months near Rio de Janeiro that Spix collected the flycatcher that he would describe seven years later as *Platyrhynchus sulphurescens.*

Flaviventris, the second *Tolmomyias* flycatcher to be described, was actually found by the Austrian prince Maximilian of Wied-Neuwied *before* Spix discovered *sulphurescens,* though it took Wied several years more to describe it.[4] Wied spent the years 1815 to 1817 traveling in southeastern Brazil. In 1831 he finally described the flatbill flycatcher he found there, and, in a moment of poor judgment, he placed the bird in the European genus *Muscipeta.* Wied was not in fact a biologist, but rather a military officer turned anthropologist who collected birds only secondarily to his work on Brazilian Indians.

Assimilis, described in 1868 by August von Pelzeln, another Austrian, was actually collected by the Austrian botanist Joseph Natterer, who had traveled to Brazil with Spix and Martius. Natterer went off on his own after arriving in South America, spending much of his time in the interior of southwestern Brazil, where he explored the sea of grasslands known as the Mato Grasso, eventually traveling overland to the town of Manuas on the Amazon. Natterer stayed in Brazil for eighteen years, collecting nearly thirteen thousand bird specimens that included thirteen hundred species. At some point during his stay at the Amazon village of Borba from 1828 to 1830, he collected *assimilis.* When his massive collection reached Austria, it took years to catalogue it and identify the species, a process that was interrupted by a fire in the Vienna Museum during the Revolution of 1848, which destroyed nearly all of Natterer's manuscripts and most of his diary. Consequently, it wasn't until 1868—forty years after the bird had been collected—that von Pelzeln published a description of *assimilis* and placed it in the Flatbill genus *Rhynchocyclus.*[5]

Poliocephalus, the last *Tolmomyias* to be described before Parker's find, was also collected much earlier than its description date, 1884, suggests. Ladislas Taczanowski, who made a specialty of Peruvian avifauna, pored over several major bird specimen collections before publishing his comprehensive *Ornithologie du Pérou*, wherein the *poliocephalus* description lies.[6] In the private collection of Count de Berlepsch, an amateur naturalist, Taczanowski came across the specimen from which he described *poliocephalus* as a new species.

From the published descriptions scattered in hundreds of books and the type specimens themselves, which were housed in museums across Europe, the English ornithologist Philip Sclater took on the mammoth chore of cataloguing all the birds in the British Museum and revising classifications where he felt it was necessary. In 1888 he published the volume that included flycatchers. There he took Spix's *sulphurescens* out of *Platyrhynchus* and put it in the genus *Rhynchocyclus,* where he also placed Wied's *flaviventris. Assimilis* and *poliocephalus,* he felt, were the same bird, so he called them both *poliocephalus* and included them with *Rhynchocyclus.* For the first time the four flycatchers were all in the same genus.[7] In 1927 Charles Hellmayr performed the same task with birds in Chicago's Field Museum, restricting himself to birds of the Americas. Hellmayr saw that several of the *Rhynchocyclus* flycatchers were consistently smaller than the others. Consequently, he erected a new genus—*Tolmomyias*—to include them. Hellmayr, however, recognized five species of *Tolmomyias* flycatchers and considered *assimilis* a subspecies of *sulphurescens.*[8] John Zimmer of New York's American Museum further revised the classification when he published his series of papers on Peruvian birds. In 1939 Zimmer separated the *Tolmomyias* flycatchers into the four species considered valid today, recognizing that Spix, Wied, Pelzeln, and Taczanowski had been the first to describe the bird that was now considered the type specimen for each of the four species. Included in Zimmer's discussion of a *Tolmomyias* subspecies (*flaviventris viridiceps*) is a reference to a specimen he examined that didn't quite match the other birds: "One specimen from the mouth of the Río Santiago is very peculiar and quite unlike a veritable *viridiceps* from the same locality. . . . For the present I am unable to give it a [subspecies] name."[9]

Parker would take note of this when he began going over the literature on *Tolmomyias* flycatchers, and would mention it to me the following spring when, Sucusari months behind us, we met in the LSU museum to talk about the final stages of his work on the newest addition to the genus *Tolmomyias.*

On the floor in the southeast corner of the range was a single specimen case with a dozen or more trays of bird skins. Each tray contained the specimens being used in a current project, most of them for descriptions of new species. Parker pulled out two trays and laid them on a worktable. There were about fifty small birds in each tray, which at first glance all looked alike. In truth, there were six different species there and two genera. Gathering these specimens together was the first step Parker would take to get an overview of the problem he was confronted with.

In one row was a synoptic series of the four other *Tolmomyias* flycatchers—one representative individual from each species laid side by side for comparison. One specimen of *Ramphotrison megacephala*, another closely related genus, was thrown in for good measure. Another row contained the seven known specimens of the new *Tolmomyias* flycatcher, which Parker plans to name in honor of the highly regarded ornithologist Melvin Traylor. With the seven *"traylori"* specimens were several questionable skins. The bulk of the remaining skins were all the other specimens of *Tolmomyias* flycatchers LSU happened to have in its collection.

When Parker first had the new flycatcher Capparella had shot in 1984 and felt it might well be a new species, he immediately called John Fitzpatrick in Chicago and Mark Robbins at the Philadelphia Academy of Natural Sciences. He asked them both to send from their collections any *Tolmomyias* flycatchers that had an "ochraceous wash on the breast," knowing that Fitzpatrick and Robbins had considerable expertise with flycatchers and would know what to look for. Fitzpatrick found two birds that were labeled *Tolmomyias assimilis obscureceps,* with a question mark on the back of the tag. They had been collected within a few days of each other in 1969 on the Colombian side of the Río Putumayo, the river that functions as a border between Colombia and Peru. Mark Robbins sent a specimen as well. Parker already had the "Zimmer specimen" from the American Museum of Natural History in New York, which O'Neill had brought back to LSU more than a year before when Parker first told him of the potentially new

A PARROT WITHOUT A NAME

Tolmomyias at Sucusari. O'Neill's sharp eye picked out this Zimmer specimen before he or Parker had even read Zimmer's description of it. With the bird Capparella had shot, that made five skins. Another one turned up in LSU's own collection, collected in 1979 in northern Peru and identified at the time as *assimilis*. For several seconds Parker stared at a seventh specimen, ragged-looking with a nearly illegible tag from the 1800s.

"I don't know where this came from," he said finally. "I can't even read the tag." He'd have to find out.

Museums are not always quick to lend their specimens, and Parker's momentary lapse in memory would make any collection manager nervous. Birds are packed carefully in several layers of cotton and placed in boxes or mailing containers which are then packaged as if they contained a Ming vase. Considering the value of a major collection, I looked about the range for a sprinkler system. Parker shook his head. It would all go up in flames if a fire got started.

After assembling the seven *"traylori"* specimens and the other related species, Parker knew he had placed the new bird in the right genus. The next thing to do was measure a series of ten to fifteen birds of each species and record the measurements on a chart. With calipers Parker showed me how he takes measurements for the wing and tail, the two critical points of comparison. Bill and tarsus measurements are often taken as well. A series of measurements from the same species should not vary by more than a few millimeters. He records the measurements for each specimen he examines, along with its museum number; the locality where it was collected; day, month, and year when it was collected; age; and sex. In this case Parker would end up with five charts that recorded the measurements for perhaps seventy-five birds. The results would be another factor to consider.

Parker stopped suddenly, in his hand a chart with roughly five hundred little boxes to be filled in.

"I shouldn't say this, but I find all of this the boring part. Some people love this, but to me it's a nuisance."

I asked how long all of this would take. Maybe a few hours a day for several days was Parker's answer. He admitted he had been dragging his feet on this. Searching for an excuse, he claimed it would be nice to have a mated pair of *"traylori"* to look at before he wrote the description. I reminded him that it took John Fitzpatrick and O'Neill more than eight years to describe the new screech owl they named after Roger Tory Peterson. Parker winced and replied that there is now some controversy over that owl, that many people think it's going to end up being a subspecies when more work is done on screech owls in that area. (Later, O'Neill would tell me that more specimens had been collected and it seemed increasingly certain that the owl *is* a good species.) But then Parker laughed:

"We're like a little group of people—the only ones in the world who care about this—so what difference does it make anyway?"

Step three is the most subjective. Parker must describe the bird in detail, noting precisely the color for every part of the bird down to the tips of its smallest feathers. He walked to the other end of the range, pulled out a drawer, and took out something wrapped in heavy black cloth. Back at the worktables he unfolded the cloth carefully to reveal Robert Ridgway's *Color Standards and Nomenclature,* a 1912 edition that is still the standard reference work for ornithologists when it comes to color. There are fifty-three plates with rectangular samples that look as if they come from a paint-swatch book, 1,115 colors in all. Parker passed his finger over a few pages, lamenting his inexperience with this part of taxonomy, then closed the book, noting that one was not supposed to expose it to sunlight for more than a few seconds at a time.

One final piece of lab work for his description would be done at Cornell. Parker would make sonograms of the songs of each of the *Tolmomyias* flycatchers to illustrate the differences in the pages of his article. He would also draw heavily on his notes to write sections on ecology, habitat, and natural history.

There were several problems he would have to deal with as he put the data together, and other issues might arise. *"Traylori,"* assimilis, *poliocephalus,* and *flaviventris* all have territories that overlap. It was

159

poliocephalus, flaviventris, and *"traylori"* that Parker had seen all in the same tree at one time. Consequently, it was now clear that *"traylori"* is not a subspecies of any of these three. They must all be distinct species—otherwise they would be interbreeding, producing hybrids, and eventually merging into one species. But *sulphurescens* it appears does not overlap with *"traylori,"* and to complicate matters *sulphurescens* is known from two separate areas. The major portion of its range covers most of Brazil, and there are large pockets in Venezuela east to French Guiana. But another form of *sulphurescens* is found in the Amazon basin, near *"traylori's"* territory. What if *"traylori"* is nothing more than a link between these two forms of *sulphurescens?* Or what if it turns out that the Amazon *sulphurescens* is a distinct species and later someone finds a link between *"traylori"* and the other forms of *sulphurescens?* That would make *"traylori"* a subspecies and make another new species out of the Amazon form. Parker laughed at the thought of this.

"To be frank," he said, "the *sulphurescens* group bothers me a little. My gut feeling is that somehow *"traylori"* is in a *sulphurescens* group. I guess the best evidence for that would be the song, and the song of *"traylori"* is rather *sulphurescens*-like, which suggests there's a relationship there."

Parker laughed again.

"But this is part of the fun. A taxonomic puzzle illuminates everything else about a bird. The thing to keep in mind—because some people here and elsewhere think finding a new species is the ultimate thing—is how much we have learned about all of these birds."

A Parrot
Without a Name

18

 On the last day of my stay at Sucusari, Parker collected a bird, but only after Remsen, who shot twice and missed, handed the gun to him and told him to give it a try. On the preceding day they had spotted a rarity high in the canopy layer among a mixed species flock—a Dugand's Antwren, a bird known from only three specimens worldwide. All the specimens were females, and this was a male, so Remsen and Parker returned to the same spot, this time with a shotgun. The antwren was still there, and, after Remsen's two misses, Parker got it on his first shot. In the two years since then, however, Parker has collected nothing else. Though Remsen cajoled him into accompanying an expedition to Bolivia last year, Parker was the only member of the group who did not prepare a single specimen. In all fairness, his role on the expedition was to spend as much time in the field as possible, listing the birds he came across and recording songs and calls, but it's unlikely that Parker would have gone had Remsen insisted he do his share of skinning birds.

It was two years ago, in the summer of 1985, that I was with Parker at Sucusari. Here at the Río Shesha camp Parker's absence sometimes seems conspicuous to me, but for the most part we live in the present moment, focused on camp chores, on swatting mosquitoes, on the spectacular birdlife in the rainforest that surrounds us. Tony and Angelo have put away the bird that they jokingly call "Ridgely's Jacamar." On the tag tied to the bird's feet it says *"Galbula tombacea"* (White-chinned Jacamar), followed by a question mark.

For three more days there is still no sign of O'Neill. We have collected fifty birds already. Most have been trapped in the nets, but Tony, Angelo, and Pete have all shot a few as well. This morning Angelo and Tony are trying to collect birds from a flock that is high in the trees above them. Tony plays and replays a tape, hoping to entice some of the birds to come closer while Angelo watches with his binoculars, the shotgun held between his legs. For twenty minutes Tony plays the tape. Several times Angelo takes aim, then lowers the gun. The birds zip from place to place, often hidden among the leaves—and leaves in the rainforest are big enough to hide an eagle. Eventually, several birds fly into the lower branches, perhaps sixty feet off the ground, and Angelo fires. The gunshot slams against the morning air. A few leaves flutter downward, but nothing else. The birds, somewhat surprisingly, remain in the lower branches, so Angelo fires again, then a third and fourth time, at which point a small brown bird drops to the ground fifteen feet away.

"Oh, I got something," Angelo says, surprised.

He quickly takes some cotton and puts it in the bird's mouth to absorb blood, then places the bird, a Thrush-like Wren, headfirst into a small paper cone that will keep its feathers neatly in place. Ten minutes later he collects a Lineated Woodcreeper out of the same flock, but the flock is moving on, so Angelo heads back to camp with the birds.

The trail leading out of camp is not hard to follow. Manuel has spent time improving it each day as he puts up new mist nets. It weaves generally northwest, rising and falling over several low ridges. This morning I have seen few birds, and in the heavy shadows of the understory even the mosquitoes are sleepy. An orange-and-black butterfly flits past me, zigzagging among the leaves and vines, disappearing with a startling suddenness when its wings close briefly and shadows engulf it. I saw a blue morpho a couple of days ago, the most famous butterfly of the tropics, with its dazzling blue wings, a creature so large and swift in flight that I momentarily mistook the first one I saw for a bird. The wingspan on a morpho can reach seven inches, not enough, amazingly, to make it the largest butterfly in the tropics, a distinction belonging to the Queen Alexandra birdwing butterfly, with a twelve-inch wingspan! But of all the tropical butterflies, the one that fascinates me the most, the glass-winged butterfly, now crosses the trail ahead of me, hanging in the still air on slow, measured wingbeats. Its wings are completely transparent, except for their edges, the ultimate camouflage. One could read a book through them. The scales on the wings are actually set on edge, like Venetian blinds that have been opened, creating the see-through effect. There is something eerie as well as beautiful about the glass-wings as they flutter along not far above the ground, repeatedly disappearing and reappearing. Some Indians believe them to be the spirits of dead children.

Half a mile out of camp, I watch Paul and Mara tear apart all the deadwood they come upon, hoping for a snake or lizard, but in the next hour they have no luck. The jungle is quiet, and we walk slowly, without much conversation. After an hour and a half we have crossed three streams. Paul wants to get to the fifth stream, which is quite a bit larger than the others and, according to Pete, contains algae-covered rocks. Paul is hoping to find frogs in the vicinity, maybe even tadpoles. But when we reach the stream, pretty as it is, there is no sign of aquatic life. It is twice as large as the other streams, about five feet across in places, and its clear, shallow water flows over a bottom of hard-packed mud and pebbles, and, in a few places, big table rocks. The stream is a hybrid: half mountain stream, half lowland stream. The presence of the table rocks is pleasing, and we walk around on them for a while, Paul peering into all the nooks and crannies along the stream edge and overturning a few stones before he gives up. He has not found one herp all morning, except for a lizard that was too quick for him. On the way back he gives in to taking insects, arriving in camp with a funny-looking caterpillar and a skinny beetle which he photographs right away. The others are all skinning birds. And the afternoon moves slowly.

"So where is this O'Neill guy anyway?" Paul asks. "Is it true what I've heard—that he's never really been out of the States?"

Saturday, June 27: one full week in camp. Paul and Mara went out last night, as is their routine, looking for snakes and frogs by flashlight. They came back with just one frog, the only herp they found all day long, and this morning as Paul tried to photograph it the frog made a giant leap for freedom and was gone.

As the morning sun begins to warm up the camp, Pete and Tony return with a pair of Barred Forest Falcons and a small flycatcher known as a White-crested Spadebill. Angelo is more excited over the spadebill than he is about the beautiful forest falcons because it is the first one from Peru for the LSU collection. Spadebills are small, dull birds that remain in the treetops, making them very difficult to collect. The bill, as the name suggests, is short and broad, and is used like a spoon to scoop insects off leaves. Pete, who collected the bird, has now made his mark on the LSU collection. He admires the bird as one might a rare gem, but unfortunately the spadebill is riddled with birdshot—detracting from its value as a good specimen—so Pete puts the whole bird in a plastic bag with cornmeal and shakes it, coating the bird with the stuff and blotting up the body fluids that will stain the feathers. This is standard procedure with birds that are shot, though most have only a few pellets in them since the fine birdshot spreads out and a tree's foliage catches much of it.

Later in the day another rarity is collected—a Red-billed Ground Cuckoo, a shy, secretive bird similar to our North American roadrunner, though fuller-bodied and more colorful. LSU has only three specimens, two of them shot by Manuel in northern Peru, and now Manuel has gotten a fourth. Angelo decides to pickle the bird whole rather than skin it, so he fills a bucket with formalin, injects it liberally into the bird as well, and immerses the cuckoo in it. This way the bird's internal organs and muscles can be examined carefully later on, something no one has done before with this species.

Camp routines are well established now, everything being centered on preparing the birds that are collected. Manuel continues to put up additional nets. The idea is to place them in a variety of habitats so that we do not miss birds that are restricted to a particular part of the forest. However, no nets have been set up southwest of camp, and no one is to shoot birds in that area either, because Pete has staked it out for his study of antbirds, which will become his Master's thesis. He spends several hours each day watching the understory antbirds along a trail Manuel cut for him. He notes exactly how each species behaves and, what is most important, how and where it forages for food. One thing he does is simply to count the number of times a given bird does something.

"Of course, Parker knows all this already," he told me. "But it's never really been quantified."

Though each of us takes time to get out of camp and explore a bit, the anticipation and excitement we felt as we made our way here has subsided. Talk of the mountains stirs everyone up now and then, but generally we seem to have settled into daily patterns. The conversations never stray far from ornithology, though Pete has hung a basketball poster on the work tent and every evening he gets out the radio and tries fruitlessly to tune in a baseball game. Since Gentry left yesterday, taking the last dugout with him, we are truly isolated, and the feeling occasionally grows stronger than anyone is accustomed to. No one talks about it, but the strain is sometimes evident. One day Cecilia was withdrawn and dreamy; another day Pete kept to himself more than usual. I'm reminded of the elder Darwin commenting on Bates's assessment of extended fieldwork in the tropics: " 'I was obliged at last,' Mr. Bates naively remarks 'to come to the conclusion that the contemplation of nature alone is not sufficient to fill the human heart and mind.' "[1] Bates came to his conclusion after a year in an isolated village with only one issue of *Punch* magazine to read, having memorized even the fine print in the advertisements. Naturalists generally don't mention this aspect of extended fieldwork, perhaps remembering how as a child one is teased for being homesick, but Alex Shoumatoff, who traveled throughout South America for eight months as he researched his book *The Rivers Amazon,* is admirably candid about it:

> I began to feel the stir-craziness which the jungle, with its constant humidity, its apparent monotonous sameness, and its claustrophobic lack of open space, can impose. . . . I had wanted to "experience the jungle" as fully as I could, but try as I might, I could never stop the internal monologue . . . which had [nothing] to do with where I was. . . . As the trip wore on, the trappings of civilization became more important than they had ever been for me. Perhaps I fell back on them as a defense against the overwhelming wildness with which I was surrounded.[2]

19

In the middle of the afternoon we hear the familiar clattering of a *peki-peki* from somewhere downriver, and ten minutes later we are all lined up along the bank to welcome O'Neill, Donna, and Marta. They are waving and shouting. They get stiffly out of the dugout and make their way up to camp amidst handshakes and some teasing. Unshaven and rumpled, O'Neill is nevertheless his ebullient self, smiling broadly and saying how glad he is to be here at last, and then, to answer the obvious question, he says that Donna got back from Lima at noon the day after we'd left, and they set off early the next morning on a speedboat, getting to Abujao around noon. We had left only two hours earlier. Oscar's wife gave them our note and let them pitch their tents on the porch. Manuel had forgotten to leave a sleeping pad for Marta, and Paul left the wrong bag for Donna, though the latter mistake turned out to be fortuitous. Had Paul left the bag Donna told him to, she would have had her clothes but no tent or sleeping bag. As it was, she had her tent, but no clothes other than the denim skirt she was still wearing from her trip to Lima.

They sat in Abujao for five days, unable to find a dugout to hire.

A PARROT WITHOUT A NAME

When they finally found one, they only got as far as the mouth of the Shesha. The water level had fallen so much in the week since we'd gone upriver that it was impossible for them to make any headway. The driver kept the gear and poled upriver while O'Neill, Donna, Marta, and the boatman's wife walked through the jungle on a barely discernible path, unsure where they were some of the time. Marta had only a pair of plastic sandals, and the boatman's wife had no shoes at all. They walked all day, made camp at a house along the river, got up the next morning, and set off again, only to discover two hours later that they'd been walking in circles. At this point a big rainstorm hit. They sat it out and then went searching for their dugout, knowing that the river would rise soon. From there, in the dugout, it still took them two and a half days. They had only a little food they'd bought in Abujao and one night traded batteries for dinner meat—a freshly shot monkey. Since this is the dry season and rains will be increasingly infrequent, it's quite certain, O'Neill says, that we will have to walk out of here. He predicts it will take seven to ten days. Paul and Mara look disturbed by this, realizing that by the time they get ready to leave the water level will have dropped again. O'Neill, who has been standing, now sits down with a sigh. He has bloody blisters on both feet from the walking.

With less than an hour till dusk, O'Neill directs Manuel to set up his and Donna's tents. Manuel immediately begins clearing the underbrush. O'Neill's Spanish is excellent, much better than anyone else's, and this, combined with his decisiveness, has already established a sense of authority here that has been missing. Of course, O'Neill wants to know what kind of birds have shown up in the nets. Angelo tells him they have three birds they are unsure of: the jacamar, a hummingbird, and a toucanet. At the work tent, O'Neill looks over the specimens. He turns the jacamar over and inspects its chin. "It's not *tombacea,*" O'Neill says almost immediately, meaning the White-chinned Jacamar. "Probably a *cyanescens.*"

Galbula cyanescens, the Bluish-fronted Jacamar, is known from southern Peru (the White-chinned Jacamar is not), but the descriptions of the Bluish-fronted Jacamar do not mention a white patch on the bird's chin, which this specimen surely has. Because of the white chin, Angelo and Tony thought it should be a White-chinned Jacamar, but they knew the White-chinned Jacamar had never been found south of the Amazon. The white patch on the chin is something characteristic of southern races of the Bluish-fronted Jacamar, the kind of thing only O'Neill or Parker would know. So, in a few seconds, O'Neill has cleared up the mystery that has occupied Angelo and Tony for several days.

O'Neill takes no more time with the toucanet.

"Selenidera reinwardtii," he says, the Golden-collared Toucanet, which in the north has a red bill, but here in the south, a green one. The problem is that in the *Birds of South America* de Schauensee only describes the northern race with the red bill. The third problem bird, the hummingbird, O'Neill ponders over. *Phaethornis bourcieri,* the Straight-billed Hummingbird, has been found in Peru only north of the Amazon, except for some specimens recently collected in the Contamana Hills sixty miles north of here. *Phaethornis philippi,* the Needle-billed Hummingbird, its near look-alike, has been known from both west and east of here, and it seems to encircle the south-of-the-Amazon range of *bourcieri,* a peculiar situation. O'Neill suspects this bird is *bourcieri,* far south of its known range, but he can't be sure until he can examine other specimens. Months later, at LSU, he will find that he is right.

Have you seen *Pipra chloromeros?* O'Neill asks. How about *Tangara gyrola?* He runs through a couple of dozen species this way, getting his bearings by the birds that are present here. Remsen did exactly the same thing with Parker after initial hellos when we arrived at Sucusari, and even in Baton Rouge this ornithological form of "twenty questions" surfaced often when the discussion of birds changed from one scene to another. If Parker mentioned a trip to Bolivia, O'Neill would run through a list of birds. Parker might well follow up by asking O'Neill if he had seen a particular bird at Balta during his first years in Peru, and thus the scene would shift again. And always Parker and O'Neill used the scientific nomenclature. On this expedition I come to hear more Latin than I have since high school. (To complicate matters, the ornithologists often use only the genus name as a kind of shorthand when it is obvious by the context of the conversation which species they are referring to.) *Pipra chloromeros,* O'Neill explains if I ask, is the Round-tailed Manakin, *Tangara gyrola,* the Bay-headed Tanager, though occasionally O'Neill is stumped, being so accustomed to using the scientific names for birds that he's entirely forgotten the common names. In the course of a conversation I may well lose track of even what family of birds is being discussed. In the end, however, I come to learn some of the genera. *Phaethornis* is a hummingbird, *Amazona* a parrot, *Xiphorhyncus* a woodcreeper, and so on.

Manuel shouts from the clearing he has made for Donna's tent. He's uncovered a nest of "twenty-four-hour ants," the largest ant in the world—over an inch long—known by this name because the pain inflicted by a bite lasts a full day. Though less well known than the infamous army ants and not as fascinating as the leaf-cutter ants, the "twenty-four-hour ant" may be more memorable. Ken Miyata, a tropical biologist, described an encounter with one:

> One of the most painful nonlethal experiences a person can endure is the sting of the giant ant *Paraponera clavata.* These ants . . . sport massive hypodermic syringes and large venom reservoirs. They call on these weapons with wild abandon when provoked, and they are easily offended beasts. Unlike the stings of honeybees and polybiine wasps, the stings of *Paraponera* are not one-shot affairs.
>
> One night as I was collecting moths at a light trap in the rain forest of western Ecuador, I felt something drop down the neck of my shirt and scurry across my shoulder. When I wrestled with my shirt to find out what it was, the ant became squeezed against my skin. It drove its stinger into my neck and shoulder flesh four times in rapid order, and each sting felt as if a red-hot spike was being driven in. My field of vision went red and I felt woozy. The shouts and nervous laughter of my companion sounded far away. After an hour of burning, blinding pain I was left with a sore back and lymph nodes in my armpit so swollen that I couldn't move my arm without pain for the next two days.[1]

We have seen several individuals at various times in camp and have given them the right-of-way, but a nest of them is a frightening thought. Manuel gets a can of insecticide and douses the ants, then stands back. Donna is not excited about having her tent put up over the nest, but since Manuel has just spent half an hour clearing the area and declares that he has destroyed the nest, she doesn't protest. A couple of days ago Paul caught one of the giant ants with a pair of forceps to examine its mandibles, which looked huge for an ant, nearly big enough to wrap around one's finger. When he cut the ant in half and tossed it into a pile of branches, it continued moving about, and two hours later I came across the front half of the creature moving steadfastly on its way and still looking quite menacing.

By nightfall the new tents are up and Manuel has turned over the cooking duties to Marta. Over dinner I ask O'Neill what he thinks the river will be like when it's time for me to leave in three weeks. Before he can answer, Donna says I should probably go out with Paul and Mara, and O'Neill is quick to agree. A week from now, when Paul and Mara are scheduled to leave, the river may still be passable, but in three weeks it could be virtually dry. Also, O'Neill doubts that Oscar will agree to come back again and get me, and, even if he does, there's not enough money to pay him, which makes the entire discussion academic. Since I must leave with Paul and Mara, it's doubtful that I will get to the mountains.

"I can't go anywhere for a while," O'Neill says, "not until these blisters heal."

I recall again O'Neill's words of wisdom before the expedition began: "In Peru it is best to count on things not going as you hope. . . . " No doubt O'Neill knows this better than anyone.

In the morning O'Neill is slow to rise, and he dawdles about the campfire for some time, but when the first birds are brought in from the nets he is eager to have a look. Without hesitation he clears a spot for himself at the worktable and selects a bird to work on, a small brown-and-gray–striped antwren of the genus *Myrmotherula.* Whether it is the Pygmy Antwren (*M. brachyura*) or the Short-billed Antwren (*M. obscura*), he is not sure. Antbirds are often as difficult as flycatchers to identify. O'Neill squeezes the bird's chest until the antwren falls limp. Then he sets it on the table and gets out his dissecting kit.

In just a few days the two aluminum folding tables have grown cluttered. In the center sits a big, unopened box of crackers, atop which is the kerosene lantern that doubles as a drying lamp for the bird and bat skeletons that hang on a string next to it. A couple of old powdered-milk cans are used to dispose of the bird flesh and other remains, emptied daily by the workers, who save a few pieces of bird meat for fish bait. Next to each person's place at the table is a small pile of cornmeal and a collection of personal items: scissors, scalpel, forceps, data tags, notebook, and so forth, except for Paul's spot, which holds a big jar of frogs, lizards, and snakes suspended in formalin. Tape recorders, bird books, binoculars, and other odds and ends lie scattered about. Pinned to the screen of the tent are several unfortunate moths that found their way inside.

O'Neill picks up the antwren and studies it. He is ready to get to work. The routine business of preparing specimens and the conversation that goes with it attract O'Neill as much as they repel Parker. The makeshift domesticity seems to please him, and he is clearly satisfied by performing a simple task that has tangible results, unlike so much of his public relations work for the museum. In addition, he knows from years of working in museums across the country the value of a well-prepared specimen. (I once saw him gluing the feathers back on a whimbrel from a West Indies collection the LSU museum had recently obtained.) The accuracy of papers on taxonomy is only as good as the condition of the hundreds of specimens those papers are based on. If a specimen has been carelessly prepared, the bird may be misshapen, appearing smaller or larger than it does in life, or the feathers may be so tattered they are difficult to examine. Data tags may contain only vague information about where a bird was collected, and say nothing at all about its stomach contents or skull ossification. So O'Neill stresses the importance of procedures that ensure good specimens.

When a bird is first taken from the mist net, it is placed in a cloth bag, then at camp transferred to a paper sack, the top held shut by a clothespin. Angelo discovered a few years ago that a paper sack, unlike a cloth bag, gives the bird enough freedom so that it is less likely to smear its own excrement all over itself in the two or three hours it may be held there. At any given time, one can walk into the work tent and find a dozen paper sacks on the ground, some of them rustling, others silent. Now and then a bird will escape, often a woodpecker that drills his way through the paper, and for a couple of minutes the ornithologists will chase the bird around the tent until they corner it.

With the antwren in hand, O'Neill places cotton in the bird's throat to stop any body fluids from leaking out. If this were a fruit-eating bird he would be certain to plug the vent opening as well. He records the specimen in his personal catalogue, noting the date it was collected, locality, weight, and the color of the eyes, beak, and feet. For O'Neill this is specimen number 7325. Every bird O'Neill has ever collected is listed in a series of these notebooks, numbered consecutively from the first bird he collected in 1960, a Brown-headed Cowbird. O'Neill will be as precise as possible in describing the color of the feet and bill since these colors will eventually fade and subsequent taxonomic work will have to depend on his description. This is an example of the kind of data that were often not recorded by professional collectors who sent birds back to U.S. museums, where ornithologists examined them in the comfort of their office chairs. The Tawny-tufted Toucanet, originally described as a species in 1835, was prepared this way and consequently Meyer de Schauensee describes the bird's bill as "reddish brown with several black vertical stripes." For a century and a half this was considered an important fieldmark on the toucanet, but when Field Museum ornithologist Dave Willard collected some of the birds a few years ago he found no such stripes on the bill. He prepared the specimens, noting this, and then several months later, when he looked at the specimens again, the stripes were present. It turns out that these marks only show up after the bird has been dead for several months.

Now, O'Neill lays the antwren on the table and with scissors makes an incision down the breast, immediately pouring a bit of cornmeal into the bird to soak up the blood. The antwren's skin is then spread apart and O'Neill carefully cuts the meat loose from the major joints at the wings, feet, and tail, picking out pieces and putting them in a pile as they come loose. Then he turns the entire bird inside out, a procedure that takes some skill in order not to tear the bird. He removes the bird's eyes and brain and notes the ossification of the skull, which in some groups of birds determines whether the bird is a juvenile or adult. Then, since this is an antwren, one of the birds for which LSU wants to obtain biochemical data, O'Neill takes pieces of tissue—liver, kidney, heart, and muscle—and puts them in a vial, tags it, and drops it in the liquid nitrogen tank, which freezes the material almost instantly.

At this point, one also checks the bird's reproductive organs to make a positive identification of its sex. Its gonads are measured as an indication of its breeding condition. O'Neill now opens the antwren's stomach and examines its contents—nothing in this case—recording this in his notebook. With the bird turned inside out, he scrapes the remaining tissue away from the skin. If something is hard to get at, he will take a syringe filled with formalin and squirt a bit where it's needed to stop the tissue from decaying. Finally, he puts the bird back to right-side-out and begins to stuff it with pieces of cotton, being careful to re-form the antwren to its natural shape. He sews up the incision, crosses the bird's legs, ties them together, and then takes his Rapidograph pen to prepare the specimen tag. These tags, no larger than a file-folder label, must hold all the essential information, which means that an ornithologist with poor penmanship will never make it in an LSU camp. O'Neill prints everything in tiny letters, ties the tag to the antwren's legs, then takes a thin sheet of cotton and wraps it around the bird. At last he pins it to a drying board with the day's other specimens. The entire process takes him about forty-five minutes. The final entry in his notebook looks like this:

> 7325 *Myrmotherula*_____? ♀, 8.5 g.; iris chestnut, bill silver-gray, base of mand. paler; feet & tarsi med. gray; netted in humid tropical forest; ovary 4×3mm, oviduct 1mm; tissue B-10533 [=B-10553]; skull 95% oss.; little fat; no molt; stomach empty

Since we have taken to having dinner in the work tent to avoid the mosquitoes, it's not unusual to be eating spaghetti next to little piles of bird flesh, or worse: last evening, as I was raising my fork to my mouth, Paul, sitting an inch from my elbow, suddenly exclaimed to Mara, "Wow, look what's in this snake's stomach. You won't believe it!"

The biologists think nothing of this. As the only nonbiologist on the trip, I find the scene in the work tent somewhat unappetizing, but when we are served the meat from a Mealy Parrot a few nights later, I eat it hungrily with my instant mashed potatoes. Fresh meat has become a rarity and Marta has made the parrot meat flavorful and tender. The work tent is especially crowded now that O'Neill and Donna have arrived. It's impossible to walk around without making people get up from their seats to move out of the way, and with the increasingly cramped quarters Tony seems somewhat irritable. He's delivered a few icy stares to Paul for jostling the table. Paul's energy level has not subsided—one night when he had nothing better to do he spent an hour chasing mosquitoes around in the work tent, clapping until his hands were plastered with blood.

O'Neill himself has remained easygoing. He wears his authority lightly. Pete didn't hesitate to joke with him when O'Neill first sat down at the table: "Hey, who do you think you are? You show up a week late and expect us to make room for you?"

Divorced since 1978, O'Neill clearly enjoys his big-brother relationship with the graduate students. "John must be a bit lonely," Parker once said, "but he never complains, and he's basically happy with himself, I think." Besides his friendly nature, O'Neill admits he took to heart the parental lecture on the necessity of sociability to one's success in life.

"One thing that has been really important in everything I've done is my meeting people," he once told me. "And in fact it's led me to develop a little saying. You know the old saying 'It's not *what* you know but *who* you know'? Well, I carry it on a little further: 'It's not *what* you know—it's *who* you know, but you got to know *what* to know *who.*' So that's why you go to school."

In Baton Rouge rarely does a day go by when he isn't on campus by nine a.m., chatting with the department secretary, checking in on whatever projects are in progress, and then attending to his own tasks, which extend from the menial (painting the crumbling ceiling in the exhibit room) to the extraordinary (writing the description of yet another new species).

In camp his manner and sense of humor are often boyish ("Well, I guess we're up a creek without a paddle," he said as the dugout that brought him turned around and headed back to Abujao, repeating the joke several times during the next few days for those who didn't hear it originally), and he will often join in the goofing around that Paul and Pete engage in, much of which is a series of insults, each one lowered to a cruder level. The mood can become infectious.

Pete comments on Paul's camera: "That's a great flash unit. How much did it cost?"

Paul: "Two hundred and fifty dollars."

Pete: "Hell, that's more than I make in a year."

Tony, looking up from his work: "And it's twice what you're worth."

20

In the morning O'Neill returns to the work tent. The blisters on his feet are bad enough that he has decided not to venture out of camp at all for a couple of days, to say nothing of going to the mountains. He has a Collared Trogon lying on the table and a square of watercolor paper propped in his lap. He has promised to do some paintings that several admirers have commissioned. He stares silently at the trogon, a studious look on his face. Though he went to college at the University of Oklahoma to be near George Sutton, Sutton did not give O'Neill any real instruction. As a painter, O'Neill is self-educated. When Sutton did make a rare comment, however, O'Neill listened.

"One of the first pictures I showed him was a Squirrel Cuckoo, and I had spent lots of time on the bird and then had sort of just slopped in a bromeliad and a limb or something in the background. He just said, 'Well, this is nice, *but...*' and then went into this friendly tirade about how the whole picture was ruined because I had spent all this time on the bird and neglected the rest of it. That was one of the first big lessons I learned."

Some years ago Roger Tory Peterson predicted that O'Neill was "going to be a first-stringer, and he's very close to it now." In fact, today O'Neill's paintings are in great demand. He has sold over three hundred of them; contributed illustrations to the *Encyclopaedia Britannica, National Geographic's Field Guide to the Birds of North America, A Guide to the Birds of Trinidad and Tobago,* among other books; and he has had his work exhibited everywhere from an LSU campus gallery to the British Museum of Natural History. Parker noted one day in passing conversation another of O'Neill's accomplishments as a painter: "John has really helped a lot of people around Baton Rouge. I think he inspired people like Gene Beckham and Doug Pratt [both men are now accomplished natural-history painters] to pursue their painting. He's always helping people and never taking any credit for it. This whole program, everything that's going on at LSU, wouldn't exist if it weren't for John."

Painting is the one purely solitary activity O'Neill engages in. At home in Baton Rouge he is always fighting to keep his afternoons free to paint. His studio is a small back bedroom where his biggest problems are finding the drawing table beneath the clutter of books, paints, brushes, and stacks of Styrofoam food containers he uses to mix paints in—and picking cat's hair out of paintings in progress. Here, however, there are no cats to bother him, and without a drawing table he must balance the stiff watercolor paper on his lap. He takes his glasses off and, with his paintbrush clenched between his teeth, he squints at the trogon. Then he swirls the brush rapidly in one of the little oval windows of watercolor in his tray of German paints, much as we all did as children. He holds the brush in his fingertips, moving his hand in even strokes. To get the stroke he desires, he may turn the painting upside down. When he rinses one color out of the brush, he invariably sticks the bristles into his mouth to re-form the point of the brush.

In two or three days, depending on his mood and what else there is to do in camp, O'Neill will have a completed painting. The Collared Trogon will make a particularly attractive painting since the bird is so colorful: its upper breast and back a shiny coppery green, a black mask covering the face and throat, its belly red as a rose, with a white collar between it and the breast. The bird's wings are finely vermiculated black and white, and the long tail feathers are a broader barred black and white. The bird is downright gaudy, just what we think of as tropical.

O'Neill looks as though he'd be happy to spend the rest of his life painting this trogon. Paul and Mara, on the other hand, are anxious to get out of camp. They want to see a small oxbow lake not far from here that Vladimiro discovered a few days ago. There is a trail of sorts and it doesn't take long to reach the lake, where we hope to observe a group of Hoatzins that were spotted there earlier. In a land of strange birds, the Hoatzin is among the strangest. Looking something like a neotropical turkey, it has a patch of bright blue skin covering its face, a startling red eye, and an unruly, comical crest of feathers sprouting from its head. Groups of the birds live together in the low trees and bushes at river or lake edge. They fly no better than a turkey, only gliding short distances and invariably crash-landing into bushes, where they usually knock several of their kind off balance and start a ruckus— loud, disgruntled croaking. What's more, they smell bad, "a strong, rather disagreeable musty smell," according to Meyer de Schauensee.

The Hoatzin is not related to the turkey, however, but apparently to the cuckoo family. It is the bird's ties to its ancient past that make it a great curiosity. Hoatzin chicks are nearly naked when they're hatched, and for their first two to three weeks they have functional reptilian claws at the bend in their wings, which they use for climbing about in the bushes. They are, briefly, a living link between reptiles and birds.

We can hear the Hoatzins as we approach the lake. From a thick stand of heliconia, a relative of the banana, we come out into an opening at the lake edge; the birds, on the opposite shore, must see us, because they become increasingly vocal. Though the lake is no more than a hundred feet across, I can barely make them out through the brush. Paul and Mara want a better look, so they decide to make their way around the lake while I wait. I've seen the birds before, with Parker, at much closer range, so I decide to wait and watch a pair of jacamars that are perched in a dead tree not twenty feet away. The jacamars remain in plain view, flying off now and then into the forest, then returning to their perch, and a pleasant hour passes before Paul and Mara return. The Hoatzins, it turns out, were frightened off, so Paul wasn't able to get any photographs. We decide to return to camp since the undergrowth is thick here near the opening made by the lake, discouraging any further exploration.

By the time we reach camp, at midmorning, my stomach is feeling queasy. An hour later, feeling worse, I chew a few antacid tablets and retire to my tent to lie down. I don't know what to blame this on (no one else in camp is ill). We have two big jugs of drinking water that are filled daily from the river, and Manuel has been adding iodine to the water as an extra precaution against bacteria, though more than once we've been told that we drank water from a jug that hadn't been treated yet. The remainder of the day I spend in my tent and fall asleep at dusk, not waking until twelve hours later. The worst seems to have passed by then, but I doze on and off all the next day, nibbling on a few vanilla wafers.

I'm sure this is nothing serious, and in fact in twenty-five years of expeditions there have been few problems with tropical diseases, though just last year Parker came back from Brazil with a case of leishmaniasis, a disease with potentially serious consequences. The leishmaniasis parasite is transmitted by sand flies (Parker often refuses to use insect repellent, feeling he has become immune to insect pests and various diseases they carry as many Indian peoples are); when it enters the body, it invades the lymphatic system and, in time, can cause extensive damage to the cartilage in the face, eventually eating away one's nose and palate entirely. The usual symptom is an open sore encircled by redness, which is just what Parker noticed on the back of his hand. In Baton Rouge he underwent the standard treatment —daily intravenous injections of antimony, a metallic element that destroys the parasite, though how or why no one knows. There can be dangerous side effects, including cardiac problems, and the treatment is not always successful, requiring a second, more dangerous, round of injections.

When I saw Parker in the spring of 1986, he was in the middle of the treatment, his lower right arm shaved, a tube with a heparin lock inserted into a vein. Every morning for a month he went to the hospital to have the antimony injected, and by midafternoon he was exhausted. The treatment worked, though Parker told me later, "You never really know." There's no definitive test for the parasite.

The year before, I heard a worse story of an encounter with a tropical parasite from a young M.A. student at LSU. In a conversation about the preceding summer's expedition, she lamented that she had to come back early. "I got some botflies and they got infected, so I had to be flown out to Lima to see a doctor."

Botfly larvae (*Dermatobia hominis*) can get beneath one's skin from a mosquito bite. The larva is encased in a hard larval sac, like a small egg, with hooks that attach to its host. Thus, trying to extract the larva is painful, and it is often not noticed until several days have gone by and it is firmly wedged in place. The larva breathes through a tiny tube that punctures the surface of the skin. Adrian Forsyth, a biologist who has worked extensively in Costa Rica, reports:

> If you pull gently on the larva, these hooks dig in deeper and bind it tightly to your flesh. If you pull harder, the maggot will eventually burst, leaving part of its body inside the host, which can lead to an infection far more dangerous to the host than the original bot. Botfly larvae secrete an antibiotic into their burrow, a tactic that prevents competing bacteria and fungi from tainting their food. A single bot in a nonvital organ thus poses little danger to an adult human, aside from mild physical discomfort and possible psychological trauma.[1]

I asked the LSU student where the botflies had attached themselves. "In the groin area," she replied.

Later, O'Neill told me that it was a bit worse than that. The botfly larvae—and there were a number of them—had embedded themselves in the vaginal walls, and the young student had naturally been reluctant to talk about the irritation she noticed, much less have someone examine it.

"I guess the girls have it a lot tougher when they have to use the *baño* after dark," O'Neill said. "They're much more exposed."

By the time she brought the matter to O'Neill's attention, she was severely infected and getting her to a hospital in Lima was an urgent matter. The doctor in the Lima hospital didn't find the larvae and it wasn't until she got back to the United States that they were removed surgically.

21

Yesterday, my stomach still a little upset, I went to sleep again at dusk and slept another twelve hours. This morning, Tuesday the thirtieth, I feel better. O'Neill has sent Manuel and Magno to set up a camp at the base of the Cordillera Divisor and they won't return until Thursday. By the time O'Neill gets ready to make the move, it will be time for me to leave. Oscar is supposed to be here on Saturday, July 4. I wonder, of course, what I will miss by leaving this early; most of all I wonder if O'Neill will indeed find a new species somewhere in the mountains. But as Parker pointed out, such discoveries are usually not as dramatic as one would expect, and often a new bird goes unnoticed until months later when it's placed in the museum collection, at which point detailed comparisons can be made.

There have been some notable exceptions, such as *Xenoglaux loweryi,* the Long-whiskered Owlet that O'Neill named in honor of George Lowery a year before Lowery's death in 1978. In late August 1976, O'Neill set up a camp on the eastern slope of the Andes in northern Peru. Moments after the tents were up, it began to rain. Manuel put up several mist nets despite the downpour, but when the

185

rain continued for twelve hours, then twenty-four hours, and nothing had turned up in the nets, O'Neill decided it was time to leave and find a drier location. In the morning, the rain still coming down, Manuel made one last check of the mist nets and brought back a small, drenched owl in a cloth sack. Assuming from Manuel's description that it was a Pygmy Owl, O'Neill did not open the sack until after breakfast; but when he did, he found an owl that looked like nothing he'd ever seen before, "shaped like an *Otus,* the size of a *Glaucidium,* and colored like a *Lophostrix*"—a mix of three different genera. That same evening, Gary Graves, an LSU graduate student, saw the silhouette of an owl and heard what he believes were its call notes, but it flew off before he could get close to it. In truth, whether or not it flew away is open to conjecture, for when one of the specimens (three birds were eventually trapped in the nets) was dissected, the muscles that control flight were found to be exceptionally small, suggesting that the owl could only fly short distances or, possibly, was even flightless. The stunted subtropical forest was filled with heavy mosses, orchids, ferns, and bromeliads, and itself had a character that seemed distinctive to O'Neill. The small, bare-legged owl with amber-orange eyes and exceedingly long whiskers remains much of a mystery today. O'Neill and Graves named the bird *Xenoglaux,* Greek for "strange owl," and presented it as a gift to George Lowery at a Christmas party later that year.

The other particularly unusual LSU discovery is a bird known as *Nephelornis oneilli.* To have a bird named after you must be the most exquisite kind of immortality under the sun. Translated from the scientific nomenclature, the common name of the bird might be "O'Neill's Bird of the Clouds," but in this case modesty overruled poetry and the bird is known by its local name, the Pardusco. The small olive-brown bird was found in an elfin forest on the eastern cordillera of the central Andes. To be precise, it was unpacked with the groceries one day in June 1973. With the expedition's supplies running low, O'Neill sent Reyes Rivera down the mountain to the nearest village to buy food. On the way back he noticed a bird that was familiar to him but not known to the Americans. He and another

Peruvian shot two of the Parduscos, and when they walked into the tent where O'Neill sat, they plopped the birds down along with the supplies. O'Neill recalls thinking aloud that it wasn't a member of the genera *Hemispingus* or *Cholorospingus,* which it somewhat resembled, and that as he and LSU graduate student Dan Tallman went through the list of possibilities and began eliminating them one by one, he had a strong feeling it was something new. Later, they would not even be able to decide what family of birds it was most closely related to. Since Tallman was working on his dissertation about the birds of that particular area, O'Neill offered to let him write the description with Lowery, even though that honor normally would have gone to the senior member of the expedition—O'Neill. In return, Tallman and Lowery named the bird after O'Neill.

If O'Neill finds a new species in the Cordillera Divisor, it will be number twelve for him. Though Angelo and Tony joked repeatedly about the "new species" of jacamar, making light of the situation, there's an undercurrent of anticipation, a serious, unspoken hope that we will find something new. Certainly, there can be very few birds left to be found, and to be present on an expedition that brings one back would be a highlight of any biologist's life.

After testing his foot around camp for a couple of hours, O'Neill decides to venture onto the trail, and Donna, who has not taken time to go very far herself, heads off with him. Four hours later Donna returns ahead of O'Neill. When O'Neill comes into camp half an hour later, he is all smiles. He sat down on a log to rest at one point and two trumpeters walked across the path right in front of him.

"They were so beautiful I didn't even want to collect them," O'Neill said.

Trumpeters look like a small rhea, with the same fine, soft feathers. Donna, who has a special fondness for trumpeters, is upset that she didn't stay with O'Neill, and now she wants to go right back out and look for the birds; but Marta has brought in the day's first birds from the nets, and there is too much work here in camp to do.

A PARROT WITHOUT A NAME

"You won't collect them before I see them, will you?"

In fact, everyone wants to see the birds, so O'Neill declares them temporarily "protected." There were two of these birds kept as pets at the Sucusari camp, and throughout Peru they are commonly kept both as "watchdogs" and because of their alleged expertise at killing snakes. The birds appear to be delicate and shy, but at Sucusari they had the habit of picking fights with a big hound dog that one of the natives kept. One of the trumpeters would sneak up on the dog when it was sleeping, peck it hard on the nose, then scurry quickly away. If the dog dared avenge himself, the trumpeters would circle him, one pecking him in the rear while he took after the other. Carol Walton of course complained that the dog shouldn't be allowed in camp, where it disturbed her pretty trumpeters, "the poor babies." (One must remember that Carol has done such things as raise a baby goat as a house pet—until, that is, Parker got tired of coming home and finding the goat on the highest object in the living room.)

It has been overcast since dawn this morning and uncomfortably humid. In the early afternoon it begins to rain lightly, continuing intermittently all day. Valdimiro has returned to camp with a small deer and made a fire of green wood to smoke the meat. Under gray skies Angelo, Pete, Gabriel, Cecilia, Donna, and O'Neill prepare specimen after specimen. The tape recorders used to tape bird calls are also the daily entertainment. Everyone has brought along his favorite music. So we sit in the jungle listening to Crosby, Stills, and Nash, then bluegrass music, then the Talking Heads, until O'Neill demands to hear something more appropriate: the soundtrack from *The Mission.* The time is filled with idle conversation. Pete complains that he's tired of doing small birds—they're too difficult to work on; but O'Neill says that large birds are too time-consuming and doing the same species repeatedly is too boring. Angelo nevertheless has been contentedly preparing one specimen after another of Wedge-billed Woodcreepers and Blue-crowned Manakins, two of the birds on which he is doing a long-term project.

Tonight, as every night, Paul and Mara disappear after dinner to make a foray into the jungle in search of nocturnal herps. Some would say this is looking for trouble, but the Freeds are careful, walking slowly and not going far off the trail. The only trouble they have encountered thus far was a big frog that leaped directly at Mara out of the darkness. "Grab it," Paul shouted, but Mara, startled by a frog bigger than her hand, screamed and jumped aside. The jungle's two most notorious snakes, the fer-de-lance and the bushmaster, are both most active at night. Despite the danger, Paul would like nothing more than to come across one or both of them. A couple of days ago, Tony advanced his theory about the fer-de-lance:

"The third person is always the one who gets it," he said. "The first person wakes him up; the second person pisses him off; the third person gets bit."

Biologists call the fer-de-lance by the name of its genus, *Bothrops.* The venom of a *Bothrops* digests muscle, destroys blood cells, and causes hemorrhaging. "You probably won't really die if you're bitten" is the standard comment; more likely, if the bite is severe, you will lose the limb on which the snake has bitten you. This was one thing that worried tropical biologist Robert Colwell when he was bitten by a *Bothrops* in Costa Rica in 1984. The episode was complete with dangerous errors in judgment (Colwell *ran* half a mile back to camp rather than lie still while his companion went for help, which would have delayed the spread of the poison); initial indecision (his colleagues came up with three different sets of antiserums that had three conflicting sets of instructions in two different languages); and a painful and worrisome ten days in a Costa Rican hospital during which Colwell's arm, then his shoulder, then the entire left side of his upper torso swelled up in reaction to the bite, followed three days later by a massive allergic reaction to the antiserum. Eventually, Colwell recovered fully, his understanding of tropical biology enhanced in a way he would never forget.[1]

Before the advent of antiserums, snakebites, of course, were even more serious. Nearly all the naturalists who wrote about their experiences in South America during the nineteenth century, the great age of neotropical exploration, included personal notes about the dangers of snakes, but I can think of no account more vivid than the botanist Richard Spruce's as related in a letter to a friend in 1855:

At 5:30 a.m. Nelson and I had our coffee, and then set off to herborize. Fortunately I indicated to Chumbi's wife the direction we should take, and we had been gone but a little while when her son came running after us to beg that we would return instantly, as his father had been stung by something in the wood and had reached home in a dying state. We hurried back, and on arriving at the house found Chumbi sitting on a log, looking deadly pale, and moaning from the pain of a snake-bite in the wrist of the right arm. He told us in a few broken words that he was creeping silently through the bush to get within shot of a turkey, when, on pushing gently aside an overhanging branch, he felt himself seized by the wrist, and was immediately attacked with so terrible a pain that he ran off in the direction of his house as fast as he could. He judged an hour might have elapsed since he was bitten, and the hand and arm as far as the elbow were already dreadfully swollen and livid, while the pulse even in the left arm was scarcely sensible. We bandaged the arm above the elbow, and as Mr. Nelson averred that his mouth was perfectly sound I allowed him to suck the wound, which was merely two fine punctures in the wrist on a line with the little finger; but the time was evidently past for either suction or bandaging, for Chumbi declared he felt excruciating pain in every part of his body. I also made him swallow three wine-glasses of camphorate rum, and we bathed the arm with the same spirit. Then we got him on his feet, and, one of us holding him on each side, we walked him up and down by the house. After a few turns he declared he could walk no more, and begged us to let him sit down; but after sitting a few minutes the pain returned with redoubled violence, and the pulse, which had beat a little stronger with the stimulant and the exercise, again became imperceptible. So we forced him up again, and made him walk as long as we could; then wrapped up the wrist in cotton soaked with spirit, and every now and then gave him a glass of the same, into which I threw a quantity of quinine. At short intervals we also gave him strong coffee, which evidently enlivened him. Still, with all we could do, and although we contrived to keep up the circulation, the swelling gained on us, and by night the whole arm up to the shoulder was so much swollen and discoloured as more to resemble the branch of a tree than anything human, and the hand was most like a turtle's fin.

Whilst this was going on, the relatives of the poor man kept up a continual wailing, as though he had been already dead; and he himself, although he submitted patiently to our efforts to procure him relief, had lost all hope of living. He indicated the spot where he wished to be buried, and gave what he considered his last directions to his wife about his children and property. He also sent off a messenger to his mother and brothers at Tabalosos, telling them that he was dying, and offering them his last adieux.

Towards evening, although the pain was still intense, the beating of the heart had become fuller and more regular, so that I felt sure the progress of the poison had been arrested, and I was now only afraid of mortification supervening in the arm. I therefore set Chumbi's wife and daughter to grind a quantity of rice, and enveloped the hand and wrist in a thick poultice, and had the rest of the arm fomented with an infusion of aromatic herbs at short intervals throughout the night. When the poultice was taken off in the morning, it was saturated with blood and putrid matter from the wounds, which had become much enlarged. The swelling was sensibly diminished, and the arm had become covered with pustules containing bloody serum, which we evacuated by puncturing them. A ready-made rice-poultice replaced the one taken off, and we kept up the fomentation and poulticing until, at the end of forty-eight hours, the swelling had entirely subsided. The blood, besides breaking out at the skin, had also got mixed with the excretions. To remedy this, I prepared a decoction of an aromatic pepper (a species of Arthanthe) that I had seen growing close by, and knew to be a powerful diuretic, and made him drink largely of it. In twelve hours the skin and the excretions were restored to their normal state.

On the second day he could take a little broth, and on the third he again ate heartily. For a month afterwards he had occasional acute pains in the arm and about the region of the heart, but at the end of two months he was quite restored, and avowed that his arm was as strong as it had ever been.[2]

Despite Tony's joking about the *Bothrops*, he called everyone together on our second day in camp and delivered a lecture on what to do if someone got bitten. We were each given a whistle to signal with if we were alone, and reminded of the basics: stay calm (rarely does anyone die immediately from snakebite; it takes two days on the average); walk slowly back to camp so as not to speed up the action of the venom in the bloodstream; get some help from someone in camp; and send someone else for El Médico. Although Tony showed us how to inject the antivenin, he stressed we were not to use it unless the victim appeared to be in serious distress. And if we did inject it we should be just as concerned about an allergic reaction, for which we've brought along adrenaline. Tony added that we should of course try to get a look at any snake that bites us so we would know how to treat the bite, and with that in mind Paul described *Bothrops* and the other deadly pit viper, the bushmaster. The bushmaster is actually the more dangerous of the two, largely because of its size—up to twelve feet—and the corresponding quantity of venom it is capable of injecting. Each fang, which may be two inches long, holds two to three cc's of venom. Fortunately, it is also the rarer of the two.

Tony finished his lecture by noting that many recent studies show that pit vipers actually inject their venom only 20 percent of the time when they bite a human. And then they rarely inject a lethal dose. It appears that the snake saves its poison for animals it intends to kill and eat. So, he said again, we should not panic if we do get bitten.

"How much antivenin do we have with us?" Paul asked.

"Enough to treat three bites," Tony said, "and if three people actually get bitten here, then I'm leaving."

Paul noted that we might have to use all the antivenin on one person if someone were to get a bad bite from a bushmaster.

"If a bushmaster injects all its venom," Tony said, "there isn't much hope anyway."

Paul and Mara have collected some snakes—several vine snakes and a colorful blunt-headed tree-snake—but the most interesting herps they've found have been a variety of poison-arrow frogs of the genus *Dendrobates.* The family, *Dendrobatidae,* contains roughly seventy-five species that are found only in the New World tropics. The common name of the frogs comes from their use by the Chocó Indians in Colombia, who dipped their blowgun darts in the poison that the frogs secrete from skin glands. Paul handles the frogs freely, but makes a habit of washing his hands afterward. Like many creatures in the tropics, the frogs advertise how dangerous they are by being brightly colored. One of the frogs has three canary-yellow stripes against a glossy black body and a bold pattern of baby-blue veins on its legs and belly that looks like a Halloween skeleton costume. Yesterday, Paul came into camp particularly excited. He'd found a *Dendrobates* (*D. pictus*) carrying its tadpoles on its back, a habit shared by all members of the genus. Unlike most frogs, *Dendrobates* care for their young after the eggs have been laid. When the tadpoles hatch, they carry them on their back to a nearby stream.

Some species of *Dendrobates* do even more to ensure that their young have a fighting chance for survival. Poison-arrow frogs generally remain on the ground, never climbing more than a few inches off the forest floor, but these species will carry their tadpoles up into the trees, climbing until they find a water-filled bromeliad where they deposit the tadpoles, out of reach of most predators. A few years ago, a tropical biologist made an even more startling discovery about the habits of these frogs. Rather than leave all the tadpoles in one bromeliad, the parent disperses them into several different bromeliads, which lessens the chances that an entire brood will fall prey to an aerial predator. Since the frog must back into the crevices of a bromeliad to release each tadpole, it cannot see if other tadpoles are already in the tiny pool of water; thus, tadpoles respond to vibration of the bromeliad by wiggling their tails vigorously, disturbing the water and letting the adult frog know they are present. Later, the adult frog will return to the bromeliad and deposit infertile eggs to augment the tadpoles' food supply. This behavior of caring for the young is strictly contrary to the very definition of an amphibian, but in the tropics definitions derived in North America often go out the window. Many species hatch from eggs as tiny frogs, dispensing entirely with the amphibious phase of development, and one species even gives live birth to its young.[3]

Paul and Mara spend the better part of each morning photographing their finds, then work during the afternoon on checking the identity of each species, recording everything in their notebooks. With a bewildering myriad of species of reptiles and amphibians in Peru, their task is no easier than the ornithologist's.

22

Today, July 1, the first bird that O'Neill prepares is a Yellow-browed Antbird, which heretofore has never been found this far south in Peru. And two days ago Angelo collected a Blue-backed Manakin, also considered a northern species. Finding birds well out of their known range is one result of these LSU expeditions, which over the years have redefined the distribution of three-fourths of Peru's birds. In some cases this may clarify the relationship of one species to another, indicating the potential for interbreeding if it's discovered that their territories overlap. There are several species pairs that O'Neill is particularly interested in because one member of each pair is found north of here and the other member to the south. In each case there is so little difference between the two species that their status as distinct species is questionable. If we were to find a bird in this area with characteristics of both, it would suggest the existence of a "cline," a distributional line along which a bird varies little by little, so that even though a northern individual and southern individual were considerably different, the birds in between the two extremes would have traits of both. The northern and southern forms and the intermediates would all be

considered the same species. This is the case with the North American Song Sparrow, with many subspecies all linked geographically and interbreeding freely. In the Aleutian Islands the Song Sparrow is a large, dark bird with a heavily streaked breast. In Baja California, the bird is only half the size and much lighter, but in between there are twenty-nine other subspecies that grow increasingly larger and darker the farther north they are found. In such a case, where all subspecies are in contact with one another and gene flow is continuous, the species is said to vary clinally.

One of O'Neill's first discoveries, the Elusive Antpitta, found at Balta near the Curanja River 220 miles south of here, is closely related to the Ochre-striped Antpitta, known only from north of the Amazon. The throat and upper breast on the Ochre-striped Antpitta are darker, rustier, but otherwise the birds appear alike. If a series of Elusive Antpittas were collected from this area with slightly darker breasts than those found at Balta, O'Neill might very well have to give up one of his species, reclassifying it as a subspecies of the Ochre-striped Antpitta instead. On the other hand, if we find Elusive Antpittas here that are identical to those at Balta, the odds are increased that the birds are distinct species. The same basic situation exists for the Semicollared Puffbird and White-chested Puffbird, the Bluish-Slate Antshrike and Cinereous Antshrike, and the Selva Cacique (another one of O'Neill's discoveries) and the Ecuadorean Black Cacique.

The subspecies concept is relatively new, and still changing. Darwin himself would have almost certainly recognized thirty-one distinct species of Song Sparrow. O'Neill, as he enters data into his notebook on the Yellow-browed Antbird, is engaged in a process that is nothing less than an attempt to explain the order of life on earth. Ernst Mayr, who has written extensively about the species concept, notes that all these ornithological matters are ultimately rooted in philosophy:

> The idea that all phenomena of nature somehow reflect an underlying order goes back to the ancient Greeks, and as a matter of fact even further back to the old religions and to the mythology of

primitive man. The study of this order—and the endeavor to explain it—is one of the tasks of science.[1]

Birds, conspicuous and widespread, perhaps best represent the diversity of life on the planet, and it is diversity (in a different mood we might call it chaos) that calls for explanation. When O'Neill has presented a description of a new species to the scientific community, he has followed an accepted set of guidelines that might seem to have evolved almost as slowly as the bird in question. O'Neill's earliest predecessor is Aristotle, the first to treat the study of animals as a worthy pursuit. In 350 B.C. Aristotle named and described roughly 140 birds, all that was known of the world's avifauna at the time.[2] He compiled information from other writers, notably Aristophanes, and from the stories he was told by fishermen and farmers, and added some of his own observations as well. His accounts were more entertaining than strictly factual and more concerned with the philosophical implications of bird behavior than with promoting verifiable, firsthand knowledge of birds. Nevertheless, by departing from the Platonic philosophy according to which the world of Ideas was completely separate from the material world of natural phenomena (the former was reality, the only thing worth contemplating—the latter, Plato's shadows on the cave wall) and asserting that ideas existed within matter, he called attention to the exact study of nature. Aristotle also asked pertinent questions about anatomy and suggested that birds could be classified according to whether they lived on land, near the water, or on the water.

With few exceptions, Aristotle's imitators focused only on the entertaining facets of his philosophy and ignored anything merely factual. Those among the literate society of the Dark and Middle Ages who were eager for enlightment had little use for those who held firsthand knowledge of animals—farmers and fishermen—but writers of fables such as Gaius Plinius Secundus (A.D. 23–79) were welcomed. For nearly fifteen hundred years his *Historia naturalis* was the major source of information about animal life. In 1544 the

Englishman William Turner set out to find and observe the birds Aristotle and Pliny had mentioned, an impossible chore, but in the process he wrote the first life histories that were based entirely on personal observation. In 1668, Walter Charleton, physician to Charles II, set out to classify all known birds systematically (the list had grown to about two hundred). His major division was between water birds and land birds (not much had changed since Aristotle) but he was faced with the complication of the motley assortment of tropical birds which had been brought back from South America by explorers and missionaries. In many cases the New World birds looked nothing like European avifauna. Charleton didn't know what to do with them. His solution was to leave most of the exotics for the back of the book. There, in the appendix, he guessed which ones might be aquatic, which ones terrestrial. Land birds were placed into groups of meat eaters, seed eaters, berry eaters, and insect eaters. Seed-eating land birds were further divided into three categories: dust-bathing, dust-and-water-bathing, and singing land birds. Charleton seemed to be grasping at whatever handles were turned his way.

Zoological and botanical science were still branches of medicine in Charleton's time. The botanist was a pharmacist-herbalist first, the zoologist a physician more concerned with human anatomy than with the structure of birds. In the eighteenth century zoology and botany would begin to establish themselves as legitimate, independent sciences. The word *ornithology* (from the Greek *ornis,* "pertaining to birds") had been first used in 1599 by the Italian scholar Ulisse Aldrovandi, and the famous English naturalist John Ray confirmed the meaning it has today when he published *Ornithologieae libri tres* in 1676. The book was also a landmark in its approach to classification. For the first time birds were classified according to form rather than function or behavior. Size, the shape of the beak, feet, and so forth were used to divide birds into categories and subcategories.

During the next few decades others made their own attempts at classification, using physical characteristics as criteria. The results were far less sensible and profitable than Ray's, and biologists often quibbled amongst themselves. In 1735 there were two events that would have a major impact on botany and zoology for the centuries to come: a Swedish doctor, Carolus Linnaeus, published the first edition of his *Systema naturae,* which contained the basis of modern taxonomy; and in May of that year a Frenchman by the name of Charles-Marie de La Condamine left France on what was the first major expedition to South America with purely scientific purposes. La Condamine, a mathematician and geodesist, set sail that spring bound for Quito, Ecuador, where his team of scientists hoped to measure a portion of the earth along the equator, part of a project intended to settle an international dispute. Was the earth slightly flattened at the north and south poles as the Englishman Sir Isaac Newton had contended, or was it elongated at the poles and constricted at the equator as Jacques Cassini, Astronomer Royal of France, asserted? At stake was the honor of France and Cassini's reputation.[3]

During the years La Condamine was tramping through the jungle (the expedition took ten years and proved, to La Condamine's dismay, that the Englishman Newton had been correct), Linnaeus was perfecting his system of nomenclature. In his study of flora and fauna Linnaeus was hampered by the hodgepodge collection of names for plants. Common names varied considerably from place to place, to say nothing of country to country (in England a woodpecker was also known as a woodspite, pickatree, rain-fowl, highhoe, hew-hole, witwall, and hickwall). Naturalists in different countries who wanted to share knowledge were required to make long descriptions of an organism just to be certain they were referring to the same plant. Some had already begun to use Latin or Greek to name plants, but the names, meant to be thoroughly descriptive, were unwieldy: *physalis amno ramosissime ramis angulosis glabris foliis dentoserratis,* or a "bladder-fruited annual, many-branched with angled branches and smooth, deeply toothed leaves." This was the common Ground Cherry that Linnaeus simplified to *Physalis angulata.*

By 1758 Linnaeus had published the tenth edition of *Systema naturae,* in which he had completely worked out a binomial system of nomenclature for all the flora and fauna listed in the book. He consistently used two words, either Latin or Greek for the sake of universality, to name all plants and animals. Genus and species, as the two categories were known, were a natural unit, he asserted, and the single Latin word designating an individual species should never again be used for any other species, thus stressing that species was a unique and basic unit in nature. The system caught on quickly in many parts of Europe. Some scientists adopted it apparently with the motive of renaming already well-known animals so as to get credit for their description under the new system. But others ignored it entirely, and in England naturalists preferred the English names of birds that had been confirmed by John Ray. Not until 1901 was an International Commission on Nomenclature founded and not until 1922 was there worldwide agreement.

In addition to giving everything a name, Linnaeus divided all living matter into two larger categories, *classis* and *ordo*. For birds, Linnaeus noted 6 orders, 85 genera, and 564 species. His classification system, however, was riddled with problems. One key to arranging flora was counting the number of stamens and pistils of a plant, but this meant lumping basswoods, poppies, and water lilies all in the same class. The nomenclature quagmire had been bridged, but there was still the problem of explaining the diversity of life and coming up with a wholly satisfactory system of classification.

During the eighteenth and nineteenth centuries there were scientific expeditions launched from every major European state. By this time, private collections in Europe were growing and the first museums were looking for benefactors. The known forms of birdlife had soared to six thousand and zoologists were arguing over a variety of pet schemes to classify them. Some said the shape of the bird's tongue was a crucial factor; others preferred the nasal glands. The problem, as Ernst Mayr summarizes, was the focus on morphological character- istics (external and internal structure), an approach that can be traced all the way back to Plato and his concept of *eidos*.[4] Every creature had an essence, Plato said, that could only be understood by the mind since the essential mold the creature was created from was in the mind of God. Ironically, one had to study the appearance of a bird in order to imagine the unseen mold. The concept also assumed that each kind of animal had continued to look the way it had in Plato's day and always would, though some individuals might vary slightly since the material world itself was not perfect; the figures from the mold might be imperfect duplicates. From this kind of thinking came the concept of species, from the Latin *specere,* "to look at," which was first used zoologically to refer to appearance. In some cases Linnaeus "looked at" the male and female (or adult and immature) specimens of a bird and concluded from their obvious differences in appearance that they were two different species.

Classifying birds was a matter of establishing the ideal type, mentally reconstructing the mold from it, laying all the imagined molds out before one, and from that trying to see certain "logical" connections. Two similar birds would be considered closely related because they shared certain visible traits. In 1859 Darwin's theory of evolution provided the key to diversity for which naturalists and philosophers had been searching for centuries. Darwin shifted the attention from the various "logical" approaches to classifying life forms to a "*bio* logical" approach. Mayr explains the difference succinctly: "We do not base the taxon [a category such as genus] on the similarity of the included species, but the included species are similar to each other because they are descendants from a common ancestor. . . . Two individuals are not twins because they are very similar, but they are so similar because a single zygote gave rise to both of them."[5] The other fundamental change was that rather than base a species on an ideal individual (Plato's essence), we now assume species refers to a population of individuals that look alike and, what is most important, interbreed.

23

 It is overcast again this morning, not an especially good day to get a look at the Cordillera Divisor, but that is what I plan to do even though O'Neill has decided not to go along. By eight o'clock I'm ready to go, and Paul and Mara set out with me for what will be our only look at the mountains we've come so far to see. Paul is disappointed that he will have no time to collect herps in the mountains, and this leads him to say how disappointed he is in general with the status of the collecting permits. (O'Neill still has no permit to collect birds here—he was not able to get one before he left Pucallpa, so we are here by authority of the permits Cecilia and Gabriel have to obtain specimens for Peru's national museum, and if O'Neill is not able to obtain a permit when the expedition is over, all the birds may have to stay in Peru.) Originally, Angelo had told Paul that he'd be able to bring back all the herps he collected. Later, he was told that some of the herps would have to be left with the museum in Lima; now he will not be able to take anything back to the States and may never again even see the specimens he has spent all this time collecting. Had he suspected this might happen, he would not have come on the trip, he says.

Given the time and trouble it takes to collect specimens on an expedition such as this, Paul's sentiments are understandable, but he's not the first naturalist to go home without the specimens he collected. There are several tragic stories of earlier naturalists losing their collections, among them Alfred Russel Wallace, Bates's companion in Brazil in 1848 and later co-author of the theory of evolution. In 1852, sailing for home, Wallace's ship caught fire in mid-ocean and had to be abandoned. Wallace lost more than three years' worth of flora and fauna collected along the Amazon and could have lost his life during the ten days he spent in a lifeboat waiting for rescue. Our tribulations on the Río Shesha certainly pale in comparison.

With more reliable transportation, modern mishaps are fewer, but they do exist. Several years ago a group of LSU graduate students made an exploratory trip to a promising region near the Peru-Ecuador border. There, the North Peruvian Low—at six thousand feet the lowest pass in the Andes between Colombia and Chile—acts as a natural distribution barrier for high mountain birds, which will not cross it. The students collected a number of birds there, among them what they felt certain was a new subspecies of the Rusty-faced Parrot and the first documented occurrence of this parrot in Peru. For some reason, no one took a picture of the specimen. A couple of days later they packed up their equipment and walked down the mountain, an all-day trek. The following day they drove to the coastal town of Piura, where at dusk they arrived tired and anxious for a shower and a good night's sleep. They parked the truck directly in front of the hotel under a streetlamp, locked it up, and collapsed in their rooms. In the morning the parrot was gone, along with everything else that wasn't bolted to the floor of the vehicle. Somewhere a petty thief was wondering what to do with a suitcase of assorted birds stuffed with cotton. Despite posted rewards—"no questions asked"—the specimens were never recovered. In subsequent trips to the North Peruvian Low, flocks of Rusty-faced Parrots have been seen flying high overhead, out of range of guns and mist nets.

O'Neill has lost specimens only once, when the Aguaruna Indians near the study site were stirred up by tales of how the Americans were taking the bats they collected back to the United States, injecting them with diseases, and then secretly releasing them again in the jungle. There was a movement afoot at the time by the Aguarunas to declare their lands, in effect, a separate nation, and leaders were using whatever means were available to unify their people against outsiders. Several Indians came into camp one day and told O'Neill and his colleagues that they had two days to pack up and leave. Without a second thought, the group did just that, but on the morning they were to leave, Parker, also on the expedition, woke up before dawn to find that the boat with all their gear on it had been sunk during the night and was sitting on the bottom of the river. Half the supplies were floating downriver, and though some of the specimens were saved, many other items—binoculars, notebooks, cameras—were never seen again.

Political instability and ecological destruction may eventually make it impossible to continue the work in Peru, which is why Parker feels it is imperative to do all the fieldwork he can now and publish papers later, but at least temporarily Peru is actually one of the safer countries to work in, assuming one avoids areas where cocaine traffickers are operating (LSU has lost several study sites this way). The only other problem is with a guerrilla organization known as the Sendero Luminoso, or the Shining Path, which controls several mountain areas in the country but has caused only sporadic violence in Lima. Much to our surprise, Donna told us that when she got back to Miraflores (an affluent suburb of Lima) to have her tooth repaired, she discovered that a car bomb had destroyed the front of the *cambio* where we had all exchanged dollars the week before.

Van Remsen, who has done much of his work in Bolivia, has had more problems. One year, an expedition was caught up in the middle of a miners' strike that put them in considerable jeopardy. Remsen was camping in the Andes with four graduate students when the local *campesinos* marched into their camp one day and told Remsen he and the others were going to be taken as hostages. Remsen reasoned with them that five American hostages in the middle of the mountains wouldn't do them any good. When Remsen pointed out that they weren't going anywhere, the *campesinos* agreed to let them be— they could always come back later.

The next day the *campesinos* began dynamiting the mountain road that led into the region to slow up any military vehicles that might be coming in. The ornithologists began to wonder how long they might be there; they had hired a car to bring them in and were depending on local *colectivo* traffic to get them back out again, but now the road was virtually impassable. Remsen decided to ration the food. The group went about their studies as best they could, trying to reason with themselves that this was just one of Bolivia's perennial miners' strikes and it would be over soon. The tension, however, grew, and eventually one of the students fell into a catatonic silence.

Two weeks went by. Remsen woke one night at three a.m. to the sound of voices on the road below them. He woke up Manuel and the two stood on the mountain ridge trying to make out what was going on. Their worst fear was that the *campesinos* had decided to come get them in the night, and when they heard something coming up the other side of the mountain—not on the trail—they woke the others and got out the one shotgun that remained. Remsen says what scared him most was that Manuel was frightened, something he'd never seen before. The sound came up the ridge a bit farther, then dissipated. Ten minutes went by. Were the *campesinos* waiting for a signal? Were they sneaking up the last few feet more quietly? A half hour passed. And nothing happened. Remsen began to wonder if they had misinterpreted the noises, as he'd hoped all along. The mountain forest remained quiet until daybreak. When they heard more voices on the road below them, they realized people from a neighboring village that had been isolated since the road had been destroyed were walking down the mountain for supplies. When the earlier groups passed during the night, they had probably scared up some peccaries, which had come half up the mountain before settling down again. Relieved, Remsen and the others went back to their work.

Ten days later they could hear the Bolivian army slowly making its way up the mountain road, stopping every hundred yards to clear a tree that had been felled to further block the road. Remsen worried over what to do. Should they keep quiet and hope the soldiers passed by without noticing them? That way they wouldn't have to answer questions about who had dynamited the road and get themselves further entangled in the conflict. But if they were found and the army thought they were hiding, that would look worse. Remsen had all the necessary government permits, but a group of Bolivian soldiers trudging up the mountain, anticipating ambushes, weary and angry from patching up the road, and just possibly looking for a conflict to let off some steam, might care little for the stamps of approval from distant La Paz. American agitators, American ornithologists—how much difference was there?

Remsen walked down to the road and waited for the approaching caravan. When the first jeep came into view, he held his passport and permits high above his head. He shouted that he was an American scientist. The soldier atop the vehicle was surprised and swung around quickly, crouched, pointing his machine gun at Remsen's chest. Remsen froze, speechless.

"I thought I would be dead in a second," Remsen says. "For that split second I thought it was all over."

But then the soldier lowered his gun and called behind him for the captain to come up. Remsen recalls how lucky they were that the captain was calm and reasonable—it might just as easily have been otherwise—and that he didn't press them when Remsen told him he wasn't sure who had dynamited the road.

The group packed their gear hurriedly, got a ride out of the mountains, made their way back to La Paz, and took the first plane to the States. Months later they heard that the troops had gone on into the next village where the rebellious *campesinos* were holed up and killed every man they saw.

As we ascend the first rise in the trail, Paul is leading the way, then comes Mara, then me. For today's walk we all have our hiking boots on and we tromp along at a merry pace. Though Paul was complaining a moment ago, he has already forgotten it. He has a buoyant spirit, and despite occasional squabbling he and Mara get along well under conditions that many couples would find impossible. Mara has dealt admirably with sunburn, insect bites, a bad cold, and a staph infection. She brushes aside a branch and holds it back until I can reach it. Paul kicks at deadwood now and then, but does not slow down to examine it. Around his wrist is a large, red rubberband that he uses to capture lizards. I've seen him knock a lizard off a leaf eight or ten feet away and then grab it before the creature knows what hit him. This child's weapon is not only effective but also seems perfectly suited to Paul's personality. He shouts with joy when he catches something and talks to the frogs and snakes when he photographs them. We walk along, making conversation, and I sense we share the same mixed emotions about this trek to the outlook—excited about seeing the mountains, disheartened that we won't get any farther than that, and aware that in just three or four days we will be returning to Pucallpa.

The trail makes a turn to the north, and I bump into one of the mist nets as I've done several times before. I know where they are and still I can barely pick them out from the broken shadows of the forest if I'm not looking for them. The understory is an unworkable puzzle of vines and shadows, the air still, quiet. The trees here reach 80 feet, where they spread out a canopy of sun-seeking leaves, broken only now and then by emergent trees that grow to 130 feet. There is leaf litter on the ground, but it's a thin layer since tropical bacteria break down all dead matter quickly. We are in the moldy basement of the tropics. The soil of the rainforest is surprisingly poor in nutrients, which the vegetation receives instead from rainwater and decaying matter. Once a section of rainforest has been cut, it is slow to regenerate. In Southeast Asia a swatch of rainforest that was cut six hundred years ago is still clearly distinguishable from the virgin rainforest surrounding it.[1] Biologists estimate it may take a thousand years for tropical rainforest to completely replace itself. This makes the reports of rainforest destruction around the world all the more disturbing. Of the fourteen million acres a year that we permanently destroy, commercial logging and agriculture take the great majority, but Catherine Caufield has noted another cause: "One reason that the Central American rainforests seem doomed to disappear is that their destruction takes five cents off the price of an American hamburger."[2] Rainforest in Central America is cleared to raise cattle. Three-fourths of the cheaper Central American beef is exported to the United States, where fast-food chains mix it with American beef to produce a less expensive hamburger. Central America hardly needs, or can afford, the beef for itself. In 1978 the average Costa Rican ate twenty-eight pounds of beef a year, less than the average amount eaten by a domestic cat in the United States.

The trail we are following here does not qualify as even a scratch on the hide of the planet, and I've heard O'Neill himself say that after flying for hours above unbroken rainforest it's hard to imagine there is anything to worry about; but if the last section of the Trans-Amazon highway cuts through this area as planned, it will provide commercial loggers access to the valuable timber all around us. It's impressive timber, certainly. Many of the trees appear gargantuan because of the buttresses at their base, which reach out from the tree like flanges on a rocket. There is one of these buttressed trees near camp. Gentry left the liquid nitrogen tanks, covered by some plastic and a few branches, well protected between two of the buttresses, which were big enough to make the walls of a small shack. In mature trees these buttresses, usually six to ten of them, may begin thirty feet up the trunk and reach away from the tree nearly as far. Because buttresses appear on many varied families of trees and irregularly on individuals of the same species, it is not clear why they develop. The obvious answer— support for large trees with shallow root systems—probably holds some truth (though sound objections have been raised to this theory), but soil conditions and other factors may have an effect also. The local people use the buttresses on smaller trees to fashion the broad blades of their canoe paddles.

The height of the trees around us, their smooth, branchless trunks, the bizzare shapes of these buttresses, and the twisted lianas that snake from one tree to the next make the jungle imposing. Tony and Manuel have been back and forth on the trail often enough that it is now well worn. In fact, there are stretches where we could follow the empty shotgun shells tied to a branch to signal a spot where several birds were collected. (From a distance the shells appear to be some strange orange flower.) Yet if we stepped off the trail, walked twenty feet, and looked back at where we had stood, no trail would be visible, and if we turned around a few times to survey the homogeneous greenery, it would not be easy to regain our bearings. One needs more experience with the rainforest and more confidence than I have to venture far away from the trail in pursuit of a bird, as Tony has done several times already. He was lost once for about an hour, but finally found his way back to the trail. O'Neill recalls being lost just once for a short time, a heart-thumping experience, and even Parker speaks in serious tones of being lost in the jungle. I cannot fully imagine Gentry's misadventure. Later, O'Neill tells me that Camilo, who has worked with Gentry for years, swore he'd never go anywhere with him again.

Distant bird calls pierce the silence. A toucan. Macaws. The familiar laughter of a woodpecker. We walk along steadily, my eyes turned up toward the occasional rustling in the leaves, Paul and Mara watching the ground. We count the *quebradas* we cross, measuring our speed this way, and by mid-morning we reach the rock-filled *quebrada* we stopped at last week. Here, I collect a few pebbles from the streambed, something to take back with me so that some day a year from now, when I'm absorbed in the routines of a civilized life, I can finger them and remember that I picked them up out of the cool water of an unnamed stream where white men had never before set foot.

During the next hour of walking, we encounter steeper rises, each one followed by a sharp descent to a stream. Atop one ridge the trail leads directly into a newly fallen tree, and it takes several minutes to find a way around it and several more minutes to find the trail again. From here on the path is harder to follow, but if we are alert we find small machete marks on the trees. Our pace slows a bit as we keep our eyes on where we're headed and huff and puff up some of the sharpest inclines. The impulse is to grab hold of branches and lianas to pull ourselves up, but I take a good look at any potential handhold before I use it, not for fear of snakes, but ants. It has been reported that each rainforest tree harbors as many as 405 distinct species of insects.[3] In some cases an insect may protect a given tree from intrusions, as is the case with a tiny ant (*Pseudomyrmex ferruginea*) and the acacia tree (*Acacia cornigea*) that it inhabits. The ants nest in the hollowed-out thorns of the tree and feed on a special nectar the acacia produces; in turn, the ants drive off other insect pests that might destroy the tree and even prevent competing plants from growing within a thirty-inch radius of the acacia.[4]

With the recent rain the steepest ascents are becoming difficult. We slip backward, fall to our knees, and struggle for a toehold, but it is all nothing more than a minor problem, perhaps a bit more than that for Mara, who has the shortest legs. Two of the deepest ravines now have bridges, thanks to Manuel and Magno. They have felled trees across the spans and even erected a hand railing for the highest bridge, which is perhaps twenty feet above the gulley. The day is still overcast, but as we walk along one of the ridges, something feels different to me. I keep looking over my left shoulder through the trees, and finally I'm sure that I can see some empty sky beyond them. I stop and look hard. It's only a faint impression, but it has to be the valley and, past it, the Cordillera Divisor. A flush of excitement rises into my face. Eager to get a better view of the mountains, I keep looking through the trees as we follow the ridge for another twenty minutes, before the trail drops steeply down into a gulley and up another rise. At the top of the rise, the path seems to go both left and right, and I suspect we are near the lookout. We turn left, which will keep us on the high ground, and sure enough, within five minutes we come to the end of this ridge where Manuel has cleared two openings, one to the west, one to the north. Across a heavily forested valley—a rumpled mass of green—the mountains rise out of the jungle. They are only 1,500 to 2,500 feet high, but, surrounded by lowlands, they appear majestic, even in this gray weather. A low line of clouds covers the peaks, giving the whole mountain range a flattop. And without any sunshine, which at this late hour of the morning would be falling on the slopes facing us, we cannot pick out any particular features.

It's hard to judge how far away they are. We guess that the valley is three or four miles across, though it looks like more. Somewhere out in the valley, to the west, a group of howler monkeys begins a chorus of disapproval at our presence. Their roar, rising and falling, rolls over the silent treetops of the valley like a storm cloud—a crazed, wild sound that seems fitting here. It continues for ten minutes, then subsides. Gentry said there are caves in the mountains, one large one that is filled with a pungent cat smell—a jaguar or mountain lion den, he speculated. And O'Neill wonders if there are oilbirds in any of the caves. A little-known, rarely encountered bird, the oilbird roosts in colonies in mountain caves. The young oilbirds become excessively fat, twice the size of their parents, before they leave the nest. They get their name because for centuries natives have used them as a source of oil. And there should be other birds in these mountains that won't be found in the lowlands. All we can do, however, is imagine what it will be like. We linger at the lookout for nearly an hour, taking our daypacks off and munching on trail mix. If the trail to the mountains were clear, we'd be inclined to keep going, but then what would we do when we got there? The mountains stand silently, a dark green wall that is appealing if not particularly hospitable. Manuel and Magno are there now, clearing a campsite and setting up tents.

After we've taken some pictures, we are ready to return to camp. Paul and Mara decide to spend some time looking for herps and I sense that they want to be alone, so I walk on ahead at a quicker pace. When the jungle is quiet, as it often is, it can be a dull place to walk, and that is what it seems like to me as I retrace the footsteps I made only an hour ago. With my head down, I plod along, the image of the mountains still clear in my mind—up one rise and down another, through a dense stand of heliconia, past a tree where ants have

211

constructed a covered vertical walkway, and up the long, slow incline to the fallen tree. Halfway back, I'm startled by a high-pitched whir and an object streaking past my head like a bullet. I stop in mid-stride, but whatever it was is gone. Five more steps, and it reappears in front of me on the path—one of the tropical hummingbirds known as hermits. Some hermits, such as this one, are among the smallest birds in the family, but are exceptionally curious and brazen. This one is darting back and forth from one side of the trail to the other. Then he hovers twenty feet before me for several seconds. It's clear that he's looking over this lumbering, two-legged mammal which appears to be out of place here. Before I can smile, the hermit shoots straight at my nose, stopping no more than two feet in front of my face, where he gives me a good inspection for a long three seconds. His boldness throws me off balance. I'm almost afraid that next he will zip forward and tap me on the forehead to see if I'm sentient. But he flips 180 degrees and shifts into high gear, leaving only a reverberation in the air around my ears.

The remainder of the walk back to camp is uneventful. In mid-afternoon I enter the clearing to the familiar sound of voices coming from the work tent. O'Neill asks about the trail and the lookout, and wonders if we ran into Manuel, who should be on his way back this afternoon. Angelo wants to know how long it took us and how fast we walked, since this will be an indication of what to expect when people begin shuttling back and forth between a mountain camp and this camp.

Shortly before sunset I take my daily bath in the river. (I am the only one who washes up so often. I enjoy the quiet time and the cool water and the flocks of parakeets that fly over with the last rays of sunlight glancing off their greenness as they tilt swiftly and dive into the trees on the opposite bank.) The water level is up over a foot because of the intermittent rain during the last few days and the current is swift. I can feel small fish nudging my legs, and a couple of flies buzz bothersomely about my head to remind me that this is not quite paradise. As I sit on the log and dry off, a swallowtail butterfly comes by to inspect my bar of soap. It reminds me of the butterfly net lying next to my tent and the promise I made to my six-year-old son to bring him back a collection of butterflies from the heart of the jungle. Three specimens, tucked carefully between the pages of my *Birds of Venezuela,* are all I have.

At dusk we are surprised to hear the motor of a *peki-peki* making its way upriver. This can't be Oscar already—he was not supposed to leave Abujao until this morning. But it certainly is. I can see the familiar cowboy hat before I can distinguish his face. He arrives with hearty greetings, having made it upriver from Abujao in just one day. With an empty canoe and high water it was an easy trip, he says, and he's eager to head back right away to take advantage of the rain-swollen Shesha. Paul objects. He has too many specimens to prepare before he leaves and there's a lot of packing to do as well. So we settle on leaving the day after tomorrow, July 4.

24

 Manuel and Magno returned last night, and in a couple of days several people will hike to the mountains and begin collecting birds there. Tony is eager to go, and Pete is torn between seeing some new birds in the mountains and staying here to continue his antbird project. O'Neill will have to decide who should go to the mountains and whether he will go in right away himself or wait for a while. This morning he asks that I take some film back to the States to be processed, and also that I write to Remsen at LSU and tell him to wire some money to Lima, which will be sorely needed by the time the expedition pulls up stakes in August. As we are talking, Tony comes back into camp after his morning walk, wearing a look of excitement.

"Look what I've got," he says to O'Neill as he takes a bird out of a small cloth bag.

It's a Scarlet-hooded Barbet, a canopy-dwelling bird that looks like a cross between a finch and a miniature toucan. The bird has a green-and-yellow body with a blood-red head. O'Neill is delighted. It's the first time I've seen him excited over a bird since he got to camp. A Scarlet-hooded Barbet has never been found this far north before—

what is more important, very little is known of this barbet since only five specimens of it exist, two of which are in the LSU collection. Tony shot the bird near the oxbow lake, and he got recordings of its call so there's a chance he'll be able to attract more individuals later. Gabriel, Cecilia, and Donna are huddled around O'Neill and Tony, marveling over the barbet. Under such circumstances any one of them might prepare the specimen, since Tony has not involved himself in this activity. To have one's name on this bird's data tag would be to garner a little piece of history.

O'Neill is sensitive to such situations. Yesterday, when a beautiful Crested Owl was collected he gave the bird to Cecilia to prepare, for which he got a big smile and thank you. Cecilia and Gabriel have the least experience of anyone here, but this is their country after all and O'Neill has made certain they've gotten their share of the prizes. He's also taken time to explain procedures to them and tell them what he knows of the birds that are being found in this area. They are both eager for the knowledge, and O'Neill for his part is glad to know there will be two more Peruvian ornithologists in future years. Now, however, he takes the barbet to the work tent and sets it down at his own place.

Over two hundred birds have been collected: hummingbirds, tanagers, antbirds, toucans, trogons, swallows, puffbirds, falcons and hawks, woodpeckers, woodcreepers, manakins, jacamars, and more. Eighty species are represented. Another thousand birds will be taken before the expedition is over. If the permit problems are cleared up, as many as 70 percent of the birds will be taken back to LSU and another piece added to the giant puzzle known as the Birds of Peru. The problem with the pieces to this puzzle is that every time O'Neill looks at one, it seems to change shape. Much earlier, O'Neill and Angelo were discussing the prevailing theories about evolution and geographic distribution in Peru. O'Neill noted that the more they learned, the more complex it seemed, "just patterns within patterns," he said.

"Yeah, but there has to be some commonality," Angelo argued.

"Sure," O'Neill replied. "None of the birds live in Africa."

A PARROT WITHOUT A NAME

In mid-afternoon, Tony and Pete renew a discussion about the small parrots they have seen every day in the tall stand of bamboo a hundred yards downriver. The bamboo is flowering and the small parrots come to it everyday to feed, but it's hard to get a good look at the birds. The thicket of bamboo is dense, growing to a healthy sixty feet or more in the morning sunlight, which it soaks up each day from its choice position at the edge of the river. Tony wants to collect some of the parrots, but because the bamboo arcs out over the river, he figures that any bird that he shoots will fall into the water and be swept downriver. Pete says that he planned on taking a bath sometime today, so he volunteers to stand in the river below the bamboo and try to catch any birds that fall his way. With that, the two of them set off—Tony through the forest and Pete, with a towel and bar of soap, down to the river. A few minutes later we hear a shot, then another. For several minutes there is silence. Finally, Pete comes into camp, breathing hard, followed by Tony. They're each holding a small green parrot. O'Neill comes out of the work tent to take a look at the birds as Tony is explaining what happened.

"It was funny," he says. "I got a clear shot at this one bird, but when I fired, it just dropped down to the branch below it and kept foraging. The other birds hardly moved either. It was like nothing had happened. So I shot again, and this time another bird fell."

The second bird dropped into the river and Pete sloshed through the water after it. Tony clambered down the bank, and as he stood at the river edge, the first bird he'd shot dropped out of the branches, alive, and landed next to him.

"Looks like a *Forpus*," Tony says, referring to a genus of small parrots known as parrotlets. All *Forpus* parrotlets (with one exception which does not occur in Peru) are green with blue on either the wings or rump.

O'Neill has been staring at the birds—looking at one, then the other—and hardly listening to Tony. Now Tony hands him the one he is holding. O'Neill turns it around and inspects it, all the while his eyes growing brighter.

"There's no blue in the wing, though," he says, gently extending the bird's wing feathers. "And look at this blue on the forehead."

Tony leans over the bird, and Pete fluffs the head feathers on his specimen to examine the patch of blue, which is no larger than Pete's thumbnail. *Forpus* parrotlets do not have blue on the forehead. And this bird has no blue in either the wings or rump. By now, Donna has joined us, and Gabriel and Cecilia, sensing something is up, are coming out of the work tent. Angelo finally gets up too, then Paul and Mara. Everyone is standing around O'Neill.

"What is it, then?" Pete asks.

"It's closest to *sclateri,*" O'Neill replies, meaning the Dusky-billed Parrotlet (*Forpus sclateri*), which is fairly common in eastern Peru and elsewhere. "But it's not *sclateri.*"

There are forty-nine species of the parrot family known to occur in Peru. Excluding the larger members of the family—macaws and parrots—twenty-five smaller species, known as either parrotlets or parakeets—can be found. Of these, only four species are *Forpus* parrotlets. Though the smaller parrots are sometimes difficult to tell apart as they stream across the sky in silhouette, in the hand there is generally no problem distinguishing one from another, assuming, of course, you know what characteristics to look for. This bird might also be confused with the Blue-winged Parrotlet (*Forpus xanthopterygius*), which in fact O'Neill and Donna saw at Abujao, but it's not a Blue-winged.

"It's nothing," O'Neill says. "It's something new."

No one says anything. Angelo leans closer to the bird O'Neill is holding. Paul and Mara exchange glances. It's as if a bomb has exploded in the distance. We see the explosion, but we have not yet felt the shock waves. O'Neill seems very sure of the startling announcement he has just made. He has spent thousands of hours looking at specimens of every bird known from South America, and now images of them have passed through his mind at high speed. A picture of this small parrot did not show up anywhere. It must be an undescribed species. Paul doesn't wait to hear anymore—he turns and walks briskly back to the work tent where he left his camera. Cecilia smiles broadly and says something in Spanish to Gabriel.

Personally, I cannot believe my luck. We have not collected a single bird from the Cordillera Divisor—O'Neill has not even seen the mountains—and here, less than eighteen hours before I must leave camp, O'Neill has a new species in his hand. I could not be more surprised and delighted if a jaguar came out of the forest and sat at my feet. O'Neill keeps the bird's legs pinched between two fingers, holding it out in front of him and turning it slowly about in the light the way one would show off a diamond ring. The bird is motionless. O'Neill continues talking about the parrotlet's plumage in a calm, purposeful voice. Pete asks another question about *Forpus* parrotlets, and O'Neill wrinkles his brow as he formulates the answer, which makes him appear to be frowning. Whatever giddy joy he might feel he holds in check. O'Neill often has a delayed reaction to such things. An hour or two later he will finally express the pleasure he had earlier reined in so as not to cloud his thinking; the moment, it appears, belonged to science. He did not want to make a mistake. And perhaps he did not want to say something that would have made him sound like an overeager birdwatcher adding one more bird to his lifelist. I recall Parker's need to mock his own excitement when we saw the new *Tolmomyias* flycatcher.

Only O'Neill, Parker, and perhaps three or four other ornithologists in the world would know enough to realize so quickly that this small green parrot—rather plain-looking at first glance—is an undescribed species. O'Neill and Parker both seem capable of instantly recalling the fieldmarks of any of the 1700 species of birds in Peru, a feat akin to memorizing *Paradise Lost.* And they know where the birds occur, where they don't, and how their markings change subtly from one region to another— this is *Paradise Lost and* three centuries of critical commentary.

"You know what this is," O'Neill continues. "This is that parrotlet Charlie Munn has seen at Manu."

Charles Munn, an ornithologist who works with Wildlife Conservation International of the New York Zoological Society, spotted an unusual small parrot a few months ago when he was leading a birding tour in Manu National Park, which is roughly 120 miles southwest of here. He photographed the bird, later showing the picture to Parker and O'Neill. It didn't look quite like any known *Forpus* parrotlet, but without a specimen in hand one couldn't be certain what it was (an immature bird? a local race?), and Munn was not disposed to collecting birds. Even if he had been, in Manu National Park he was not allowed to. This is another case, O'Neill claims, of discrimination against ornithologists: "Don't touch the birds or mammals [in Manu], but sure you can catch some fish to eat."

The parrotlet that O'Neill is holding is still alive but fading fast. Paul, who has come back with his camera, is already taking pictures. Since the sky is gray, O'Neill walks over to the riverbank where the light is better. Cecilia, Pete, and Donna have all gotten their cameras as well and formed a half circle about O'Neill, who holds the parrotlet out in front of him. O'Neill, in blue jeans and T-shirt, with a two-day beard, looks as disheveled as the bird, but he lets a slightly self-conscious smile cross his face before he strikes a serious pose for science and history. The parrotlet is pretty, green as the jungle, darker above, lighter below, like a new leaf. The color on the forehead is a pale, powdery, cobalt blue.

Paul asks if he can photograph the bird in the tent he has rigged up to provide a "natural" background. "Don't lose this one," Pete says (a bird escaped from Paul last week). O'Neill hands the bird to Paul, then asks Donna to prepare the other parrotlet. Donna smiles briefly at this honor, then is all business. She takes the bird into the tent, lays it on the table, and powders it lightly with cornmeal, then gets out the color chart and holds the bird's bill against the squares of color. O'Neill looks over her shoulder and they confer, settling on what is known as "pale horn" for the color of the bill. The toes are "salmon," they decide, and the tarsi "vineaceous pink." Cecilia and Gabriel, who have left half-prepared specimens on the table, go back to their own work, and Pete remembers that he was about to wash up. Someday, one imagines, he will talk about the time a new species of parrot fell into his bathwater.

Angelo looks at Tony. "Some pretty neat birds here, huh? Makes it worth pushing the boat?"

Tony smiles in response, then heads off in the direction of his tent. To my surprise everyone seems to be savoring the excitement of this moment privately. A shout of joy, it seems, would be undignified. And maybe the jungle itself with its shadows laid upon shadows is pressing in on us a bit. It strikes me as ironic, however, that these biologists are here in the jungle in the first place because they have never lost the insatiable curiosity and adventurous spirit they had as twelve-year-olds, but now at this moment of high excitement they have fallen back into their earnest grown-up selves. I'm surprised also at how quickly the camp returns to normal. Paul and Mara have gone back to their work of cataloguing their last few specimens, which they must finish before they can begin packing for tomorrow's departure. With only an hour of daylight left, Manuel has gone off to check the mist nets, and Marta, who had only watched the commotion over the parrotlet from a distance, is now busy starting the fire for tonight's meal. The scientific world may have one more known species of bird today, but we will still be eating beans and rice tonight.

And so we are. We stand around the campfire, holding our bowls in one hand, slapping at mosquitoes with the other. Headlamps and flashlights have been turned off. The glow of the fire falls short of our faces so we speak without being able to see each other's expressions, and inevitably the conversation turns to the parrotlet. O'Neill speculates about the bird's distribution. If this is the same small parrot that Munn saw in Manu National Park, then the bird may be quite widespread. Where else might it be found? And though Pete and Tony casually referred to the birds as parakeets initially, we are now calling them parrotlets since they appear to be closely related to the *Forpus* parrotlets. This is a somewhat arbitrary distinction, however, that ornithologists have not always applied uniformly. Joseph Forshaw, author of *Parrots of the World* and regarded as the world authority on the parrot family (332, now 333, species), has noted that "there is no biological basis for distinguishing parrots from parakeets," let alone parakeets from parrotlets. The bird collected today has the appearance of the parrots we are accustomed to seeing in pet stores, except it's no bigger than a house sparrow: a miniature parrot, thus a parrotlet. Later, O'Neill will explain the distinctions succinctly: "If it's medium to big and it has a short tail, it's a parrot. If it's medium to small and has a long tail, it's a parakeet. If it's huge and has a long tail, it's a macaw. And if it's little and has a short tail, it's a parrotlet."

There are more similarities among members of the parrot family, however, than differences. And parrots do not seem very closely related to any other family of birds. Their closest relatives seem to be, of all things, pigeons. When I question O'Neill about how certain he is that this is a new species, he says he'll feel better when a male bird is collected also (both birds today were females). There is no doubt in his voice though, only a bit of caution at expressing his announcement as a certainty. O'Neill once told me that in retrospect he feels that he and Lowery made a mistake in deciding that the Orange-throated Tanager should be a new genus as well as a new species. Because they had only the one specimen to base the description on, they were forced to assume that it was a representative individual, but in fact when more birds were collected several years later, O'Neill noticed that their bills were not nearly as large as that of the original type specimen, and it was the unusually large bill that had convinced him and Lowery that the bird represented a new genus.

It seems doubtful that O'Neill is wrong about this parrotlet, though. The blue on the forehead is unmistakable and no other all-green parrotlet has it. O'Neill marvels at our good fortune. He hoped to find a new species on this expedition, but did not expect to find it here in the lowlands. That we found this bird unexpectedly only confirms O'Neill's basic assumption that you don't know what birds are in a given area until you go there. "John has a great knack for picking a likely spot," Parker once told me. "He just seems to know where there's going to be something." I think of the Long-whiskered Owlet that showed up in the mist nets after two days of steady rain, of the Pardusco carried into camp with the supplies, of the Elusive Antpitta and Black-faced Cotinga both collected in the same forest near Balta. O'Neill is modest about his accomplishments in this regard, but is always pleased when someone else points out that he has been directly involved in the description of more new species than any other ornithologist alive. This parrotlet will be number twelve.

Though Tony and Pete collected the specimens, they will have only a small part in describing the parrotlet as a new species. In the first place, neither of them has enough experience with the process of classifying a new species to be directly involved, but moreover, neither of them would be here were it not for O'Neill. Most likely, Charles Munn will co-author the description since he saw the bird first and because Munn is highly regarded for the work he has done on neotropical birds over many years.

After dinner, in the work tent Pete makes another hopeless attempt to tune in a baseball game on the radio. One night he got a play-by-play of a soccer game, but the only thing we could make out was the excitement in the announcer's voice and the roar of the crowd. Usually, at nine o'clock we manage to pick up a Voice of America broadcast that fades in and out unpredictably, which is what that whole other life has done in memory and dream since I've been here. In the middle of the table the bug-splotched kerosene lantern hisses and casts its decaying yellow light to the edge of the clearing where, against the thick darkness of the jungle it may as well give up. The night air is soft and damp, standing beneath the trees in pools that never dry up completely. Some evenings the jungle is quiet, on others it is filled with sound—the rough-edged din of enough frogs to fill a stadium. Any bird call will be identified: Common Potoo, Least Pygmy Owl, Ladder-tailed Nightjar. Often O'Neill will play the teacher: "Cecilia, what's that?" If she doesn't know, the question goes to Gabriel or Pete. On the drying boards on the north side of the work tent are two small parrots for which, as yet, there is no answer to such a question. This is the strangest thought of all to me. One of the most basic impulses we have is to ask the names of things. Young children associate the name of something with the phenomenon so closely that their eyes widen with fear as they say the word *fire,* their faces brighten with astonishment when they point to the sky and say *bird.* And if you grew up with a field guide in your pocket, you assume that every bird has a name. In the twentieth century, who would doubt this?

Tomorrow, after Paul, Mara, and I have left, Angelo, Donna, and Tony will pack up some of their personal belongings and, the following day, hike to the Cordillera Divisor to begin collecting birds there. Later, two crews will shift back and forth between the mountains and the lowlands to give everyone an opportunity to experience both habitats. Though they will come across some interesting birds in the mountains, today's parrotlet will remain the highlight of the expedition—the new species O'Neill hoped he might find. As more of the small parrots are collected—eighteen in all, including several males—O'Neill will begin to suspect that the bird is even more unusual than he first thought, that perhaps it does not belong to the genus *Forpus* at all. A feeling that the bird doesn't look quite right for a *Forpus* will keep coming back to him. All *Forpus* parrotlets have a brightly colored rump, a trait clearly absent in this bird, and *Forpus* parrotlets are a bit darker green in the chest. It is a very subtle distinction, but O'Neill dwells on this, believing that in this case it means something. Later he would tell me that before he left Peru, an idea came to him: "Boy, it would be amazing if this new parrotlet turned out to be related to the Tepui Parrotlet."

The Tepui Parrotlet belongs to another genus altogether, *Nannopsittica,* and it lives not in the Amazon basin, but in the strange, flat-topped mountains in Venezeula, Guyana, and Brazil known as tepuis. It was first described as a species in 1883 and was placed in the genus *Brotogeris,* but later it was moved into the genus *Bolborynchus.* In 1916 Robert Ridgway reviewed the parrotlet genera and expressed astonishment that the bird had ever been placed in either of those genera.[1] There were a number of significant traits that separated the Tepui Parrotlet from all other parrotlets, Ridgway felt, and so he erected a new genus for the bird, *Nannopsittaca.* Until now the Tepui Parrotlet has been the only species in this genus.

When O'Neill begins reading the descriptions of the genus, he will feel increasingly certain that the new parrotlet belongs to *Nannopsittaca.* Two months later, at LSU, he will measure the bird's bill and discover it conforms to Ridgway's description of the Tepui Parrotlet's bill: "depth of the maxilla at the base equal to much less than one-half the length of the culmen." Other traits fit *Nannopsittaca* also. The bird's undertail coverlets come all the way to the tip of the tail, whereas in *Forpus* parrotlets they are distinctly shorter. The paler green of the new parrotlet's breast is also very similar to the Tepui Parrotlet. The new parrotlet is close enough to the Tepui Parrotlet to include it in the same genus, but it differs from the Tepui Parrotlet in having no yellow around the eye, only a slight yellow tint to the forehead, and, most conspicuously, the blue on the head.

"The characteristics of the species really are just a slight difference in color," O'Neill will tell me six months later. "When I get the whole group back [to LSU] and can measure them all, there might be a slight size difference, but it's going to be millimeters if it's anything. But I have no qualms about making it a separate species because of the fact that there's such a big gap in range and there's a difference in color. The big question is what is the history of it. And now I'm sort of thinking . . . well, was there originally some sort of little parrotlet like this that was all around the Guayana Shield mountains and then in the eastern foothills of the Andes and in the Brazilian Shield mountains too? So now the interesting thing would be that maybe there's another population over in Bolivia and Brazil." Once again O'Neill is faced with the scientist's paradox: the more you know, the less you know. He has added a new piece to the puzzle, but the pieces next to it no longer look the same, and the gaps between pieces look larger rather than smaller.

During the night I fall into the restless sleep that so often precedes a journey. In the early morning hours the air cools down and I zip up my sleeping bag halfway. The nighttime temperature has been ideal for sleeping. The low has been fifty-nine degrees, the daytime high, eighty-one. (We don't know exactly how much rain has fallen because in an enthusiastic spree with the machete Manuel cut down the tree that Angelo had attached a rain gauge to.)

I get up at dawn and immediately set to stowing everything in my duffel bag. Taking the tent down gives me an odd feeling—what should I do with the palm fronds that I cut and laid over the tent and which have served so well to give me shade during my afternoon note-taking sessions? But there's no time for reflection. Paul and Mara are dismantling their tent and clothesline. Except for Tony, the others are all lingering about the campfire, where Marta is making the day's pancakes and coffee. The sun is rising through the trees across the river as if someone is slowly turning up the flame. In an hour Yellow-headed Vultures will lift from those trees as they do every morning and sail into the tropical sky. As I mix a cup of hot chocolate to have with my pancake, I hear O'Neill's voice in my head: "It's nothing. It's something new."

A few moments later, there is a round of picture-taking—even Manuel gets out the new camera O'Neill gave him—and farewells, and then we haul our stuff down the bank to the river and hand it to Oscar, who places it in the dugout. I take my seat, feeling small and untethered. Miguel, the boatman, pulls on the rope several times and the engine takes hold, the propeller kicking up water as he lowers it into the Shesha. A little cloud of blue smoke drifts upriver on the breeze. Over the clatter of the *peki-peki* we shout good-bye and wave. Oscar digs his pole into the bank and pushes us out into the current where Miguel wastes no time getting us on our way. He opens the throttle wide, and we shoot quickly downriver, laughing at the difference between his point of view on this moment and ours. While we are still shifting about in our seats, we pass the soon-to-be-famous bamboo thicket, round the first bend, and slip out of sight of camp.

I look back once. There is no sign that anyone ever passed this way.

O'Neill, I expect, is already sitting down at the worktable. This is his twenty-second expedition in twenty-five years. He has led LSU groups to every region of the country, which altogether have collected more than twenty thousand specimens, and completely overhauled the literature on Peruvian birds, and by extension, on all neotropical avifauna.

"The Orange-throated Tanager was a turning point," John Fitzpatrick told me one day at the Field Museum. "It led to a giddy two decades of discovery in Peru," most of it in the eastern Andes, which Fitzpatrick called "the last heartland of unexplored wildlife."

Judging by this expedition, it isn't over yet. But while O'Neill, Parker, and colleagues continue to find the last unknown birds on earth, they themselves seem to be a vanishing species.

"Only a handful of individuals in the United States is competent to supervise and undertake large-scale studies of tropical ecological systems," says Peter Raven, who chairs a committee on research priorities in tropical biology for the National Research Council, part of the National Academy of Sciences.[2]

Parker once said that he was mystified as to why so few ornithologists were working in South America: "I knew from reading that I was seeing South America in the same condition that Bates and Darwin had seen it. And it's that way right now, I tell my friends. And they still don't go!"

Although O'Neill has said many times how much easier fieldwork is today than it was for someone such as Darwin or Bates (mist nets, microcassette tape recorders, plastic tarps, lightweight nylon tents, medicines, and so forth ease many of the burdens), the fact remains that on an expedition such as this, one is truly cut off from civilization. Paul told me that in all their previous fieldwork he and Mara had always been near a road where they could hop into a jeep at night and drive to town for a meal and cold drink. Here, a sudden illness or an otherwise minor accident with a machete or one of the guns could be fatal. And it's not melodramatic to say that the misadventures in the jungle that Al Gentry shrugged off so quickly were a matter of life and death.

Now, sitting cross-legged in the dugout, the morning sun laying a heavy hand on my shoulder, I lean back and trail my fingers momentarily in the Shesha. Behind us is the newest bird known to science, a parrot without a name. The thought that I carry such news with me, that for the moment I know something that Ted Parker doesn't, is delicious. Ahead of us are puffbirds and kingfishers, sunbitterns that again elude Paul's camera, and a King Vulture sitting on the bank and watching unperturbed as we pass by. When we reach Abujao, we will spend a night at Oscar's house, then be up early and sent off with two young villagers to the mouth of the Río Abujao, where we board the *colectivo* that will take us to Pucallpa. The following evening at dusk, a tea-colored band of sky hanging above the jungle sunset, our plane will rise into the night and spirit us back to Lima and the known world.

Epilogue

Although O'Neill did not come across any new species in the Cordillera Divisor, there were some exciting moments and valuable discoveries. Four trails were established in the mountains so that birds could be collected from various altitudes and habitats, and during July and early August people shuttled back and forth between the mountains and the Río Shesha camp. One morning in the mountains Donna was sitting quietly beneath a fruit-bearing tree, hoping to see a group of trumpeters that had been coming there to feed. She caught sight of some movement out of the corner of her eye and turned to see a jaguar moving toward her. The animal never noticed Donna and continued on through the forest. The same morning, only a couple of hundred yards from the main camp, Angelo had the same experience with a second jaguar. The jaguar stood still for so long and at such close range, perhaps fifteen feet, that Angelo began to feel nervous and slowly backed away from the creature. The jaguar took a few steps and disappeared in the undergrowth.

The mountains held several other prizes, among them a huge leaf-cutter ant colony (the largest O'Neill had ever seen). The expedition also recorded twelve species of monkeys as well as river otters, giant anteaters, tapirs, and deer. Late in July, Tony collected a Violaceous Quail-Dove, the first time the bird had ever been found in Peru (though O'Neill had long suspected its presence there). Ten species of birds were recorded that had never been found so far north before, including O'Neill's Elusive Antpitta. Six other species had their known ranges extended southward.

After a month in the mountains, the group broke camp and returned to the Río Shesha. Three days later, on August 8, they set out for Abujao, having collected nearly 1,500 birds representing 426 species. It had taken Oscar and his crew seven days to get upriver from Abujao. The Shesha was reduced to a small channel a few feet wide and Oscar had brought just four dugouts with him, which meant there was barely enough room for the gear. O'Neill decided that only he and Donna would go with the canoes; the others would have to walk. The idea was for the dugouts to meet up with those on foot at the end of each day since all the food and tents were in the canoes, but a series of mishaps that included people walking in circles and canoes repeatedly hung up on sandbars left the group that was walking without food or shelter on the third night out. It took eight days to get everyone and everything to the mouth of the Shesha. The boatmen who had spent a week walking barefoot in the river as they pushed and dragged the canoes, had ground the soles of their feet down to the last layer of skin, and an encounter with a stingray left Vladimiro, camp assistant and hunter extraordinaire, in considerable pain for several days (his brother was nearly bitten by a *Bothrops* that struck at him).

It was two weeks later that O'Neill and Angelo, the last to leave Peru, finally returned to the States—with only four of the specimens they had collected, including two males of the new parrotlet. Everything else remained in Lima. Since the necessary government permits had never been approved, "we couldn't take anything out because officially we had never collected it," O'Neill later said.

O'Neill returned to Peru in May 1988 to meet with the new Dirección General Forestal y de Fauna and discovered that all of the scientific reports LSU had sent to Peru during the past ten years had disappeared. No wonder this new director had doubted LSU's sincerity about working *with* the Peruvians. After several days of talks O'Neill gained the trust of the new administration, and a new agreement was reached regarding future expeditions. But to acquire the birds from the 1987 expedition, LSU will have to get them on long-term loan from the museum in Lima. Until recently O'Neill was making plans to return to the Río Shesha area, but the economic situation in Peru has worsened and terrorism has spread. At this point, O'Neill has put all fieldwork in Peru on hold.

Notes

THE ORANGE-THROATED TANAGER

Chapter 1
1. Catherine Caufield, *In the Rainforest* (New York: Alfred A. Knopf, 1985), p. 37.
2. Norman Myers, *The Primary Source* (New York: W. W. Norton, 1984), p. 178.

Chapter 2
1. Edward J. Goodman, *The Explorers of South America* (New York: Macmillan, 1972), p. 3.
2. Ibid., passim.
3. Henry Walter Bates, *The Naturalist on the River Amazons,* 4th ed. (New York: Dover, 1975), preface.
4. Manuel A. Plenge, *The Species of Birds Described in Peru by Decade.* Unpublished monograph.
5. John T. Zimmer and Ernst Mayr, "New Species of Birds Described from 1933 to 1941," *The Auk* 60 (April 1945), p. 249.
6. Erwin Stresemann, *Ornithology from Aristotle to Present* (Cambridge, Mass.: Harvard University Press, 1975), preface.
7. George H. Lowery, Jr., and John P. O'Neill, "A New Genus and Species of Tanager from Peru," *The Auk* 81 (1964), pp. 125-31.

Chapter 3
1. Peter Matthiessen, *The Cloud Forest* (New York: Viking Press, 1961), p. 236.

Notes

Chapter 6

1. Myers, *The Primary Source,* p. 11.
2. Ibid., p. 72.
3. Jurgen Haffer, *Avian Speciation in Tropical South America* (Cambridge, Mass.: Nuttall Ornithological Club, 1974), passim.
4. Theodore A. Parker III et al., *An Annotated Checklist of Peruvian Birds* (Vermillion, S. Dak.: Buteo Books, 1982), pp. 13–27.

Chapter 7

1. Raymond Bonner, "A Reporter at Large: Peru," *The New Yorker,* January 4, 1988, p. 31.
2. Bates, *The Naturalist,* p. 84.

ON THE RÍO SHESHA

Chapter 8

1. By "large," I mean the snake's total size, not its length. The regal python of Malaysia is reported to reach thirty-three feet, while the anaconda is thought not to reach more than twenty-five feet; but the anaconda is much bulkier than the python. One nineteen-foot anaconda was recorded as weighing 236 pounds.
2. Myers, *The Primary Source,* p. 35.
3. Caufield, *In the Rainforest,* p. 37.
4. Ibid., p. 76.

Chapter 9

1. Rodolphe Meyer De Schauensee and William H. Phelps, Jr., *A Guide to the Birds of Venezuela* (Princeton: Princeton University Press, 1978), p. 45.

Chapter 11

1. John P. O'Neill, "The Subspecies Concept in the 1980's," *The Auk* 99 (July 1982), pp. 609–12.
2. Ernst Mayr, *Evolution and the Diversity of Life: Selected Essays* (Cambridge, Mass.: Belknap Press of Harvard University Press, 1976), pp. 493–94.
3. Quoted in Mayr, *Evolution,* p. 495.
4. Joel Carl Welty, *The Life of Birds,* 3rd ed. (New York: Saunders College Publishing, 1982), p. 12.
5. John W. Fitzpatrick and Nina Pierpont, "Specific Status and Behavior of

Cymbilaimus sanctaemarae, the Bamboo Antshrike, from Southwestern Amazonia," *The Auk* 100 (July 1983), pp. 645–52.

6. Thomas S. Schulenberg and Laurence C. Binford, "A New Species of Tanager (Emberizidae: Thraupinae, *Tangara*) from Southern Peru," *Wilson Bulletin* 97 (1985), pp. 413–20.

7. François Vuilleumier and Ernst Mayr, "New Species of Birds Described from 1976–1980," *Journal für Ornithologie* 128(1987), pp. 137–50.

Chapter 12
1. O'Neill, "Subspecies Concept."
2. Ibid.
3. Myers, *The Primary Source,* pp. 66–67.
4. Caufield, *In the Rainforest,* p. 59.
5. Ibid., p. 220.
6. Ibid., p. 219.
7. Ibid., p. 212.
8. Myers, *The Primary Source,* p. 190.

TED PARKER'S HOUSE

Chapter 13
1. John P. O'Neill, "A New Species of Antpitta from Peru and a Revision of the Subfamily Grallariinae," *The Auk* 86 (1969), pp. 1–12.

Chapter 15
1. Bates, *The Naturalist,* p. 339.
2. George V. N. Powell, "Sociobiology and Adaptive Significance of Interspecific Foraging Flocks in the Neotropics," in P. A. Buckley et al., eds., *Neotropical Ornithology* (Washington, D.C.: The American Ornithologists' Union, 1985), p. 722.
3. Ibid., p. 724.
4. Charles A. Munn, "Permanent Canopy and Understory Flocks in Amazonia: Species Composition and Population Density," in Buckley et al., eds., *Neotropical Ornithology,* pp. 683–712.

Chapter 17
1. John W. Fitzpatrick and Melvin A. Traylor, Jr., "A Survey of the Tyrant Flycatchers," *The Living Bird,* 19th Annual (1980–81), p. 7.

Notes

2. Johannes Bapt. von Spix, *Iter Brasiliense Aves,* vol. 2, p. 10, plate 12, fig. 1.

3. Goodman, *Explorers of South America,* p. 300.

4. Maximilian Wied, *Beitrage zur Naturgeschichte von Brasilien,* vol. 3, part 2 (1831), p. 929.

5. August von Pelzeln, *Zur ornithologie Brasiliens,* vol. 2 (1868), pp. 110, 181.

6. Ladislas Taczanowksi, *Ornithologie du Pérou,* vol. 2 (1884), p. 285.

7. Philip Lutley Sclater, *Catalog of the Passeriformes, or Perching Birds, in the Collection of the British Museum* (London: British Museum of Natural History, 1888).

8. Charles Hellmayr, *Catalog of Birds of the Americas and Adjacent Islands* (Chicago: Field Museum of Natural History, 1927).

9. John T. Zimmer, *Studies of Peruvian Birds,* no. 33 (October 11, 1939) (New York: American Museum Novitates, 1045, The American Museum of Natural History), p. 15.

A PARROT WITHOUT A NAME

Chapter 18

1. Bates, *The Naturalist,* preface.

2. Alex Shoumatoff, *The Rivers Amazon* (San Francisco: Sierra Club Books, 1986), p. 162.

Chapter 19

1. Adrian Forsyth and Kenneth Miyata, *Tropical Nature* (New York: Charles Scribner's Sons, 1984), p. 108.

Chapter 20

1. Forsyth and Miyata, *Tropical Nature,* p. 155.

Chapter 21

1. Robert K. Colwell, "A Bite to Remember," *Natural History,* April 1985, pp. 2–8.

2. Richard Spruce, *Notes of a Botanist on the Amazon and Andes* (New York: Macmillan, 1908).

3. Forsyth and Miyata, *Tropical Nature,* p. 181.

Chapter 22

1. Mayr, *Evolution,* p. 408.

2. Stresemann, *Ornithology,* p. 3. This chapter, in general, owes much to Streseman's account of the history of ornithology.

3. Goodman, *Explorers of South America,* pp. 183–200.
4. Mayr, *Evolution,* pp. 485–88.
5. Ibid., p. 427.

Chapter 23
1. Myers, *The Primary Source,* p. 45.
2. Caufield, *In the Rainforest,* p. 108.
3. Ibid., p. 60.
4. Forsyth and Miyata, *Tropical Nature,* p. 110.

Chapter 24
1. Robert Ridgway, *Birds of North and Middle America,* Part VII, Bulletin of the United States National Museum, 50 (Washington: Government Printing Office, 1916), p. 114.
2. Quoted in Caufield, *In the Rainforest,* p. 81.

Index

237

A NOTE ABOUT THE AUTHOR

Don Stap has published a book of poems, *Letter at the End of Winter,* and, in 1986, received a creative writing fellowship in poetry from the National Endowment for the Arts. His prose has appeared in the *North American Review, Sierra, International Wildlife,* and elsewhere. A native of Michigan, he now teaches at the University of Central Florida.

A NOTE ON THE TYPE

This book was set in a type face called Garamond. Jean Jannon has been identified as the designer of this face, which is based on Garamond's original models but is much lighter and more open. The italic is taken from a font of Granjon, which appeared in the repertory of the Imprimerie Royale and was probably cut in the middle of the sixteenth century.

Composed by Superior Type,
Champaign, Illinois

Printed and bound by Fairfield Graphics,
Fairfield, Pennsylvania

Typography and Binding Design by
Valarie Jean Astor